Halos and Avatars

HALOS AND AVATARS

Playing Video Games with God

Edited by Craig Detweiler

WESTMINSTER
JOHN KNOX PRESS
LOUISVILLE · KENTUCKY

First edition
Published by Westminster John Knox Press
Louisville, Kentucky

10 11 12 13 14 15 16 17 18 19—10 9 8 7 6 5 4 3 2 1

Book design by Sharon Adams

Library of Congress Cataloging-in-Publication Data

Halos and Avatars : playing video games with God / edited by Craig Detweiler.
    p. cm.
    Includes index.
    ISBN 978-0-664-23277-1 (alk. paper)
    1. Video games—Religious aspects—Christianity. I. Detweiler, Craig, 1964–

GV1469.3.H35 2010
794.8—dc22

2009033750

PRINTED IN THE UNITED STATES OF AMERICA

∞ The paper used in this publication meets the minimum requirements of the American National Standard for Information Sciences—Permanence of Paper for Printed Library Materials, ANSI Z39.48-1992

Westminster John Knox Press advocates the responsible use of our natural resources. The text paper of this book is made from 30% post-consumer waste.

To Zoe and Theo and the next generation of gamers

Contents

Introduction

Halos and Avatars

CRAIG DETWEILER

> Prepare for unforeseen consequences.
> *G-Man*, Half-Life 2

It all started innocently enough with a teddy bear and a stuffed monkey. Nana was at the Hallmark store, choosing a Valentine's Day card for her grandchildren. She overheard two senior citizens talking about how much their grandkids loved their Webkinz. So my children didn't just receive a plush toy from Nana. No, they received an invitation to enter a virtual world, unlocked by the password attached to their new stuffed animals.

First they needed to choose a name for their Webkinz. Then, their online profiles came with a cache of virtual cash. Evidently, virtual monkeys need to be fed, just like real pets. And what happened when the account ran out? Winning online games earns rewards that can be devoted to virtual decorating. After all, what teddy bear doesn't want new wallpaper or a matching carpet? Yes, a grandmother who had never played a video game in her life ushered my preschool kids into the world of avatars, competition on the Internet, and virtual economies.

As a parent, how should I have responded? Should I have tossed Nana's gift in the trash? Should I have denied my kids the opportunity to enter their password into the Webkinz database? Resistance sure felt futile. Perhaps the wise parent gets involved in online games, helping children make smart purchases with their virtual winnings. It is an opportunity for youngsters to learn budgeting, grasp stewardship, and try on the responsibilities of parenting.

Webkinz turned out to be just a warm-up for the even larger realm of Club Penguin. Now my kids could gather in Disney's icy, online discotheque,

1

bumping into hundreds of other penguins operated from home computers around the world. My children could challenge their virtual friends to some type of online game in which only one would emerge victorious, earning rewards like pet "Puffles." My children were learning how to win. Their interest grew so passionate that a timer had to be set before every session in Club Penguin. Unless interrupted, they would spend an entire afternoon hopping from snowscape to sea. Before my children reached second grade, they already had a second life and multiple projected selves. They were two of the 12 million user accounts within this MMOG—a massively multiplayer online game. Academic research failed to keep pace with the virtual takeover of our household. Teddy bears and penguins had already been colonized.

As a person of faith, I wonder, "What would Jesus play?" He challenged his disciples to " 'Let the little children come to me, and do not stop them; for it is to such as these that the kingdom of God belongs' " (Luke 18:15–17). Many concerned parents consider video games a hindrance to schoolwork, social ability, and spiritual growth. The Wii may cause kids to get cranky, competitive, or withdrawn. But there is also the sense of childlike wonder that overtakes even casual gamers. Our family loses track of time, responsibility, and our burdens while we're playing. Games make us miraculously free from everyday concerns. They are a consolation, a respite, an escape. And isn't that desirable, even spiritual? Jesus warned that "Whoever does not receive the kingdom of God as a little child will never enter it." Perhaps the finest video games can help us reacquire a playful, childlike faith.

WHITHER VIDEO GAMES?

I have recently learned something quite interesting about video games. Many young people have developed incredible hand, eye, and brain coordination in playing these games. The Air Force believes these kids will be our outstanding pilots should they fly our jets.

President Ronald Reagan, 1983

While video games began in arcades, they have now expanded to consoles for the home, computers, portable handheld devices, and cell phones. In 2008, the Pew Internet and American Life Project found that 94 percent of teenage girls and 99 percent of teenage boys play video games.[1] The same research indicates that 90 percent of parents often play along with their teenage children. Teachers vacillate between confiscating the Nintendo DS and incorporating games into learning activities. Violence is a legitimate concern in video games, with the bloody *God of War* earning its M (for Mature) rating. Yet educator James Paul Gee sees games as "action-and-goal-directed preparation for, and simulations of, embodied experience."[2] In an effort to reach younger voters, Barack Obama's presidential campaign bought ad space on billboards within eighteen games, including *Grand Theft Auto*, *Madden NFL 2009*, and *Guitar Hero*.[3] Unfortunately, far too many adults remain unaware of games' social importance and educational possibilities.

Gaming cannot be considered a new phenomenon. *Pong* (1972) beeped across my childhood living room almost forty years ago. *Ms. Pac-Man* (1981) gobbled up my little sister's quarters at many an arcade, and my baby brother

---

Scientists have concluded that video games can cause violent behavior, inferior test scores, trauma, and deteriorated values and morals. While such studies merit consideration by adults and children, other research suggests that video games can help make teens smarter and more productive in society. The gaming generation can multitask, handle large amounts of work, think more clearly, distinguish the lines between reality and fantasy, and relate in community better than prior generations. One hundred percent of the gamers I interviewed and observed all functioned highly in society, could articulate their points well, were excellent at problem solving, could diagnose problems as they came up, and were very aware of "real" life and "second life" as it related to both their micro and macro worlds.

The 2008 Pew Internet and American Life Project offered these conclusions in their study of teens, video games, and civic culture:

Almost all teens play games.

Gaming is often a social experience for teens.

Close to half of the teens who play online games do so with people they know in their offline lives.

The most popular game genres include games with violent and nonviolent content.

There are civic dimensions to video game play.

The quality of game play is not strongly related to teens' interest or engagement in civic and political activity.

Teens who take part in social interaction related to the game, such as commenting on Web sites or contributing to discussion boards, are more engaged civically and politically.

Civic gaming experiences are more equally distributed than many other civic learning opportunities.

Video games are thus not the devils that popular news outlets paint them out to be. Second, these conclusions suggest that something bigger is going on in video game culture that requires our attention. Third, gamers are not the stereotypical socially awkward, anticommunal, antisocial, violent personalities that society has painted them out to be. In fact, they are quite civic minded and use games as a social outlet.

—Daniel White Hodge

was raised on *Donkey Kong Junior* (1982). By the time I became a parent, I expected somebody to offer some tangible answers. Unfortunately, psychological and sociological research swings from incendiary ("Pathological gamers did worse in school, had trouble paying attention in class and reported feeling 'addicted' "[4]) to enthusiastic ("Video games are beneficial and can have positive effects on children's civic and social development"[5]). Rather than lament the conflicting signals, I invited my fellow contributors to enter the fray as agents studying agency.

Magazines and Web sites devote ample space to which games to buy and which to avoid. But cultural observer Chuck Klosterman wonders how, given games' cultural cachet and economic impact, "there is no major critic who specializes in explaining what playing a given game *feels* like, nor is anyone analyzing what specific games *mean* in any context outside the game itself. There is no Pauline Kael of video-game writing. There is no Lester Bangs of video-game writing."[6] When will video games, or at least reflection on games, grow up?

This book is an effort to take games seriously, to wade into an emerging field and make sense of an expanding phenomenon. Its authors take elements from the latest academic theories and research, but endeavor to speak to gamers, designers, and parents in everyday language. (We even draw upon the wisdom of parents who are game designers!) We explore questions of meaning, teasing out trends and themes with theological implications within virtual worlds. This collection is not limited to the religious reader, but is aimed at anyone interested in thoughtful reflection on the video gaming experience.

The finest games draw from substantive wells in philosophy, mythology, and theology. Hard-core gamers recognize the nihilistic underpinnings behind *Fallout*'s conclusion that "War never changes." *Halo* raises pertinent issues of religious authority and its potential abuse. *BioShock* causes players to reflect on the blind trust they may have placed in characters and even the game designer. Games rarely venture into overtly religious territory. Those that do, often mix their sources across cultural lines. Norse mythology may bump up against Buddhist practices. Japanese games like *Neon Genesis Evangelion* (1995), *Xenogears* (1998), and *Final Fantasy X* (2001) adopt biblical characters like Cain and Abel or concepts like "sin" to craft their own original stories.[7] But we are not on a search for Christ figures in video games. We're far more interested in what lies behind, beneath, and within the most compelling games. In many series, religion is something to be feared, resisted, and even overthrown. For example, *Assassin's Creed* wades into the messy history of the Crusades with characters vying for a piece of Eden. So are game designers (and players) generally skeptical toward religious institutions? While that may make gamers wary of churches and temples, it may also make them open to the radical redefinition of faith embodied by the rebel Jesus. Rather than focusing on religion within games, this book will focus on the theological implications of both the stories being told and the structure of the games.

OVERCOMING OBSTACLES

The sheer volume of games, formats, and genres can create a basic barrier to entry. How does an outsider sort out the various abbreviations that dominate online reviews? We attempt to refrain from too much insider jargon, taking time to at least break out various acronyms like FPS (first-person shooter games like *Doom*, which incorporate the players' P.O.V.—point of view) or RTS (online games like *EverQuest* that incorporate live, real-time strategy). Multiple abbreviations may be applied to a single game like *World of Warcraft*. It is an MMORPG, a massively multiplayer online role-playing game, that incorporates real-time strategy (RTS) and is often abbreviated as WoW.[8] (For parents desperate for practical advice, skip straight to the appendix.)

Lest the uninitiated become overwhelmed by the possibilities, let us begin by identifying the most pervasive contemporary home console formats: the PlayStation (from Sony), the Xbox (from Microsoft), and the Wii (from Nintendo). Like BetaMax versus VHS tapes, they are each proprietary and incompatible. They each have competitive advantages (graphics, speed, ease). Broadly speaking, the PlayStation and the Xbox cater to teenagers, adults, and "hard-core gamers" while the Nintendo appeals to children, families, and more "casual gamers."

Hundreds of companies produce video games for these consoles, home computers, and handheld devices. Sony, Microsoft, and Nintendo each publish games for their consoles. Nintendo brought *Mario* into the world and keeps bringing him back (with his brother, Luigi!) for various sequels and spin-offs. Sony Computer Entertainment's most popular title is *God of War*. Microsoft purchased Bungie Studios in order to bring *Halo* exclusively to its Xbox. Bungie is just one of hundreds of independent companies designing and producing video games. The largest suppliers of games include Electronic Arts (*Madden NFL*, *The Sims*), Activision Blizzard (*Guitar Hero*, *Call of Duty*), and Japan's Capcom (*Resident Evil*). A single, massive hit like *Grand Theft Auto* can sustain a company like Rockstar Games for years. However, many of these companies are one failure away from takeover or bankruptcy.

The fastest-growing segment of the gaming business is mobile games. Ever since *Snake* was first offered on Nokia cell phones in 1997, over 1 billion people have played its variations.[9] Apple's application store for the iPhone is stocked with over thirteen thousand games, and the price is right: the average game download costs just $1.79. But with 40 million iPhones and iTouches in circulation (at the time of this writing), they represent quite a pervasive delivery system. Classic games like *Tetris* and *Scrabble* have been adapted to cell phones. The upstart company Tapulous has attracted 10 million users of "Tap Tap Revenge."[10] Such eye-popping possibilities have attracted major game makers like Electronic Arts to mobile gaming. *The Sims 3* was simultaneously released to PCs and iPhones.

Select game designers are singled out for their genius and innovation. Among the most revered pioneers are Shigeru Miyamoto (*Donkey Kong, Mario, Legend of Zelda*), Will Wright (*SimCity*), Sid Meier (*Civilization*), and Rand and Robyn Miller (*Myst, Riven*). In the early days of video games, designers tended to serve as their own computer programmers. Russian computer scientist Alexey Pajitov created *Tetris*, yet Pajitov's rights to the game were routinely ignored in the various knockoffs that flowed from Hungary to the United States. It often takes years to create a single game, so increasingly the roles of designer and programmer are divided among an extensive creative team. These departments now include writers, animators, art directors, engineers, sound designers, and music composers. Gaming production is a decidedly masculine world; fewer than one in five workers in the business and just 3 percent of game programmers are women.[11] The Academy of Interactive Arts and Sciences has presented annual Interactive Achievement Awards and initiated a new member to its Hall of Fame each year since 1998.[12] The first ten honorees have all been men.

Film fans are used to identifying movies by genres like musicals, science fiction, and fantasy. Games are often subdivided in similar ways. Broadly speaking, games range from violent action and adventure (*Gears of War, Grand Theft Auto*) to family friendly (*Little Big Planet, Rock Band*). As with television, racing (*Gran Turismo, Need for Speed*) and sports (*Tony Hawk's Pro Skater, FIFA*) earn separate designations. The most detailed characters and stories are often found in role-playing games like *Final Fantasy, The Elder Scrolls*, and *Fallout*. Stealth games like *Metal Gear Solid* reward unarmed players who avoid detection. Strategy games (*Civilization, Command & Conquer*) often allow the user to play God, deciding who survives and thrives under trying conditions. The goal is to promote technology and innovation within a culture (starting with something as simple as a wheel), lest it turn into a revolt against your divinity. *SimCity* was billed as the ultimate experience in planet management. This volume touches upon virtually every format and genre of games, exploring who plays them, how, and why.

"God games" are more about playing video games *as* God than *with* God. While a film like *Bruce Almighty* turned such a scenario into comic relief, Peter Molyneux's games like *Populous* and *Black & White* hearken back to pre-Christian eras, when capricious gods struck terror into villages. *Populous II* developer Jeff Haas suggests that "God as a buddy, or even an ally, is hopelessly modern. [Before that] you kept out of the gods' way, appeased them when needed, and prayed that your god would vanquish the other gods."[13] *Second Life* offers the godlike ability to fly and teleport. It's comparable to living like mythological minor gods, who "get drunk, have sex, fight, and cast spells."[14] Futurist Kevin Kelly explains the allure: "Stripped of all secondary motives, all addictions are one: to make a world of our own. I can't imagine anything more addictive than being a god. . . . Godhood is irresistible."[15] But do such game experiences create a greater understanding of the divine or a more insatiable hunger for power? In this book, we want to tease out those temptations and trace the broad fingertips of God across the gaming world.

ANCIENT PARALLELS

Let my playing be my learning and let learning be my playing.
                                                    Johan Huizinga

To those who consider video games a new phenomenon, I suggest a more modest line of continuity. Video games may be seen as the electronic evolution of the penny arcade, and companies like Sega trace their roots to the first coin-operated amusements. Pinball machines clanged and chimed during the 1930s. Wii bowling is not too distant from arcade games like Skee-Ball. First-person shooter games echo shooting galleries of an earlier era. Only the technology (and the targets) changed. My grandparents had the ring toss; I had *Tetris*. My kids have both within the cozy confines of Webkinz. Each venue offers prizes from stuffed animals to extended play. Grandparents may play Bally slot machines in a Vegas casino while their grandchildren enjoy Midway's *Mortal Kombat* in the arcade. It all involves a form of keeping score.

The creation of virtual spaces for Webkinz also has echoes in ancient toys like dollhouses. My children are learning how to match carpet and drapes. They're considering the relative costs of a new bed versus a desk set. Instead of paper cutouts and two-dimensional costumes, kids can dress their virtual bears and monkeys in clothes they've earned through the hard work of gaming. A god game like *The Sims* places participants above the action. The game is a vibrant and dynamic dollhouse where each choice matters, a world in miniature.[16] *Second Life* allows participants to dress up, play house, and build with blocks. While they may be perceived as infantile, these games allow us to practice building a life, a culture, a community.

Games are an ancient part of the human experience. Nabatean board games have been uncovered in Petra. The Chinese game Go began thousands of years ago and is still played with great enthusiasm in Japan and Korea. Greece's original Olympic Games are restaged as a massive global spectacle every four years. We are seemingly born to play. In his classic study, *Homo Ludens* (Man the Player), cultural theorist Johan Huizinga analyzes the play element of culture. He argues that it's not just a matter of how we play within our everyday settings, but to what degree play itself defines our culture and our humanity. Huizinga traces play back to animals. From household pets like puppies, we discover that animals require no special training or permission to play. It is innate. Huizinga sees play as a form of freedom, beyond ordinary life. But he finds elements of play in the legal system (with all the dressing up and speeches), in political campaigning (even more dressing up and speeches), and also in fields of war (albeit a serious and often deadly form of play). So what does *Homo Ludens* contribute to our understanding of video games? Plenty!

Writing in 1938, Huizinga described play as "a stepping out of 'real' life into a temporary sphere of activity with a disposition all of its own."[17] Nearly every video game attempts to create a sphere with a unique and magical disposition. He also identified how a play community forms: "The feeling of being 'apart together' in an exceptional situation, of sharing something important, of mutually withdrawing from the rest of the world and rejecting the usual norms, retains its magic beyond the duration of the individual game."[18] Surely this describes the clannish behavior associated with *World of Warcraft* or *Madden Nation*. Huizinga also identified the enduring appeal of hiding behind avatars, noting that "The 'differentness' and secrecy of play are most vividly expressed in 'dressing up.' Here the extra-ordinary nature of play reaches perfection. The disguised or masked individual 'plays' another part, another being. He *is* another being."[19] Did the creators of *Second Life* read Huizinga? Perhaps they, along with Huizinga, invited the desire to play that is planted in our hearts?

Why do we get so immersed in our games, whether via *Madden*'s virtual football or an extended session of *Half-Life*? Huizinga connected the dots between our play and our most sacred rituals. Both take place within the magic circles that we demarcate. For Huizinga, what happens within those circles is "actualization by representation." Whatever we perform or play within our rites takes on a mystical quality, elevating us to a higher plane. We become our virtual "Mii," whether participating in Wii boxing or *Super Mario Kart*. Our online challenges take on cosmic significance (which explains why we may toss a game controller when we lose). Huizinga suggests our sacred rituals are "played or performed within a playground that is literally 'staked out,' and played moreover as a feast, i.e. in mirth and freedom. A sacred space, a temporarily real world of its own, has been expressly hedged off for it. But with the end of the play its effect is not lost; rather it continues to shed its radiance on the ordinary world outside, a wholesome influence working security, order and prosperity for the whole community until the sacred play-season comes round again."[20] Is that why video games exert such a powerful pull? When we win a virtual contest online, the euphoric feelings of victory spill over into our everyday world. My son still beams at recollections of mastering *The Original Adventures of Lego Indiana Jones* on the Wii. It was a moment of father-son bonding, of shared accomplishment, a rite of passage for an excitable seven-year-old (and his dad).

Huizinga studies games as a religious ritual, an essential cultural phenomenon. But video games can be studied in myriad ways. For example, as the costs shifted from a quarter per play to $250 for a console, economists began to take notice. Interactive entertainment became a $50 billion global business, with consumers spending more on video games than movies or music each month.[21] Subscription-based games like *EverQuest* and *World of Warcraft* now generate huge monthly income, but they also have become intriguing laboratories for studying economic decision making and economies of scale. *Second Life* created its own currency, "Linden Dollars." Scholar Edward Castronova has noted that such virtual currencies are now trading on eBay's Category 1654 (Internet Games) at higher rates than the Japanese yen or the Korean won.[22] We cannot overlook the business of gaming in any discussion of why certain games rise above the avalanche of options.

So, a short list of methodologies for approaching games includes:

1. Economics—Games serve as a real-world business or virtual economy simulator.
2. Science—Complex math and engineering skills create computer games.
3. Art—Innovative design informs games' settings, costumes, and graphics.
4. Music—Game soundtracks have become an arena for new symphonies.
5. Education—Games can be a teaching tool for math, science, ethics, and so on.[23]
6. Sociology—Fans and clans/patches and mods embody participatory culture.
7. Gender and race—Games raise issues of empowerment and representation.[24]
8. Psychology—Game playing affects brain waves, moods, and so on.

To this growing list, we wish to add theology. We want to talk about God as experienced and revealed in, around, and through video games. What ancient theological conundrums may arise from the game design or the game playing experience? What terminology may have to shift to accommodate the new styles of thinking and learning that follow virtual technology? How is spirituality expressed by the gaming generation? How are the timeless teachings of Jesus seen and heard by those wired to a joystick?

SERIOUS GAME PLAYING

We had the experience, but missed the meaning.
T. S. Eliot

As a relatively recent phenomenon, the study of video games is still in its infancy. Popular Web sites like IGN, GameSpot, and 1UP offer previews and reviews. Magazines like *GamePro, Game Informer*, and *Edge* provide a graphic format that matches the games themselves. Blogs like Joystiq and Kotaku offer rumors of upcoming releases and fast-breaking news, while academic journals like *Game Studies* offer thoughtful analysis.

Game theorists offer competing approaches to this topic. Narratologists see games as the next stage of storytelling, tracing the continuity from campfires to theaters to video arcades. Scholars such as Henry Jenkins celebrate the convergence where new media (like video games) incorporate the styles of old media (like movies) by relying on cut scenes to advance the game story.[25] The history of video games (both the technologies and the personalities) is just starting to be written.[26] Forty years after *Space Invaders*, efforts are under way to develop a canon of classic video games.[27] The emerging consensus of gaming breakthroughs includes *Tetris* (1985), *SimCity* (1989), and *Doom* (1993).[28] As a live, online phenomenon, *World of Warcraft* introduced real-time strategy to video gaming in 1994. In 2007, the Library of Congress funded a project dedicated to preserving virtual worlds like *Second Life*.

Nintendo's *The Legend of Zelda: Ocarina of Time* (1998) demonstrated the sweeping narrative potential of games. *Edge* magazine rhapsodizes about Shigeru Miyamoto's creation: "The world of Ocarina is multifaceted, and like all great works is a magpie, grabbing plot details and visual cues from hugely varied influences: *The Sword in the Stone, Peter Pan, A Christmas Carol*, the Pied Piper and even something like Maurice Ravel's *Bolero*."[29] Breakthroughs like *Fallout 3* (2008) allow a player to witness (and even create) the entire history of a character. What special stats and skills that develop in childhood will prove essential in the postapocalyptic landscape of *Fallout 3*? Choices that players make affect the karma of the onscreen persona. All these massive technological and thematic innovations suggest we're living through a golden age of video games, where technology encourages more detailed and imaginative storytelling. Professor Janet Murray optimistically envisions *Hamlet on the Holodeck*.[30] Will Lara Croft someday be seen as a character with the complexity of Lady Macbeth? Or are we witnessing the demise of storytelling, from subtlety to pure sensation?

Ludologists (rooted in the Latin word for play, *ludus*) suggest that how a game is played matters more than whatever content or characters inhabit the screen. The pioneering play theory of Roger Caillois led to explorations of how the apparatus of games (the gameplay) may undermine attempts to tell an overarching story.[31] Early game theorists like mathematician John Nash (of *A Beautiful Mind* fame) focused upon game strategies to explain economics, politics, or even biology. To recent scholars like Jesper Juul, video games are an engineering problem, dependent upon mathematical algorithms and computer processors to resolve their narrative conflicts.[32] How a programmer structures a game may trump whatever story it allegedly serves. Ludologists wonder, "Are our brains now wired to run down certain video rabbit trails that may be divorced from serious reflection?" The finest Guitar Heroes may have memorized patterns rather than hearing the heart and soul of the music. Children clicking across Club Penguin may think they are earning points, but they are actually being taught how to shop by a self-contained Disney delivery system. For ludologists, the medium serves as a more important message than any narrative arc.

Denver Post game reviewer David Thomas notes how the structure of games includes theological assumptions. Players are usually dropped into a universe that operates under a firm set of rules. Those rules may be masked, like a puzzle to be solved, but Thomas suggests that that situation approximates our experience with God. We must learn how to navigate the mysterious side of life. Games are created by a programmer with a firm master plan, but we experience that plan as remarkable freedom. Thomas surmises, "If you believe there is theological structure with rules, purpose, and an ethical system, you're telling people there is a purpose."[33] We must consider how a game unfurls as an occasion for theological reflection.

Unfortunately, these competing schools of thought often overlook the pure pleasures that video games afford.[34] While the story and structure of games matter, surely the look, feel, and sound of games are each worthy of serious reflection and praise. Mario's bushy moustache accounts for some portion of his fame. The squeals of Toad and roar of Bowser are an essential part of *Super Mario Kart*'s popular embrace. Lara Croft's idealized body fueled teen boys' fantasies and feminists' valid rants. We must acknowledge the artistry inherent in lighting, costumes, and set design. The research and attention to detail poured into every frame of *Call of Duty* deepen the gaming experience. Engineer Hao Chen spent months working on the water-tech programming for *Halo 3*—"basically, making sure that any water appearing in the game hyper-realistically eddies, flows and creates turbulence around objects."[35] The same care goes into the score. Composer Koichi Sugiyama elevated game music when he recorded his *Dragon Quest/Symphonic Suite* with the London Philharmonic Orchestra in 1986. Nobuo Uematsu's soundtracks to *Final Fantasy* have been turned into orchestral concerts that have toured Tokyo, Los Angeles, and Stockholm.

Fine art museums have also started to recognize games as art. Hard-core gamers have adapted the graphic engines from video games to create computer animation called "machinima." Fans will sometimes overhaul a beloved older game, creating a mod (modified) version. *Half-Life* underwent a total conversion before reemerging as the even more popular *Counter-Strike*. Artist Riley Harmon connected a *Counter-Strike* Source server to a sculpture for a gallery installation titled "What it is without the hand that wields it."[36] When a character dies within the game, a physical approximation of blood streams across the gallery wall, creating a tangible encounter with game violence. The Barbican art gallery gathered 125 games across the history of interactive entertainment for the retrospective show "GAME ON." Since opening in 2002, the exhibition has toured from Finland to Israel, from Chicago to Hong Kong.[37] Video games are both art and craft. We must study their story, structure, and style.

HALOS AND AVATARS

Halos and Avatars examines both the medium and the message. We trace the history of gaming consoles and the significant change that Nintendo's Wii introduced. While images of couch potatoes haunt television viewers, virtual tennis players have replaced sedentary gamers. *Halos and Avatars* also wrestles with the stories themselves, from the ethical dilemmas inherent in *BioShock* to the high stakes of *Halo*. To the nascent field of game studies, we add the combustible element of theology. It may not be an easy fit. We resist the temptation to baptize gaming as inherently good or evil, attempting to bring nuance to an emerging phenomenon. But to parents and players, we suggest that divine fingerprints remain embedded in the experience. Our Creator comes alongside the game-making and game-playing process, taking us back to the original ethical choices. Will we set aside a sacred space in the center of our garden? Will we serve as our brother and sister's keeper? The civilizations we build will either be sustainable or destined for self-destruction. What ethical choices will we make? What games are we playing with—or as—God?

Our first chapters explore the tensions between the games' story and technique. Aspiring game designers must match form and function. As a filmmaker, Chris Hansen is intensely interested in how video games are affecting cinematic storytelling. In chapter 1, he traces the similarities and differences between movies and games, from *Tekken* to *Kill Bill*. Why have so many exhilarating games like *Doom* been turned into lousy movies? Maybe games are not as adaptable to the movies as Hollywood would like. They're still developing that essential part of riveting drama: character. In chapter 2, Mark Hayse celebrates *Ultima IV* and the work of game designer Richard Garriott. As an educator, Hayse is interested in the process of learning and the structure of games. How does the form of *Ultima IV* correspond to the process of religious discipleship? And what can educators and ministers learn from the systems that Garriott creates?

In chapter 3, Rachel Wagner suggests that Christian resistance to video games may reside in the form itself. Does the interactive nature of gaming conflict with the notion of a closed canon of Scripture? Perhaps Christians don't want to be placed in the position of manipulating Jesus. We will follow Jesus anywhere but the arcade.

In chapter 4, Heidi Campbell traces how some Muslims have embraced interactive entertainment. Having been reduced to the role of villain in countless first-person shooter games, Muslim game designers have seized the opportunity to counterprogram. Can positive portrayals of a faith be transmitted through game and character design?

Kutter Callaway concludes the first portion of the book with the history of gaming consoles. To this end, chapter 5 considers the rise of the Wii as a theological desire. A more embodied game may correspond to the longing for a more embodied faith. What kind of games might we play in our sacred spaces?

The Halos section of the book deals with how games are made and how games are played, offering firsthand accounts of particular games and genres. How do we master a game? If we cannot beat the computer, how does the game master us? We discover what creative questions drive game designers, and also what drives the most dedicated gamers to keep playing. For chapter 6, Lisa Swain interviews two significant pioneers in interactive entertainment: Rand Miller, who with his brother, Robyn, created the groundbreaking games *Myst* and *Riven*; and Marty O'Donnell, who composed the evocative score for the *Halo* trilogy. Miller and O'Donnell discuss the origins of their best-selling series, connecting their faith and their art in surprising ways. Creating such vibrant virtual worlds gives them particular insight into the theological tension between predestination and free will.

Matthew Kitchen draws upon his experience working at ESPN to discuss the enduring popularity of the *Madden NFL* series. In chapter 7, Kitchen explores our competitive nature. Do video games allow us to process those desires in a healthy manner, or do they fuel our insatiable hunger for victory? Kitchen suggests that with the rise of Major League Gaming, competitive gaming has barely begun. As gaming becomes a job, players may lose the joy of playing. What does a robust theology of play include?

As a professional musician, Andrew McAlpine is both intrigued and repelled by the growth of *Guitar Hero*. Chapter 8 wrestles with the nature of art and music making. As art simulators, *Rock Band* and *Guitar Hero* may give participants a false sense of accomplishment. Will more creative music arise from a generation raised on classic rock riffs, or will future musicians be content to ape those who've gone before?

Psychologist Kevin Newgren concludes section 2 with an appreciation of *BioShock*. The ethical conundrums introduced in its underwater city of Rapture provide ample fuel for discussion. So why do Christian games like *Left Behind* often place less faith in their audience? In the face of ongoing debates about stem cell research, Newgren explores the complexity and critique embedded into the core of *BioShock*.

The final section of *Halos and Avatars* focuses upon the role playing and virtual selves inherent in interactive entertainment. James Cameron's blockbuster film *Avatar* put the concept into popular parlance. "Avatar" has roots in Hinduism and is associated with the descents of the Supreme God, Vishnu. It is often translated in English as "incarnation," inviting interesting parallels to the Christian notion of Jesus' bodily incarnation. Are we taking on divine characteristics when we descend into a game? (Or are we at least understanding what it feels like to "condescend" to another plane?) This section builds upon the groundbreaking work of scholars such as Sherry Turkle, who asked, "Are we living life *on* the screen or life *in* the screen?" She pointed out how we've learned to take things at *interface* value. So what are the implications for people of faith? How much of ourselves are projected into each new Mii we create for the Wii? We consider how pastors might talk about conversion to gamers who've been born again and again and again.

In chapter 10, Jason Shim recounts his initiation into *Second Life*, taking us inside a virtual wedding. It raises interesting questions of the arrangements, the ceremony, and the officiant. And what kind of participation is required of guests? As the happy couple type, "I do," the real complications begin. In chapter 11, Dan Hodge interviews dedicated gamers, studying the many roles they play. Rather than being isolated individuals, as the media stereotype portrays, many gamers view their activities as inherently communal and even spiritual. Hodge suggests that violent games raise issues of eschatology. They allow gamers to escape the travails of today and envision a victorious future. Doesn't religion offer a similar hope of rising above our circumstances? One problem: what happens when life gets more complicated than a game (or a Bible promise)? Hodge challenges dedicated gamers and committed believers to embrace the mystery and ambiguity that accompany the God-given gift of life.

For our final chapter, John Morehead considers the implications of virtual and projected selves. Drawing upon sociology and theology, Morehead wonders if our humanity might be getting lost on the holodeck. However, he finds that the cybersociality inherent in online gaming exceeds potential worries. We are becoming more human even in our virtual worlds. Morehead challenges us to develop more thorough theologies of play, fantasy, and community.

Finally, we offer an appendix for parents and youth leaders who are wondering how to think about interactive entertainment. From their work with Fuller Seminary's Youth Institute (FYI), Kara Powell and Brad M. Griffin offer practical ways for families to both talk and play. They bring communication theory into the kinds of conflicts that are playing out in countless living rooms. We are grateful for the interviews conducted by Noah Lau Branson, a high school senior who talked to other students about their gaming practices. Their quotations are distributed throughout the book, allowing gamers to speak for themselves.

I am so grateful for these brilliant partners on this collaborative endeavor. Their collective wisdom exceeds their relative youth. Almost five years ago, Kevin Newgren asked why my book *A Matrix of Meanings: Finding God in Pop Culture* didn't discuss video games.[38] His question undoubtedly started this process. My codirector of the Reel Spirituality Institute, Rob Johnston, enthusiastically encouraged this far-flung research. My colleagues at Fuller Seminary's Brehm Center provided the generous infrastructure to gather these bright voices. My editor at Westminster John Knox, Jana Riess, brought a keen eye and sharp insights to this multifaceted manuscript. I am indebted to Rand Miller and Marty O'Donnell for taking time out of their hectic game production schedules for an engaging interview. My wonderful wife, Caroline, endured my many late nights of reading, writing, and editing. She remains my greatest friend, ally, and partner. Finally, my energetic children, Zoe and Theo, were willing to serve as delightful case studies. They dove into the world of Wii whenever I needed to put another theory to the test. May they always play with such infectious enthusiasm.

The field of game studies is so open and the games themselves are still developing, so it is tough to draw conclusions from such a moving target. But we are taking at least a screenshot of interactive entertainment circa 2010. With the arrival of James Cameron's all-digital *Avatar*, more people have begun wondering how to navigate virtual worlds and video games. With so many projections of ourselves on so many screens, getting scared or confused is easy. But those searching for a cautionary tale will be disappointed by this book.

We are concerned by the desensitizing aspects of video games. They often objectify women and glorify violence. Yet the rise of game culture coincided with a striking decline in teen violence and teen pregnancies. By many measurements, the gamer generation is the best behaved cohort in fifty years. We're intrigued by this counterintuitive phenomenon.

Halos and Avatars aims to demystify the gaming universe and dignify the passions of the most active gamers. We believe in the theological possibilities contained within even the most debased pop culture.[39] Jesus dared to descend into our everyday situations and struggles. He seems like the type of person who would come alongside a group of gamers, grab a controller, and join the fun. While we may rightly question whether games can become addictive or depressing, *Halos and Avatars* chooses to focus on the divine footprints found in virtual worlds. When we play games, we return to life as it was intended—full of joy, wonder, imagination, and freedom. So grab your joystick and find the chapters that click with you.

SECTION 1

Playing Games with God

1

From *Tekken* to *Kill Bill*

The Future of Narrative Storytelling?

CHRIS HANSEN

In *The Nines*, a 2007 independent film written and directed by John August, a seemingly normal man (played by Ryan Reynolds) learns that he is actually a godlike being who has created the world in which he now resides as a sort of living video game. August has said that he "had a bit of a *World of Warcraft* problem," which was clearly his inspiration for the film. His protagonist is the ultimate game designer, creating a completely functioning world to be used as his plaything—*World of Warcraft* writ large(r). Characters can do anything they want to do and can be anyone they choose to be. But the all-powerful designer of the game—who can end it with a thought—is also subject to the rules of the game. He must live out the destiny set out for him as a character within it.

This godlike control over the narrative defines the attraction of gaming for many people. And while true control comes from designing such a world, even the protagonist of *The Nines* chooses to shed his godlike powers and his memory to enter the game in order to play it. Evidently, designing isn't nearly as satisfying as becoming a player—an interactive character within the game. It's God as the ultimate beta tester (or has that been done already?).

So why are video games so important to people? How does a filmmaker like John August get addicted to what gamers refer to as "World of War-crack"? He admits it sucked up "most of my waking hours" for "a period of about four months."[1] Having written major Hollywood films like *Big Fish* (2003) and *Charlie and the Chocolate Factory* (2005), August chose to make his directorial debut in a film in which the whole world is a video game. If games replace films as our preferred stories, how will they alter our understanding of narrative arcs, character development, and our own sense of calling?

The cultural impact of games continues to rise. According to a 2003 study by the Pew Internet and American Life Project, 70 percent of college students reported playing video games (from console-based games to computer and online games) at least once in while, and 65 percent reported being regular or occasional game players.[2] By 2008, the Pew study revealed that "fully 97% of teens age 12–17 play computer, web, portable, or console games."[3] More and more people are immersing themselves in imaginary worlds for longer periods of time. Reports of diminishing box office attendance for the film industry are juxtaposed with a burgeoning video gaming industry; game sales alone rose to $1.33 billion in February 2008. So what is it about video games that draws in so many for repeated game play?[4]

Many (if not most) video games draw heavily on story. Like movies, some have more developed stories than others. *Tekken* or its many derivatives might be likened to a mindless action film in that the story doesn't matter as long as the action holds people in thrall. Many role-playing games might be said to have a better story than a fighting game or a first-person shooter game, but nearly every nonsports game possesses some semblance of story, however thin the plot might be. Games don't sell without a story hook, which also explains why games with movie tie-ins are such an easy sell. If a movie does well at the box office, the video game company can move a lot of copies of a game with the same characters, even if the action of the game has little to do with the original movie. For example, classic films like *The Godfather* (1972) and *Scarface* (1983) have been reimagined as popular video games. Some movies, like *Kill Bill* (2003 and 2004), appear as if they were designed as previews for a game (and might even be more interesting in that format!).

NARRATOLOGY VS. LUDOLOGY

Video games have developed their own rules and conventions. Clues and passwords to advance the game are not offered until a player has demonstrated a level of mastery. Some scholars argue that the structure of the game (how it is played) is more important than the story being told. Ludologists like Dr. Janet Murray insist "that games, unlike other cultural objects, should be interpreted only as members of their own class, and only in terms of their defining abstract formal qualities."[5] In other words, ludologists are more interested in the rules and structure of a game than the narrative or story elements. Examining a game from the ludologist's perspective, your interest would be less on the story events and more on the abstract rules of the game and how those rules compare and contrast with other game-playing experiences. In contrast, narratologists reject the notion that *how* the game is played supersedes *what*

Best Movie-to-Video Game Adaptations

What makes a great licensed game? A great licensed game needs to be fun to play as well as a faithful representation of the movie/television/comic universe it utilizes. This list is tough to build because determining whether a game is empirically a better game than another, or whether it's just a better representation of that movie as a game, is a difficult task. To that end, I've attempted to present the games that are empirically the best (sound, game play, graphics, etc.) that are also based on movies.

1. *GoldenEye 007* (N64)—Considered by many to be the greatest game for the Nintendo 64, this game also tends to top the list of best movie games. Great four-player game play enables people to enjoy the game in large groups, making it a must-have. The Rumble Pak support left me "Shaken, not Stirred."

2. *Chronicles of Riddick: Escape from Butcher Bay* (PC/Xbox)—This one surprised a lot of people. The movies weren't exactly cinematic masterpieces, but the game turned out to be nonstop action. A combination of highly tense stealth and white-knuckle action makes this game a strong recommendation.

3. *Blade Runner* (PC)—This game is a near-perfect trip into Ridley Scott and Philip K. Dick's masterpiece. With a gripping story and technology that was ahead of its time, this title is considered by many to be one of the greatest adventure games of all time.

4. *Tron 2.0* (PC)—Whether you're an obsessive fan of the movie or not, this game rocks. Monolith blew us away with a truly polished first-person shooter, with excellent characters, fantastic music, breathtaking environments, and a truly immersive experience.

5. *Aladdin* (SNES/GEN)—In the early 1990s, almost every movie video game was garbage; in fact, the genre had become a joke. *Aladdin* marked the first real movie game that was a blast to play.

Runner-Up: *The Matrix: Path of Neo*
—*Jonathan Sears is a Master of Divinity student at Fuller Theological Seminary and the cofounder of HSL Editorial, a boutique film and television post-production company.*

the characters within the game may be saying or doing. This chapter sides with the narratologists in citing the important similarities between games and films. While I can appreciate the formal aspects of game design, for the average user, the story still reigns supreme.

As watching movies on portable devices transforms cinema from a communal experience to a solitary one, video games are becoming the social story-based entertainment of choice—and they are social. The 2008 Pew study found that while 82 percent of teens play games alone, "76% of teen gamers play games with other people in some way, either online or in person," and that "nearly two-thirds (65%) of teens say they play games with other people who are in the same room with them." Perhaps more significantly, "Of teens who play games in more than one way (with others online, in person, or alone), equal numbers say they play most often with others in the same room and by themselves."[6] Games are apparently often more communal than movies.

The *New York Times* reported that some theaters in Europe have converted at least one screen to a video gaming cinema experience. Avid gamers can compete against each other in a modified screening room, complete with multiple video game screens—or simply watch others do so while enjoying a tub of hot buttered popcorn. The large movie screen serves as a backdrop, showing game footage and scores from gamers in the room. According to the commercial director for Electronic Arts in Spain, "Now you can play with your friends or your 'clan.'"[7] Over the past decade, games have begun to challenge the centrality of movies to the popular culture, even threatening to replace them. The Pew studies suggest that gaming is to today's teens what movies were to the previous generation (or two): social activities based around a shared narrative experience.

CONNECTIONS BETWEEN GAMES AND FILMS

If games have dethroned movies, it is due in part to the willingness of game designers to adopt cinematic narrative strategies and styles. As a filmmaker and professor, I am keenly aware of—and have studied and taught my students about—the methods we use to draw in the audience. Video games do many of the same things, but with the added bonus of interactivity. If you're watching a movie about, for example, adventuresome scientists fighting genetically engineered dinosaurs on a remote island, you can have a thoroughly enjoyable experience (assuming you've placed yourself in the hands of a skilled filmmaker). However, if you're playing a game about the same close encounters with dinosaurs, you have the added benefit of being able to determine the outcome, based at least in part on your own skill level. And you can probably choose to play as one of a number of characters, any one of whom might accurately reflect your personality or differ so much from you that the experience can be freeing. You are creating, managing, and even dominating your own Jurassic Park.

What are the distinguishing characteristics of classical Hollywood cinema? I teach my filmmaking students to engage their potential audiences with a number of tactics:

1. *Make sure there is conflict.* Aristotle understood that conflict is the essence of drama. As I tell my students, if you don't have conflict in every scene of your film, you have a situation, but you don't really have a story.

People carry out their lives with conflict every day—on the job, at home, in school. We often see our lives as little dramas, with each of us starring as the central character in our own personal narrative, what Neal Gabler playfully described as "lifies."[8]

Films and games both depend upon interesting, high-stakes conflict. Otherwise, the audience simply ignores the fictions and pays attention to the problems of their own lives. Also, one must present conflict that rises as the stakes get higher. James Bond has to deal with myriad henchmen before facing the mastermind behind the plot, and the scientists in *Jurassic Park* (1993) have to deal with various dinosaur-related challenges before facing the insidious velociraptors. In much the same way, gamers work through increasingly difficult challenges in game play. They defeat minor threats before facing a "big boss" like Psycho Mantis from *Metal Gear Solid* or Ganon from *The Legend of Zelda: Ocarina of Time*. Gamers' success involves building upon progressive knowledge. They use skills learned by defeating the lesser villains to assist them in the battle against the more powerful enemies (not unlike a movie character learning the weaknesses of a nemesis in order to defeat him or her).

2. *Write a story with a unique hook.* One of the appealing aspects of any entertainment experience is novelty: providing audiences something unexpected. Hollywood has made an industry out of slight changes to proven formulae. Although summer blockbusters have been reduced to a series of sequels, new franchises like *The Matrix* (1999) invariably break through via audience interest. A unique hook for a film brings in new audiences. The same thing happens with games. Dedicated gamers want something original and different with a new game, and are even less satisfied than movie audiences with the same old game play repackaged with new settings or characters.

One might argue that sports games and the incredibly popular *Guitar Hero* series are not story-oriented at all. But these games are created and marketed in a way that is no different from other more obviously story-filled games. In most sports games, the player takes on the role of a member of a specific team (or the entire team). Interest is generated through a backstory for the characters and teams involved, whether they are actual professional or collegiate teams or simply products of the game creators' imaginations. Even *Guitar Hero* has a story: You become a character like Axel Steel, choose his clothing and guitar, and enter into competition to become the titular "guitar hero." You accrue dollars after successful gigs, unlocking new venues and the possibility of better gear. This narrative is, admittedly, a little thin, but so is the narrative in some engaging action movies.

3. *Provide the potential for visual interest.* People go to the movies for spectacle, but visual interest also includes other ways of seeing. That might be the dark and rainy streets of a good film noir or expansive western vistas. The New York of a Woody Allen comedy differs from the New York of a Martin Scorsese gangster picture. Pixar takes us to colorful, animated worlds whether under the sea in *Finding Nemo* or in the sky with *Up*. Video games not only provide the same opportunities for visual delight, but they actually extend the possibilities because the entire world of a game is a digital creation. Unlike film, there is no possibility of using practical, preexisting locations. Gamers expect a visually rich, digital experience. Players look forward to deep exploration of the worlds within pioneering titles like *Myst* or the fantastic realms of *God of War*. In vivid experiences like *World of Warcraft*, the setting isn't simply a background for a game but a place to get lost during game play. Participants engage the game on a visceral and visual level, in ways that are less goal oriented and more exploratory in nature.

Games increasingly adopt cinematic aesthetics and camera movement in their game play. They often use a subjective point of view, a necessity when the gamer controls a character who must navigate through the game. Movies more commonly use a neutral point of view, and only rarely employ a completely subjective first-person point of view (except for moments when the audience is placed in the role of the stalker/villain/monster). Films are about individuals learning to situate themselves within the context of a larger world. The visual style usually echoes this concern by situating the character, visually, in the midst of an active mise-en-scène. The audience sees the character as he or she interacts with other characters and with the environment. In contrast, games often represent the opposite point of view (P.O.V.), with a story and visual focus on an individual's dominance over the world that he or she inhabits. We see the world quite literally through the eyes of the game character, through his or her point of view, able to see and hear only what the character sees and hears.

4. *Create an interesting but relatable main character to guide the action.* After a century of storytelling, movies have nearly perfected this process of building a rooting interest for the protagonist. Lead characters in popular movies often resemble audience members in key ways. They share demographics and typical life choices, although they're usually quite a bit more attractive (even when trying to hide behind glasses or frumpy hairstyles). Other heroes serve as fantasy figures, presenting an idealized version of life: what the audience members want or already imagine themselves to be. In either case, the audience identifies with and follows the heroes as they undergo the challenges that the narrative presents.

Audience identification may be even more important in video gaming. The gamer isn't simply an audience member watching an unfolding story, but is actively engaged in making that story happen through choices and skillful play. One might argue that the lead characters of video games are decidedly unlike the game players, but I contend that they often represent wish-fulfillment identities, whether as a criminal doing unthinkable things in the *Grand Theft Auto* games or as a super-soldier in the *Halo* series. Note, too, that Master Chief in the *Halo* games doesn't have identifiable facial features because of his uniform, making it easier for any game player to see him- or herself as the face behind his helmet.

Game creators can glean another character tip from film storytelling: in addition to making the lead relatable, they also need to *make that character psychologically defined*. David Bordwell identifies the psychologically defined character in classical Hollywood cinema as "a discriminated individual endowed with a consistent batch of evident traits, qualities, and behaviors" who is "the principal causal agent" of the narrative.[9] In other words, the main character's every trait arises for a reason from his or her psychologically defined personality. Such characteristics become either benefits to be used to the character's advantage or weaknesses to be overcome on the road to success. In *Signs* (2002), Rev. Graham Hess (played by Mel Gibson) struggles to understand why his wife died tragically. The film raises ancient questions of theodicy, asking how a just God can prevail over such a seemingly random universe. Why do bad things happen to good people? In the end, Graham learns that events and character traits are clearly part of a larger plan; in this case, he and his family are able to use all of their clearly defined traits to survive an alien attack. Whether it's his brother's massive baseball swing, his daughter's predilection for leaving half-filled glasses of water on every available surface, or his son's asthma, everything has a purpose and each trait plays a significant role in the resolution of the plot. That baseball swing (and the bat mounted on the wall in celebration of some past baseball glory) is perfect for bashing in an alien's head; the glasses of water make for convenient weapons when it is learned that the aliens are averse to the liquid; and even the asthma is a positive, as the asthma attack prevents the alien's poison from entering the son's lungs, thus sparing his life. Everything happens for a reason, and it becomes clear that filmmaker M. Night Shyamalan's entire plot has been building toward a foreordained conclusion—precisely because this is a well-planned movie that is designed to tie up loose ends and show how every story element has a purpose in the larger narrative.

Video games use the same storytelling tropes for characters. They are equipped precisely with the tools, knowledge, and skills needed to complete the game—or at least those tools are provided within the game in order to be found. These essential skills will be learned and the knowledge will be acquired. Of course, some of these skills and often much of the character's background and the initial plot information are provided beforehand via a game's instruction manual, not unlike the communicative work performed by a film's trailer, which provides a basic story line to viewers so that they know what the film is about before they even enter the theater.

5. *Follow rules of cause and effect.* In *Narration in the Fiction Film*, Bordwell says that "causality is the prime unifying principle" in classical Hollywood cinema, adding that all other elements of storytelling are "subordinated to the movement of cause and effect."[10] In other words, a character acts, and that action causes a reaction. Movies are built around this concept; the protagonist's every action has consequences, and the accumulation of effects leads him or her to the resolution of the plot through action. Coincidence is shunned in narrative storytelling, because it is an effect without a cause, an entirely unsatisfying way to conclude a narrative. Without the human element of causation, the conclusion becomes a contrived deus ex machina, and this uncaused effect defies our ability to see our destinies as being determined by our own actions.

Video games employ the same causal structure. The relationship between the actions of the protagonist in a game and the consequences of those actions displays an even stronger example of causality because the game simply doesn't progress until the video gamer—playing as the protagonist—does something. Without that action, there is no effect, and thus no game.

6. *Make use of a linear progression of events to tell the story.* Movie stories unfold, with some exceptions, in a linear fashion. Hollywood films play out using cause and effect in a linear fashion; *this* action causes *this* consequence, and we see the results play out in order. Of course, some films make use of flashback, puzzle-box, or nonlinear storytelling, but these tend to be art films, or at least films with ambitions toward that sort of artistry.

Few games allow a player to roam and meander without pursuing the game's objectives. (The *Elder Scrolls* series would be a notable exception.) Unlike film, video games struggle to tell a story in a convincingly nonlinear fashion. Gamers can only make sense of their roles in a game if they understand what happens directly after their actions. In this way, linearity is coupled with cause and effect. A gamer has to see the results of his or her action immediately after taking such an action in order to comprehend what he or she must do to complete the game and arrive at a satisfactory resolution to the game's conflict or dilemma. Agency is essential to game play.

CONTRASTS BETWEEN GAMES AND FILMS

How do games and film differ? Why do classic games like *Final Fantasy* or *Resident Evil* often make forgettable movies? And why have amazing movies often been reduced to lamentable gaming tie-ins? The string of failures prompts regrets and laments within both industries. James Newman and Iain Simons have this take on the matter:

> The world of licensed-product games remains an area of deep suspicion for the gaming audience. The franchise tie-in has given games a few true gems (*Star Wars*, *Spider-Man 2*) but a vastly larger number of poor cash-ins (*E.T.*, *Superman 64*). This has always been the area where the videogames establishment becomes most insecure, most

---

Worst Movie-to-Video-Game Adaptations

It's tough to say that these are the worst movie-to-game adaptations of all time because there are literally hundreds, if not over a thousand, movie-based games. Fellow gamers have their own strong opinions about what's actually the worst. I've included some of the most commonly referenced ones, as well as a few that I can't stand.

1. *E.T. the Extra-Terrestrial* (Atari 2600)—According to Wikipedia, "Many copies of the game were returned to stores, which led to the Atari video game burial, in which Atari dumped truckloads of *E.T.* cartridges into a landfill in New Mexico after they failed to sell."* That should speak for itself.

2. *Street Fighter The Movie: The Game* (PSX/SATURN)—I've never understood this release. Why make an absolutely wretched movie of a fantastic series of games, and then adapt a game based on that *terrible* movie? Fail.

3. *Ghostbusters* (NES)—I'm an avid *Ghostbusters* fan. I've seen the movies tons of times, and I even liked the second movie. But playing this left me hoping I could trap the game and keep it in the Ecto Containment Unit.

4. *Back to the Future* (NES)—The only things that connect this pointless game to *Back to the Future* are the title screen and the fading picture in the HUD (Heads-Up Display). Great Scott, someone find me a DeLorean and a Flux Capacitor, and we can save the world from this disaster.

5. *Superman* (N64)—How do you ruin a *Superman* game? Turn it into a flight simulator with bad controls, bad story, bad everything. Even Lex Luthor would consider playing this game a cruel and unusual punishment.

Runner-up: Almost every other movie game.

—*Jonathan Sears*

*http://en.wikipedia.org/wiki/Atari_video_game_burial

unsure—almost apologetic about what it is. Strangely whenever the games world moves in proximity to Hollywood, it transforms into a fawning ingénue of its former self. Movies appear to represent everything that games wish they were, the ultimate aspirations of the industry being often cited as "interactive cinema."[11]

What can be learned from so many embarrassments? Perhaps the surface pleasures of gaming can only reduce the complexities of film. Do games offer filmmakers too little dramatic material with which to work?

Consider the cinematic version of the revered game *Doom*. The *Doom* game brings multiple players directly into the action. It is a first-person shooter game, where the player's point of view is situated behind the barrel of a weapon. Players kill all manner of villains and creatures; the entire object of the game is to destroy all comers. What it lacks in complexity it makes up for with sheer, visceral interactivity. *Doom* exploits horror filmmakers' favorite tricks: shadows and sound. Newman and Simon suggest, "The game thrusts the player into disorienting darkness at key stages, forcing them to begin to orientate themselves by dim door signs and to identify the location of the enemies purely through the stereo depiction of their grunts."[12] What could be more cinematic?

But translate this concept into a movie, and you have a story about the Rock killing villainous creatures. It becomes an episodic snore rather than a dynamic, first-person test of grit and wit. In *Doom* (the movie), director Andrzej Bartkowiak tries to re-create the game experience by framing a large portion of the movie from the perspective of one standing behind the gun. Reviewing the *Doom* movie, film critic Roger Ebert notes, "There is a lengthy point-of-view shot looking forward over the barrel of a large weapon as it tracks the corridors of the research station. Monsters jump out from behind things and are blasted to death in a sequence that abandons all attempts at character and dialogue and uncannily resembles a video game." It is, in essence, the first first-person-shooter movie. Ebert explains one of the chief problems with this strategy of storytelling: "I know how it feels not to play [the game], because I've seen the movie. 'Doom' is like some kid came over and is using your computer and won't let you play."[13] In essence, the movie version preserves the very limiting narrative simplicity of the game but removes (by necessity) the interactivity that makes it worth experiencing in the first place. The film didn't even bother to respect the original (and preferable) story line from the game.

While screenplays often start with character studies of psychological depth, games seem to add history as more of an afterthought. Games' primary strengths are spectacle: dropping characters into extreme situations with little advance warning or narrative through-line needed. Visual scholar Andrew Darley connects video games to the early days of silent film, suggesting that digital effects have revived the "spectacular" appeal of the movies. He writes, "As the corpus of films attached to this rejuvenation of special effects has developed and expanded—from *Star Wars* to the likes of *True Lies* and *Titanic*—so has the narrative element of such films receded in favor of the stimulation, impact and astonishment that can be produced by new and revamped techniques of image-capture and fabrication."[14] Perhaps the gaming experience has conditioned filmgoers to demand more bangs (and less depth). Darley considers, "The pleasures of reception in visual digital culture are direct, sensual, and quasi-ritualistic, considerably removed from the interpretative dimension of meaning and significance."[15] We get the bigger, louder, and faster movies we want. Large-scale action films with big budgets but little in the way of depth—such as *Spider-Man 3* (2007), *Indiana Jones and the Kingdom of the Crystal Skull* (2008), and *Transformers: Revenge of the Fallen* (2009)—continue to do well at the box office in spite of critical panning because they offer spectacle, and that's why many people go to the movies.

Note how the structure of video games has influenced the cinematic storytelling style of Quentin Tarantino. His earlier films, like *Reservoir Dogs* (1992) and *Pulp Fiction* (1994), were violent tales rooted in character, and *Jackie Brown* (1997) focused upon the eponymous stewardess trying to overcome her vexing circumstances. But Tarantino's two-part epic *Kill Bill* (2003 and 2004) is highly episodic, driven only by the next kill. It resembles the arcade game *Tekken*, or its countless rip-offs with better-known characters like Godzilla or the Marvel comic heroes. One character matches up against another, defeats him or her, and then takes on the next, slightly more powerful or dangerous fighter. *Kill Bill* could be likened to games like *Metroid Prime* or old four-armed Goro in *Mortal Kombat*. The gamer must defeat a variety of unskilled henchmen on increasingly difficult game levels, all leading up to a confrontation with a "boss" character, who is the hardest to kill. The flashbacks that reveal elements of the history of the main character in the movie are like the cinematic interludes in many games, which many seasoned gamers skip so we can get back to kicking and punching. *Kill Bill* is at its most dynamic in the extensively choreographed fight sequences. Interest drops when it attempts to explore the various characters and the motivations for their violence. The threadbare plot and surrounding narrative serve only as vehicles to serve up yet another stylized fight sequence with opponents of increasing skill.

Does *Kill Bill* represent the future of cinema? Tarantino's *Inglourious Basterds* (2009) borrows heavily from the Nazi hunting in the *Wolfenstein* video games. *Kill Bill* and its game antecedents both depict a singular heroine (like the Bride) who must face a series of unique antagonists (the Deadly Viper Assassination Squad) in increasingly exotic settings (from a suburban Pasadena home to the temple of Pei Mei). She must defeat those villains using increasingly complex weapons and martial arts (like the Five-Point Palm Exploding Heart Technique). But each sequence is a discrete, closed piece of the narrative—a separate chapter. Once an exotic villain (Vernita Green, O-Ren Ishii, Elle Driver) is dispatched through violent confrontation, the protagonist (Beatrix Kiddo) may move on the next one, with no implications from the last. There is almost no complexity and no rising conflict, aside from the ultimate villain (Bill) who awaits. Perhaps because of this, cleaving the narrative in half to make two films out of it presented little difficulty. It was simply a matter of finding the end of one of the confrontations and then adding a little bit of voice-over at the start of "Part 2" to refresh the audience's memory.

But simplicity of storytelling is not necessarily a vice, and narrative complexity is no guaranteed virtue. Video games might be seen as inferior as stories not simply because of a lack of complexity (after all, some good stories are very simple ones) but rather because of a lack of a *possibility* of complexity. It's not like anyone is about to make a video game out of Charlie Kaufman's fractured *Synecdoche, New York* (2008). Video games seem to function best if they have a rather uncomplicated narrative; they stick to the surface. What makes a film like *Synecdoche, New York* so interesting—the lack of clarity in the main character's life, and its lack of a clear objective or goal that he can pursue—is exactly what would make it a dreadful game. How can a gamer play a game in which there is no clear objective?

Movies generally unfold in such a way that the end, while occasionally surprising, seems inevitable, almost fated. Movies present us with the single possible solution to a problem, usually determined by the ingenuity of the main character. But the video gamer, in contrast, does not always possess the ingenuity of a movie's main character. After all, he or she hasn't had the benefit of a highly paid screenwriter to provide that ingenuity. In other words, by adding interactivity to this storytelling mix, and by putting video gamers at the center of the narrative as the protagonists and chief causal actors, video games don't present us with a single path to the resolution of a story, but rather a meandering series of choices and possibilities. The solution to a game *might* be the same when experienced on different occasions, but the choices made by different gamers to get to that conclusion (or even the choices made by the same gamer upon replaying the game) almost never will be. The ability to change the experience through different choices makes video gaming attractive. The more variety and complexity in the narrative, the more likely the game will be a hit.

Yet movies remain the same every time we watch them. While we might look for subtle nuances that we've never noticed before (and the best films invite such reconsideration), we will never expect the narrative itself to change, except by our own interpretation of the characters' choices. Films become predictable, but games seem to present a world of possibilities.

THEOLOGICAL IMPLICATIONS

How might the structures of films and video games influence—or be influenced by—belief systems? The Bible is, at its core, a story about humanity and its relationship with God (or God's relationship to humanity). But our take on storytelling impacts our reading of Scripture. If we approach a story from the classic view represented by cinema, we will view the gospel story through that lens, as a tale of destiny, with one main character who is like us but also an idealized version of us, whose actions drive the plot, and whose choices are destined to bring the linear story to a single possible resolution. Jesus becomes the central hero, enduring suffering, taking on religious authorities, leading a band of outsiders. The cinematic view of storytelling affects our understanding of the story told to us through the Bible.

But what if we view the biblical story via video game narratives? Two possibilities come to mind. First, if gamers' view of storytelling involves multiple paths to the same conclusion, then their view of biblical truth might be seriously altered. We already see a move toward religious pluralism, or the belief that, ultimately, all roads lead to God. Religion becomes just an individual's personal choice of how to get there. Video gaming's multiple-path narrative style matches a pluralistic impulse. If we relate to the world through our stories, and our stories show us that we can play the game a different way every time *and still come to the same resolution*, then will the generation that experiences storytelling through this lens eventually come to accept that as reality? Allow me to suggest a more positive outcome. Video games may push us toward religious pluralism or relativism, but people raised on video games might not lose their belief in the singular truth of the Bible. They may simply develop a more tolerant view of the different paths people take that lead them to that truth.

Christians profess to believe in the statement, often attributed to Augustine, but whose actual source is unknown, "In essentials, unity; in non-essentials, liberty." Video games might push the next generation toward a fuller understanding of that concept. Understanding the world through a multitracked storytelling lens does not necessarily have to lead to pluralism, but it might lead to more tolerance among Christians for differences in the paths that other Christians take. In a culture where Christianity has been commonly associated with the religious Right, Sunday church attendance, and living comfortably in the suburbs, a little tolerance for different ways to follow Jesus might prove beneficial. If video gamers are able to see social-justice oriented Christianity as a viable interpretation and application of the gospel story, is that a bad thing? Could we look at other Christians and think, "*Well, those aren't the choices I'm going to make, but we believe in the same God and are trying to achieve the same ends.*" The narrative peculiarities of video games might initiate newfound respect for others.

After all, it's not as if there aren't opposing and clashing styles within the Bible itself. Take, for example, the book of Proverbs, with its cut-and-dried view of cause and effect and the right way to live, versus the more uncertain tone of Ecclesiastes. That book refutes the simple wisdom of Proverbs by saying, essentially, that earthly life can prove ephemeral, whether we are wise or foolish, since the lives of both the wise and the foolish will ultimately end in death.

Beyond these two books, the Bible, through its authorship at the hands of many people (guided by God), embraces multiple styles, from traditional narrative, to poetry, proverbs, letters, songs, and philosophizing. It would seem that God realized long ago that humans experience stories in many ways and provided for that by crafting the Bible in such a way that many different storytelling styles and genres are represented. By implication, this would seem to indicate that multiple storytelling styles might be useful for us in understanding our world.

And what are we to make of the oft-reported decline in mainline denominations? The National Council of Churches reported, on its Web site and in its *2009 Yearbook of American and Canadian Churches*, that the two largest Christian communities, the Roman Catholic Church and the Southern Baptist Convention, "join virtually every mainline church in reporting a membership decline." Though the declines were small—0.59 percent for the Roman Catholic Church and 0.24 percent for the Southern Baptist Convention—they still represent an interesting trend among Generations X and Y (the Millennials) regarding church membership.[16]

It could be that the next generation isn't looking at differences, but rather similarities across faith. Active gamers understand that Presbyterians and Baptists and Roman Catholics might each have viable ways of relating to God. Whereas a moviegoing generation might study each tradition individually, drawing comparisons and contrasts afterward, the gaming generation seems to dive straight into the belief pool and sort things out as they go. As Eileen Lindner, the editor of the *2009 Yearbook of American and Canadian Churches*, writes, this is a generation of people who "attend and support local congregations but resist joining them."[17] Perhaps the reason for this resistance is that the video gaming generation is slow to commit to one method of reaching God.

Gaming might also provide a bigger challenge to theologies that emphasize the sovereignty of God over free will. Calvinists might find growing resistance to their notions of predestination from a generation that has adopted multiple means to solve a game. Free play—the ability in a game to play as the gamer chooses, free of the objectives or rules set up by the game designers—is a hallmark of the game experience. It is a chance to apply in creative ways all that you've learned. The singular focus of movies can frustrate gamers who expect to choose their own route or adventure, to find their own path.

What is especially interesting in this discussion—and an area ripe for further exploration—is the possible manner by which video games might bridge the gap between predestination and free will. Most games do have a predetermined endpoint, the point at which—when victory is won—the game ends. But most games also leave the gamer with plenty of room to roam around and explore the confines of the world that the game designer created. That is, the game ultimately has a point, and you can feel the game designer's hand guiding you toward that point, toward a destination or a goal, but you can also choose how fast or slow you get there. Plenty of rabbit trails are offered along the way, and gamers who are so inclined can journey down those trails to explore the complexity of the designer's creation. More goal-oriented gamers can plow through to determine the endpoint before doubling back to enjoy the rabbit trails from a very different perspective.

Movies, by contrast, simply don't give this freedom of choice to the viewer. Movies are predestined to end the way their creators saw fit when they made them, whereas video games, in their own way, point toward a resolution of the seemingly incompatible notions of predestination and free will.

With all of these considerations in mind, perhaps it is time to move beyond fearing video games only as a medium that contains too much violence. Video games and movies are clearly about more than just their content. They also reflect and influence, through their methods of telling stories, our understanding of our own experiences as Christians. And because the strength of video gaming is the very interactivity that separates it from movies, perhaps the strengthening of this participatory aesthetic among a generation that prefers games to movies will deepen our understanding of the human role in God's story—shifting us from passive observers of the unfolding events to active participants engaging with the stories around us as we move toward the ultimate conclusion.

2

Ultima IV

Simulating the Religious Quest

MARK HAYSE

INTRODUCTION

As a young ministry undergrad in the 1980s, I eagerly anticipated and purchased the computer role-playing game *Ultima IV: The Quest of the Avatar* (1985), even though I did not have a personal computer of my own.[1] In its day, *Ultima IV* transformed the video game landscape not only in terms of its scope and size but also in terms of its story and structure. Unlike other games, *Ultima IV* begins by launching the player upon a quest to (1) rediscover forgotten virtues, (2) contemplate moral perfection, and (3) become a messianic figure who saves Britannia not through hack-and-slash combat but through spiritual enlightenment. *Ultima IV*'s designer Richard Garriott referred to this savior for the first time in video game history as an "Avatar."[2] For weeks, I delightedly explored the ethical landscape of *Ultima IV* in our campus computer lab. Soon enough, however, another ministry student abruptly interrupted my virtual adventure by calling me back to the straight and narrow. He saw *Ultima IV* as an occult phenomenon and my infatuation with the game as, at best, a waste of time. However, I did not share his perspective. I experienced *Ultima IV* as a philosophical and religious conversation, despite its low cultural status as a video game. Nevertheless, I dutifully set aside *Ultima IV* as an act of faith, refocusing myself upon the study of Scripture, theology, and pastoral ministry. Now I find myself returning to *Ultima IV* in that same spirit—as an act of faith. This chapter intends to explore the question, can video games effectively function as religious educational media?

The capacity of video games to function as religious educational media depends upon what scholars describe as the "explicit curriculum" and the "implicit curriculum."[3] The explicit curriculum consists of publicly identified educational aims, objectives, and content. In contrast, the implicit or hidden curriculum consists of value-laden rules, processes, and procedures that subtly shape an educational environment. In a classroom, for example, the explicit curriculum may consist of a worksheet on American colonial history. However, a teacher's direction to complete the worksheet in small groups reveals an implicit curriculum of cooperation and interdependence. Even without extended explanation, students still learn how to work together because of the implicit curriculum. The implicit curriculum can make or break the best-laid plans of an explicit curriculum. The best teaching utilizes both the explicit and the implicit curriculum.

Similarly, video games teach their lessons and values through both the explicit and the implicit curriculum. In the case of *Ultima IV*, its story and its structure reflect Garriott's curriculum of ethical reflection. *Ultima IV*'s story presents the player with a complicated matrix of ethical dilemmas—the explicit curriculum. However, a set of hidden rules and programmed equations quietly govern game play within *Ultima IV*—the implicit curriculum. Today, video game narratologists and ludologists argue about which matters more within video games: stories or rules, the explicit narrative or the implicit procedures. However, role-playing games like *Ultima IV* manage to integrate both aspects into one very compelling experience.[4] *Ultima IV*'s ethical game design—novel in its day—establishes its historic significance within the video game canon.[5] This chapter contends that Garriott's use of the explicit and implicit curriculum in *Ultima IV* serves as a better model for religious educational video game design than that of more contemporary evangelical Christian video games such as *Left Behind: Eternal Forces* (2006).[6]

A MORAL ECONOMY

As *Ultima IV* game play begins, players generate their characters by answering a series of ethical dilemmas, each juxtaposing two of *Ultima IV*'s virtues. In this example, the ethical dilemma juxtaposes the virtue of Compassion with the virtue of Honor: "Thou art sworn to uphold a Lord who participates in the forbidden torture of prisoners. Each night their cries of pain reach thee. Dost thou A) show Compassion by reporting the deeds, or B) Honor thy oath and ignore the deeds?" Upon answering, players receive no evaluative feedback. Instead, the game immediately proceeds to the next ethical dilemma. The answers that players give shape the profiles of their in-game characters. However, *Ultima IV*'s documentation does not explain this relationship. Game play simply begins with players' characters standing outside of a hometown that reflects their ethical preferences, as depicted in table 1.

Table 1: Corresponding Virtues, Classes, and Towns in Ultima IV

Dominant Virtue	Player Character Class	Starting Town
Compassion	Bard	Britain
Honesty	Mage	Moonglow
Honor	Paladin	Trinsic
Humility	Shepherd	New Magincia
Justice	Druid	Yew
Sacrifice	Tinker	Minoc
Spirituality	Ranger	Skara Brae
Valor	Fighter	Jhelom

Source: *Ultima IV: Quest of the Avatar* (1985)

For example, if players tend to value honesty more than the other virtues, then they begin game play as mages in Moonglow, the hometown of honesty. Garriott explains that this implicit curriculum in his game design is intended to link players' self-understanding with their in-game characters:

> In role-playing games, people generally don't want to take responsibility for the action a character takes, so they can separate themselves from the person who's going around slaughtering everyone. And that's something I changed in *Ultima IV*. I said, you don't get to be the puppeteer. I want this to be *you*. . . . I'll let you transmute your physical essence any way you want. But the spiritual essence is still you. Your life force is what's driving that character. You are responsible for the actions of that character.[7]

As players wander through Britannia, seeking perfection in each virtue, *Ultima IV*'s internal karma counter keeps a running total of their progress toward enlightenment. The hidden numerical value assigned to each virtue ebbs and flows, moving up or down in response to the ongoing ethical choices and behaviors of players, as depicted in table 2. As players perform these virtuous actions, their corresponding point values increase or decrease until all virtues are perfected at one hundred points each, at which point full Avatarhood is attained.

Ultima IV's virtue system functions as a moral economy.[8] Here, the word "economy" refers to the network of reciprocity by which players interact with

Table 2: Point Values for Virtuous Actions in Ultima IV

Virtuous Actions	Point Values		
Attacking a Non-evil Creature (animal)	Compassion −5	Honor −3	Justice −3
Being Honest to the Herbs Woman	Honesty +2	Honor +2	Justice +2
Cheating the Herbs Woman	Honesty −10	Honor −10	Justice −10
Fleeing from a Non-evil Creature	Compassion +2	Justice +2	
Fleeing from an Evil Enemy	Valor −2	Sacrifice −2	
Getting Killed	Sacrifice +1		
Giving Blood at the Healer	Sacrifice +5		
Giving to a Beggar	Compassion +2	Honor +3	
Killing an Evil Enemy	Either Valor +0 or	Valor +1	(random)
Letting Non-evil Creatures Flee	Compassion +1	Justice +1	
Meditating at a Shrine for One Cycle	Spirituality +3		
Refusing to Give Blood at the Healer	Sacrifice −5		
Solving Quests by Finding Special Items	Honor +5		
Stealing a Chest	Honesty −1	Honor −1	Justice −1
Talking "Proud"	Humility −5		
Talking "Unproud"	Humility +10		
Talking to Hawkwind the Seer	Spirituality +3		
Throwing Mondain's Skull into the Abyss	All Virtues +10		
Using the Power of Mondain's Skull	All Virtues −5		
Using the Wrong Mantra at a Shrine	Spirituality −3		

Source: Dan Simpson, *Ultima IV: Quest of the Avatar FAQ/Walkthrough*, version 1.61. http://www
.gamefaqs.com/computer/doswin/file/562660/1807.

the virtual world of Britannia and its inhabitants: for example, engaging in combat, making peace, offering a fair price, or taking advantage of another. The word "moral" describes the particular values that Garriott embeds within that economy.[9] Throughout game play, *Ultima IV*'s moral economy monitors all player interactions in Britannia, coding and storing them in a simple database. In short, *Ultima IV* is a game about ethical choices and their consequences. Right choices produce an Avatar. Wrong choices do not.

Garriott's pioneering design for a moral economy now stands as an industry standard, especially within role-playing games. Examples abound. In Peter Molyneux's *Black & White* (2001), players assume the roles of deities who live in deeply reciprocal relationships with tribal people. Divine kindness produces a faithful people who serve out of gladness. Harshness produces fearful, resentful people. More recently, Molyneux's *Fable* (2004) and *Fable II* (2007) confront players with a moral economy in which every choice brings a long-term consequence—not only in social reputation but also in physical appearance. A heroic life well-lived earns beauty and admiration. A dastardly life of evil brings only disfigurement and scorn. Similarly, LucasArts' *Star Wars: Knights of the Old Republic* (2003) tracks the choices that players make, gradually turning them toward either the light side or the dark side of the Force while an easily accessible "alignment meter" offers ongoing feedback. Bethesda Softworks' *The Elder Scrolls III: Morrowind* (2002) and *The Elder Scrolls IV: Oblivion* (2006) both utilize a moral economy of "Fame" and "Infamy" in order to determine alignment and reputation. Depending upon players' choices, their experiences in the world produce either sympathy or opposition as the game progresses. Even Rockstar Games' notoriously violent *Grand Theft Auto IV* (2008) operates according to a moral economy. Its protagonist, Niko, faces unavoidable ethical dilemmas. The murders that he commits return to haunt his mind throughout game play. *Grand Theft Auto* offers a cautionary tale, a way not to be.

Although many video games today incorporate moral economies, their designers tend to make them more explicit than implicit. Players discover quite easily—perhaps too easily—what they should or shouldn't do in order to fix problems, make friends, exploit resources, and win the game. Wrong turns and bad choices weigh very little in such games. Players quickly detect them, returning to the last saved game in order to try again. In contrast, Garriott's decision to largely conceal the moral economy sets *Ultima IV* apart from other video games. Although players come to understand the importance of virtue early in the game, the means of practicing virtue remain ambiguous. As game play progresses, Garriott's curriculum of virtue gradually moves from the implicit to the explicit, from mystery to clarity. This gradual movement can be described as "unfolding revelation."

UNFOLDING REVELATION

In *Ultima IV*, Garriott skillfully uses unfolding revelation to gradually introduce players to the moral economy of Britannia. As game play begins, players experience a sense of uncertainty and anticipation. They do not yet hear virtue calling. They feel tentative about where to go or what to do. This tension enhances *Ultima IV*'s initial aura of mystery, inviting the player to wander toward hidden horizons. Throughout game play, Garriott slowly reveals bits and pieces of *Ultima IV*'s moral economy through player dialogue with Britannia's inhabitants. Step by step, players come to understand the importance and complexity of virtue.

Of course, many video games conceal critical information from players as game play begins. Video games often function as complex puzzles that only hidden information can solve. Advanced levels of play remain locked away. Quests are not yet completed. Artifacts remain hidden. Access to power is restricted. The puzzle-completing nature of video game play invites players into a problem-solving adventure of active agency. However, Garriott's use of unfolding revelation within the context of a moral economy transforms *Ultima IV* from an ordinary puzzle into a deeper, philosophical journey.

As *Ultima IV* begins, virtue remains a mystery. Gradually, players come to realize that the quest for virtue demands ongoing ethical self-assessment. Every interaction with the subjects and objects of Britannia requires critical reflection. The game forces players to roam across Britannia in search of wisdom, seeking answers to questions such as these:

- What is the right thing to do when I am attacked by others? Should I fight back? Should I turn the other cheek? Stand my ground? Flee for the sake of my life (or theirs)? What interrelationship exists among Valor, Justice, Honor, and Compassion?
- What belongs to me, and what does not? If I find something of value on my journey, under what conditions may I claim it as my own? What is the nature of Honesty?
- When asked to share financial or physical resources with others, how much should I share? Is there any amount that is too little or too large? According to what criteria should I practice the virtue of Sacrifice?
- When strangers ask about my character, what should I say in response? Should my speech be forthright, honest, and plain? Should I speak instead with modesty, even if at times my Humility is false?
- Are there certain tools that I should not employ in the service of virtue? Or does the virtue sanctify every tool in order that the end justifies the means?

Ultima IV provides very little explicit guidance on these issues, yet they remain critically important to the outcome of the game. Britannia's hope rests upon the Avatar's success in attaining virtue through Garriott's moral economy. At the same time, players can do little but contemplate, seek counsel, and forge ahead in the midst of unfolding revelation.

Although *Ultima IV* provides players with feedback on their progress in virtue, the feedback rarely fully satisfies. For example, players never discover that, behind the veil of *Ultima IV*'s moral economy,

- Fleeing from evil enemies loses Valor points twice as fast as defeating evil enemies earns Valor points.
- Fleeing from non-evil (animal) enemies costs no Valor points, but earns two Compassion points and two Justice points instead.
- Allowing non-evil (animal) enemies to flee earns one Compassion point and one Justice point.

In other words, the attainment of valor requires contextual practice, and must be tempered by compassion and justice. However, Garriott's use of unfolding revelation conceals these relations and equations. Although the citizens of Britannia gladly instruct players about virtue, their advice is somewhat rare and often opaque. Players also receive spiritual direction from Hawkwind the Seer in Castle Britannia and from mystical shrines hidden throughout the land. Even so, the advice from Hawkwind and the shrines tends to raise as many questions as it answers. Most important, players cannot gain access to their own karma counters.[10] Thus, players soon realize that unless they play with critical reflection, they will likely violate the virtues without knowing it. Instead, they must play with intuition and discernment, trying to grasp the subtleties of a moral economy essentially hidden from view. In summary, unfolding revelation coupled with a moral economy combines to produce a sense of sacred quest within *Ultima IV*.

As philosopher Alasdair MacIntyre points out, the medieval notion of a sacred quest can provide a sense of direction for human life. The medieval quest began in pursuit of the Good, yet the precise nature of the Good remained unknown at the quest's onset. Only through searching, groping, and fumbling for the Good could the Good finally be identified and known:

> It is clear the medieval conception of a quest is not at all that of a search for something already adequately characterized, as miners search for gold or geologists for oil. It is in the course of the quest and only through encountering and coping with the particular harms, dangers, temptations and distractions which provide any quest with its episodes and incidents that the goal of the quest is finally to be understood. A quest is always an education both as to the character of that which is sought and in self-knowledge.[11]

The sacred quest of which MacIntyre speaks sounds very much like Garriott's quest of the Avatar. A moral economy awaits discovery. Players vaguely sense its shape, seeking to live in congruence with its contours, yet the unfolding revelation of that moral economy forces players to thoughtfully—even reverently—contemplate each choice that they make along the way. Garriott describes this in his own words:

> You don't know any of this [about the virtues] when you start the game. You don't even know you are in Britannia. You wake up in Britannia and wonder, "Why am I here?" There is a period of discovery. You wonder why you're in Britannia—there doesn't appear to be any great world-saving thing to do. Since nobody ever says, "Go on the quest of the Avatar!" your discovery that you're going to go on the quest of the Avatar, and exactly what that is, is a completely self-generated thing.[12]

The tension that exists between a moral economy and its unfolding revelation creates an occasion for intense reflection. As it turns out, the hyperactive imaginings of *Ultima IV* players turn out to be just that—overdone. Although the moral economy of *Ultima IV* feels quite sophisticated, that impression owes more to unfolding revelation than to mathematical complexity. As seen above in table 2, the equations of virtue are simple and straightforward once revealed. Video game theorist Ian Bogost describes this tension between the known and the unknown as a "possibility space" within which players must reconcile their own perceptions with the game designer's system.[13] Bogost describes the exploration of a possibility space as an experience of "self-reflection, debate, dispute, and a host of other contentious activities."[14] In other words, Bogost maintains that when players encounter a model of the world through video game play—even a fictional world such as *Ultima IV*'s Britannia—they critically compare that model with their own worldviews. To the players of *Ultima IV*, the possibility space in which they wrestle consists of the distance between Garriott's ethical system and their own moral commitments.

Garriott's implicit curriculum for *Ultima IV* consists of his hidden moral economy and his intention to foster critical reflection within players. As the game progresses, however, Garriott's implicit curriculum gradually becomes explicit. Players slowly discover how to faithfully practice the complexities of virtue by paying attention to the cues within their virtual environment. Interestingly, Garriott admits that while creating *Ultima IV*, he feared that it would not be well received due to its "ethical, moral, parable stuff."[15] Nevertheless, players discovered that the philosophical journey could be a pleasurable one indeed. Garriott's curriculum of virtue allowed players to explore thoughtful questions at their own pace. By refusing to reveal too much too soon, Garriott created a virtual environment in which heightened critical analysis became a joyful pursuit.

LEAVING PLAYERS BEHIND

Religious education hinges, in part, upon the interplay of morality and mystery. In religious terms, morality reflects the nature and character of an infinite Creator. However, divine morality remains difficult to discern when trapped within the limitations of a finite Creation. The religious quest consists—at least in part—of the search to reconcile the finite with the infinite, the Creation with the Creator. Arguably, religion needs mystery. Mystery calls for contemplation and elicits a spirit of discernment. When religion minimizes mystery, religion tends to degenerate into a rationalistic system or a set of legalistic rules. In his essay "The Aims of Education," Alfred North Whitehead famously declares that education evokes within students a religious sense of "duty *and* reverence" (italics added).[16] By this, Whitehead means that religious education addresses not only one's moral obligation to others but also one's appreciation for infinite mystery. Following Whitehead, religious education aims learners toward a never-ending horizon that seeks to guide everyday life. In short, faithful religious education necessarily maintains a tension between morality and mystery.

Similarly, video games that couple a moral economy with unfolding revelation reflect the curriculum of religious education. Apart from unfolding revelation, even the most exquisite moral economy quickly degenerates into a mere rule system to exploit. Video games undermine the need for contemplation and discernment when they reveal their essential mystery up front in the instruction manual or tutorial level of play. Players need not struggle to understand the meaning of a moral economy when its questions are answered through on-screen meters and graphical displays. Players can dismiss any sustained reflection upon the ethical implications of their choices when their consequence is immediately and explicitly revealed. Without unfolding revelation, a moral economy becomes nothing more than a system of "virtual virtue points" similar to other economies, like gold pieces or experience levels. Only the process of unfolding revelation can transform the game play experience of a moral economy from statistical manipulation into poetic spirituality. Without unfolding revelation, a video game's moral economy is more likely to elicit yawning Sunday school answers from players instead of sponsoring electric "aha" moments. As a case in point, consider the implicit and explicit curriculum of the evangelical Christian video game *Left Behind: Eternal Forces.*

Left Behind is technologically superior to *Ultima IV* in every way. Its visual effects dazzle the eyes while *Ultima IV* utilizes only the sixteen-color palette of 1985's archaic Apple II. The game play of *Left Behind* speeds along in real time while *Ultima IV* requires repeated floppy disk swapping

---

Gamers Speak

The Fuller Youth Institute interviewed teenagers about their gaming habits.
  Patrick, seventeen years old, white/Hispanic, 2.7 GPA

- What do you wish your parents realized about video games? *That they aren't just brain rotters. They are entertainment and a source of fun.*
- How would your life be different without video games? *I'd be doing way better in school, and I'd be a little more focused on the things going on around me.*
- What else would you want to say about video games? *I wish they would make video games a little cheaper so people that don't have their parents' support can buy them.*

Melkon, seventeen years old, Armenian, 3.7 GPA, Honor Roll

- How much do you game each week? *21 hours.*
- Why do you play? *It's a fun way to kill time, and spend time with friends.*
- What else would you want to say about video games? *I think it's up to the kid to use games to their right potential. Some kids get obsessed and games give them anger problems, and they tend to resolve their conflicts with violence, like they see in video games.*

---

in order to move from place to place. *Left Behind* immerses players within a three-dimensional environment, but *Ultima IV* allows players only a two-dimensional, top-down view of the game. The world of *Left Behind* contains a population of hundreds and hundreds—even thousands—of unique virtual individuals, while *Ultima IV* features only 256 virtual characters. The soundtrack of *Left Behind* plays like a Hollywood film score, but the soundtrack of *Ultima IV* humbly limps along in tinny two-part harmony. Despite its strengths, *Left Behind* reflects a much weaker religious educational curriculum than does *Ultima IV*, primarily because it fails to couple its moral economy with unfolding revelation.

Left Behind visibly displays its moral economy through an arrangement of on-screen color bars and numerical scores, right down to the last point. By clicking on each character in *Left Behind*, players can immediately see whether the character is part of the Lord's army, part of the Antichrist's army, or unaligned. "Good guys" show a green "Spirit" bar over their heads, "bad guys" a red bar, and "neutrals" a gray bar. After clicking on a character, a numerical "Spirit" score appears at the bottom of the screen. When players' Spirit bars are green and Spirit scores are high, they can "lock on" to a neutral character with one mouse click. From there, it is a simple matter to perform coercive personal evangelism on the neutral character. Resistance is futile. Once "saved," the character flashes brilliantly, joining the Lord's army. Throughout game play, all Spirit points decrease over time. Thus, players must frequently mouse-click a "Pray" icon to replenish their Spirit points. If players shoot and kill bystanders, their Spirit points immediately and dramatically drop. However, by clicking the Pray icon repeatedly, players can restore their Spirit scores to normal levels with mechanical efficiency. While playing *Left Behind*, players never need to wonder, "What are we supposed to do now? How are we supposed to treat others? What do we need to do in order to practice virtue? What is the nature of right and wrong?" Instead, players only have to click buttons, monitor scores, manipulate variables, and manage units in order to win the game. In the absence of unfolding revelation, the moral economy of *Left Behind* serves only as a thinly wallpapered statistical system in which moral practice is vulgarized.

In addition, the eschatology (theology of the future) in *Left Behind* fails to engage players' imaginations at the depth found in *Ultima IV*. In *Ultima IV*, players possess only a vague sense of what awaits in the future. Only one thing is certain: the world needs a savior. Although the path is uncertain, the hope is sure. *Ultima IV* forces players to adopt a watchful spirit, actively searching the eschatological horizon for hints of what they are called to become. Through careful discernment, players work to align their choices with that emergent future. Although Garriott has already determined the conditions for winning the game, those conditions are revealed only incrementally, thus maintaining a feeling of openness, wonder, and anticipation. In contrast, the eschatology of *Left Behind* is not only fundamentally determined but also fundamentally revealed. Players proceed through the game according to task-oriented levels, not through an open-ended process of playful discovery. Each new level in *Left Behind* provides a detailed outline of conditions for success. The path to achieve those goals is literally linear. In *Left Behind*, the absence of unfolding revelation produces a feeling of eschatological foreclosure. The future becomes nothing more than a predetermined path, prohibiting players from doing anything other than playing out a story that has already been told. *Left Behind* fails even to initially evoke the sense of morality and mystery that *Ultima IV* sustains across game play. Instead, *Left Behind* functions as just another resource management game beneath an incidentally Christian skin.

The curricular flaws of *Left Behind*'s game design plague both the general and evangelical Christian video game markets today. Video game designers are immersed within a culture of cheat codes, walkthrough guides, and instant gratification. In light of this, perhaps they deem players incapable of the patience required to work through the process of unfolding revelation. Conversely, evangelical Christians include a vocal theological contingent which is convinced that divine mystery has been sufficiently disclosed in Christ and in the book of Revelation. Perhaps this approach animates the evangelical preference for declaration more than contemplation. Indeed, those who design video games for the evangelical Christian market tend to favor the explicit and the literal over the implicit and subtle.[17] They choose narratology over ludology, trying to isolate the message from the medium.

With this in mind, the time is right to revisit the Christian tradition's curriculum of salvation history. Although God's hidden economy of Christ-as-messiah was designed from "the foundation of the world" (Eph. 1:3–5; 1 Pet. 1:18–21), it was revealed only within the "fullness of time" (Gal. 4:3–6; Eph. 1:9–10). In fact, Christ was—and still is—the "mystery" of God (Rom. 16:24–26; Eph. 1:8–10; 3:3–9; Col. 1:25–27; 1 Tim. 3:15–16). Although the terms of Christ's first coming have been revealed, the terms of the second advent remain at least partially hidden (Rev. 10:6–8). The church now lives within a possibility space between the explicit and the implicit; the past, present, and future; the moral economy and unfolding revelation of salvation history. Within that space, Christ calls the church to keep watch (Mark 13) and to faithfully anticipate the kingdom come (Matt. 6:9–10). If religion encompasses the making of meaning from mystery as the apostle Paul suggests (1 Cor. 13:11–12), then perhaps video games that engage players in a similar possibility space might provide an effective platform for religious educational media.

CONCLUSION

If video game designers want to create effective religious educational media, then they must learn to think like educators. Effective education requires more than mere lecture, drill, and review. Similarly, religious education entails much more than an explicit curriculum of heavy-handed morality lessons and Scripture quizzes. Subtlety matters. Religion consists of the possibility space between the hidden and the revealed. Within that possibility space, we strive to live in harmony with the Transcendent through ethical action. Without this struggle, do we really encounter the Divine, or do we meet merely a false god of our own design? The effectiveness of religious education hinges upon its implicit curriculum—the fashioning of a subtle environment within which the contemplation of Mystery can occur.

Richard Garriott designed a brilliant prototype for religious video game play in *Ultima IV: The Quest of the Avatar*. Although largely unsophisticated by the standards of today's marketplace, *Ultima IV* effectively paired a moral economy with unfolding revelation. In so doing, Garriott demonstrated that video games could treat the possibility space of religion as a serious subject, even if this was not his primary intention.[18] Among the many "god games," ethical role-playing games, and explicitly religious games that have followed *Ultima IV*, few have incorporated Garriott's unique blend of morality and mystery—a blend that can transform video game play from mere puzzle solving into a reflection of God's unfolding work of salvation history in Christ.

3

The Play Is the Thing

Interactivity from Bible Fights to Passions of the Christ

RACHEL WAGNER

What is distinctive about the story of Jesus that makes it so popular in film, but so unusual in video games? This peculiar question is the focus of my analysis. What might seem strange at first—that Christian filmmakers repeatedly visually depict the passion of Jesus, and yet video game designers do not do so except as parody—comes into sharp focus when we consider how harshly the notion of interactivity clashes with the notion of theological inevitability.

In their tacit refusal to create interactive versions of the story of the crucifixion, Christian media designers seem to have understood intuitively what theorists are just now beginning to recognize: a game and a film can do very different things with a story. Game theorist Henry Jenkins acknowledges that games and films are increasingly difficult to distinguish due to the phenomenon of media convergence, which is part of an increasingly apparent convergence culture. However, even Jenkins admits that "if some games tell stories, they are unlikely to tell them in the same ways that other media tell stories."[1] If a story is transformed generically into a game, some of the most critical changes can be illuminated by considering four important concepts: narrativity, immersion, intent, and play. In this chapter, after exploring the theoretical foundation of these concepts, I move to an analysis of a series of new media artifacts dealing with the life of Jesus and exhibiting increasing levels of player-viewer interactivity.

NARRATIVITY

What is a story, anyway? Eric Zimmerman broadly defines narrative, characterizing it according to its overall structure:

47

> A narrative has an initial state, a change in that state, and insight
> brought about by that change. You might call this process the "events"
> of a narrative. . . . A narrative is not merely a series of events, but a
> personification of events through a medium such as language. . . . The
> representational aspect of narrative . . . is constituted by patterning
> and repetition.[2]

According to this broad definition, examples of narrative could include a book,
a game of chess, even a marriage ceremony, a meal, and a conversation.[3] Texts
are one of the most rigid forms of narrative, because "when immersed in a
text, readers' perceptions, reactions, and interactions all take place within the
text's frame, which itself usually suggests a single schema."[4] Although games
and films are both narratives in the broadest sense, the way they enact the
telling of a story is quite different.

The Christian preference for narrative over game is traceable back to early
Christian insistence on the fidelity of the Jesus story as the fulfillment of biblical prophecy. The story of Jesus hinges for Christians precisely on his willing
death and resurrection. Paul makes this point in an early letter, when he urges
the Corinthians to hear the story of Jesus' death rightly: "For I handed on to
you as of first importance what I in turn had received: that Christ died for our
sins in accordance with the scriptures, and that he was buried, and that he was
raised on the third day in accordance with the scriptures, and that he appeared
to Cephas, then to the twelve" (1 Cor. 15:3–5). For Paul, the death of Jesus
was the culmination of all of history. His death is to be understood in one way
and one way only: as the means to salvation for humans. Tampering with the
story, especially in terms of imagining that things could have unfolded otherwise, is not an option for Paul or his followers.

We see a similar resistance to experimentation with the narrative in the
harsh rejections by the church fathers of the creative interpretation and new
storytelling of the gnostics. One of the main reasons that Irenaeus objects to
the gnostics is their willingness to "play" with Scripture:

> Such are the variations existing among them with regard to one [pas-
> sage], holding discordant opinions as to the same Scriptures; and
> when the same identical passage is read out, they . . . all depart [from
> each other], holding so many opinions as to one thing, and bearing
> about their clever notions in secret within themselves. . . . For, though
> holding wrong opinions, they do in the meanwhile, however, convict
> themselves, since they are not of one mind with regard to the same
> words.[5]

By contrast, Irenaeus praises those who accept the view that there is only one
reading, one divine narrative that "has come even unto us, being guarded and

preserved without any forging of the scriptures" and which consists in "reading without falsification" and engaging in "lawful and diligent exposition in harmony with the Scriptures."[6] The developing notion of apostolic succession is itself a very early version of Christian insistence on linear narrative over the playful interpretive "games" engaged in by gnostics and others.

Augustine, writing centuries later, sees himself as the bearer of the authentic tradition, and urges other readers of the Scripture to accord to the same interpretation: "Whoever takes another meaning out of Scripture than the writer intended, goes astray, but not through any falsehood in Scripture." The Scriptures contain only one right interpretation for Augustine, so to read rightly is to read the way the author intended and, more important, the way that God intended. Some people may engage in freer interpretations, Augustine admits, but so long as these are harmless and ultimately corrected, a little play is acceptable "if [the reader's] mistaken interpretation tends to build up love." Such a reader "goes astray in much the same way as a man who by mistake quits the high road, but yet reaches through the fields the same place to which the road leads." However, a reader who wanders from the intended interpretation of Scripture should be corrected eventually, even if the misreading is harmless, since "if he get into a habit of going astray, he may sometimes take cross roads, or even go in the wrong direction altogether. . . And if he should once permit that evil to creep in, it will utterly destroy him."[7] For Augustine, to read right is to see the straight path of interpretation intended by God and to limit the "play" of free interpretation as much as possible.

Film, due to its own fixed trajectory, is thus more suitable to theological inevitability than games, since film more readily parallels the Christian view of time as shaped by God in a predetermined linear trajectory. Films are input-driven (i.e., they come into us as recipients) just as Augustine's view of God's desire for us is input-driven. Video games are output-driven (i.e., they come out of us) and therefore are more akin to the narrative experimentation in which the gnostics engaged. Markku Eskelinen would likely agree; he argues that the relationship a viewer has with a film, play, or story is different from the relationship a player has with a game:

> The dominant user function in literature, theater, and film is interpretative, but in games it is the configurative one. To generalize: in art we might have to configure in order to be able to interpret, whereas in games we have to interpret in order to be able to configure, and proceed from the beginning to the winning or some other situation. Consequently, gaming is seen here as configurative practice, and the gaming situation as a combination of ends, means, rules, equipment, and manipulative action.[8]

Game players would be "frustrated, rather than satisfied, if the game unfolded in an altogether predictable fashion."[9] This kind of predictability, however, is precisely what many Christians want. A film director presents for us a single trajectory of how the story will turn out, and it doesn't change upon repeated viewings. A game designer, on the other hand, "design[s] worlds and sculpt[s] spaces." Events in a story become environments in a game, producing an experience that Jenkins calls "environmental storytelling."[10]

No matter how many twists and turns a film takes or how creative its use of time, or how expansive its depiction of space, it remains a fixed piece. Whereas film producers present us with dramatic stories in their entirety, game designers "cannot create drama; [they] can only create the circumstances from which drama will *emerge*."[11] So Jenkins is right to say that "stories are not empty content than can be ported from one media pipeline to another."[12] The medium shapes the story.

IMMERSION

Another way that films and video games are distinctively different is in the degree and quality of immersion generated. In films, certainly there can be rich identification with a character, what Ken Perlin calls "transference." He says that "as I watch a movie, I am continually testing the protagonist's apparent inner moral choices against my own inner moral measuring stick, looking for affirmation of higher goals and ideals, or for betrayal of those ideals." For Perlin, the very reason this transference works is that we "give over our choice-making power" and "passively allow the narrative to lead us where it will."[13]

Instead of developing a solution to the problem posed in the film, the viewer must simply hope that the character portrayed in the film has the strength or skill to overcome the challenge, and to rejoice if he or she succeeds.[14] Such a passive identification with the characters onscreen works well with the Jesus story, since the grateful Christian is intended to see the events unfolding inexorably for his or her eternal benefit. In a film, Jesus is represented as permanently "other," never inviting our identification with him except as grateful recipients of salvation.

In video games, immersion is typically accomplished through identification with an avatar, that is, with "textual or graphic representations of users that include a character designed to fit into the fictional environment in question, complete with a set of personality traits, skills, and health status."[15] When playing a game, a player's virtual identity "becomes one of the many 'selves' included in the user's identity, perhaps the one in which the user realizes himself in the most complete way because of the lack of limitations."[16] It's easy to see why films about Jesus are generally more acceptable than video games with Jesus as an avatar, since most Christians believe that Jesus is qualitatively different from us in meaningful ways and therefore beyond the possibility of intimate identification through immersion. To make Jesus one of many selves that we try on is to diminish Christian belief in his divine nature.

Another problem with the notion of Jesus as avatar is that avatars are left behind when the game is left behind. Perlin argues that when he plays as Lara Croft he cannot "sustain the fiction" that "an actual Lara Croft continues to exist offstage" because he has "not actually experienced her agency." Rather, he says, "All I have really experienced is *my* agency."[17] Games, he says, are about challenges, and a "character" in a game is "merely a convenient vehicle for framing and embodying these challenges." To play as Jesus, then, would be to suggest that we act for him; that we are the agency that informs his actions; and we are what remains as "real" when the story of the game is finished being told.

For Richard Bartle, the most immersive form of identification with one's avatar is to see one's avatar as a "persona," that is, a real version of oneself. Players in this stage of immersion describe themselves as actually being "*in a world*" as the avatar. According to Bartle, in the "persona" stage, "You're not assuming an identity, you *are* that identity; you're not projecting a self,

---

Gamers Speak

Roberto, seventeen years old, Mexican American, 3.3 GPA

- Why do you play? *Boredom of the everyday stuff.*
- What characters do you tend to assume? Why do you choose those characters? *Handsome Mexican characters, because that best represents myself.*
- If I asked your parents about the effects of video games on you and your relationships, what would they say? *They don't care.*
- What do you wish your parents realized about video games? *They are slowly killing me.*

Christopher, fourteen years old, Caucasian, on Honor Roll

- What characters do you tend to assume? Why do you choose those characters? *I tend to pick complicated magical creatures, especially the ones that have more power. It's fun to be powerful. . . . You can kinda associate yourself with the character. . . . You can be something great and you won't get hurt.*
- How would your life be different without video games? *I think there would be more time to spend on anything really . . . school, music, friends, and other hobbies.*
- What else would you want to say about video games? *They help intuitive thinking, like coming up with new ideas to entertain people.*

you *are* that self. . . . There's no level of indirection, no filtering, no question: *You* are *there*."[18] Interactivity, says Ian Bogost, produces "user empowerment," and "the more interactive the system, the more the user can do, and the better the experience."[19] For Christians, however, the more interactive the story of Jesus, the less theologically acceptable it is. Christian games like *Left Behind: Eternal Forces* (2006) avoid the problem of agency and immersion in relation to Jesus by not depicting him at all, and instead give Christians a sort of agency that supports God's control over history. As helpers in the end time, the players in *Left Behind* fight in support of the theological inevitability of the Christian story, and their enemies are those who refuse to accept it.

REFLEXIVITY

Wade Clark Roof defined in 1999 what he calls "reflexive spirituality," seeing in today's multimediated world "a situation encouraging a more deliberate, engaging effort on people's part for their own spiritual formation, both inside and outside religious communities." Roof points out that in today's world, "Responsibility falls more upon the individual— like that of the *bricoleur*— to cobble together a religious world from available images, symbols, moral codes, and doctrines, thereby exercising considerable agency in defining and shaping what is considered to be religiously meaningful."[20] That is to say, the individual must "play" with received traditions and decide what to believe. There is no predetermined goal or end to reflexive spiritual work; it is, by definition, ongoing and transformative.

Acknowledging the personal nature of religion today, Jolyon Mitchell and Sophia Marriage argue that religious identity "is not *absolutely* any of these, but tends to be more *private, subjective, implicit*, and *reflexive* than in the past." Today, they say, "Autonomous selves tend to pick and choose from among traditions, and this has the effect of making the symbols of those traditions . . . less embedded in their received histories."[21] The selection of selves from a spread of religious options sounds not so different from the careful design of one's avatar in a role-playing game online.

In addition to choosing what one will use in the development of religious identity, today's media users must also decide how to read received media. In other words, it is no longer self-evident if something is to be read as a story, a ritual, a game, a film, or several of these at once. The fact that some scholars today are arguing for the ritual function of media means that the user's intent in reception is increasingly important. One of the ways that people interact with films and video games is through the level of emotional involvement with them, and what this emotional investment suggests about the degree of interactivity allowed.

Films, by contrast, can certainly create a strong sense of emotional arousal "related to the viewer's expectations of what will happen to the central protagonists."[22] The idea of "fate" here is crucial. Despite how emotionally involved viewers may become in the story, they have no power to determine its ending. For Christians watching a Jesus film, such a limitation is actually a strange theological comfort.

According to Perlin, "linear narrative forms" like films and games serve different purposes, in that the "traditional goal of a linear narrative is to take you on a vicarious emotional journey, whereas the traditional goal of a game is to provide you with a succession of active challenges to master."[23] The first play of a game is typically disorienting, whereas in a second or third play of the game, emotional arousal is caused by anticipation of events one has already seen so that "what was surprising in the first playing of the game is transformed into a suspense-like coping anticipation in subsequent playing."[24] Whereas in films, emotional investment comes through awareness of impending inevitability, in a video game, the outcome "is in principle just as uncertain the second time through as it is the first time."[25] Therefore, as Torben Grodal notes, video games "are mostly able to evoke those emotions that are supported by the sympathetic nervous system (fight and flight-related emotions)."[26] Christian responses to the suffering of Christ could hardly be compatible with such emotional uncertainty.

Ritual, then, offers us a compelling means of comparing the experience of interactivity in films and video games, highlighting for us the distinctive differences in player choice. The deep connection between ritual, games, and films also highlights why the intentional decision by some game makers to transform elements of the Jesus story into a game format is so problematic. For Christians the appropriate response to the Jesus story is humble gratitude and the acceptance of grace, an emotional position reinforced by the rigidity of the narrative. The act of choosing to play a Jesus video game, then, can have theological implications, too—as a rejection of the inevitability of Jesus' death as salvific for all of humanity. In this way, interactivity can function as a form of cultural critique.

PLAY

In games, play is the "space of possibility" afforded a player to explore the world of the game and to make choices within it. Even in a game, play is dependent upon rules or some other defined baseline against which play

moves. For Christian interpreters like Augustine, play is the theological interactivity allowed using the "system" of the Bible and assumptions of salvation
history. For Mel Gibson as director of *The Passion of the Christ*, play consisted
of the choices he made in additional dialogue, and in costuming, lighting, and
music. But for Gibson and for Augustine, the system was nonnegotiable and
play was limited to those interpretive processes that maintained the predetermined Christian rules of play.

It seems most useful to think of the notion of play as experimentation and
innovation in response to a rigid system or structure. In this case, then, we
could think of theology as the most basic level of play with the biblical text,
directing a film about Jesus as exhibiting a greater degree of play with the
biblical text, and a video game about the Bible as having the greatest degree
of play with the biblical text. Play, then, can be a characteristic of stories,
films, games, and rituals. What differs is the degree of play, who is allowed to
engage in play, and what results from play.

PLAYING JESUS

The four concepts examined here—narrative, immersion, reflexivity, and
play—are useful in analyzing the few existing interactive new media artifacts
that utilize the Jesus story, and they help to explain why there aren't more
examples of Jesus interactive media. Considering forms of media that range
from hypertext to first-person shooters to online role-playing games, I examine how different degrees of user interactivity affect how we receive narrative,
how we immerse ourselves in the experience, how we reflexively incorporate
it into our sense of identity, and how we play.

Stations of the Cross

The stations of the cross exist online in several forms for faithful Catholics
and curious visitors to navigate as a hypertext collection of linked pages. As
Douglas and Hargadon note, "Readers of most hypertext fiction are merely
exploring the narrative, not constructing its links and rearranging its structure, or even generating lexia and links themselves."[27] In the online stations
of the cross from Catholic Online, the penitent begins by reading a prayer of
contrition, then clicks to move through the stations.[28]

Bernstein and Greco use the example of an imagined hypertext *Hamlet* to
explain how hypertext works, and why it might be more suitable to telling a
predetermined story than a game would be. "Tragedy," they say, "requires
that the characters be blind."[29] In other words, no matter how much the

viewer-participant may wish to, in order for *Hamlet* to be *Hamlet*, he or she cannot be allowed to change the trajectory of Hamlet's demise. Similarly, for believers, one cannot be allowed to derail the story of Jesus' passion and death.

With the stations of the cross, the viewer's interactivity is limited to clicking to go to the next station. Richard Schechner asks of hypertext, "How much really do the participants contribute? They participate for the most part in games that are fixed, making choices that are extremely limited: they agree, that is, to be manipulated."[30] In experiencing a hypertext, there are choices involved, just as if in a real experience of the stations of the cross, one might choose to wander back to a previous spot, or sit and meditate in another. However, as Schechner says of hypertext, choices are offered only "within a strictly defined and tightly limited field."[31] Furthermore, any unorthodox contemplation that one might engage in while clicking a hypertext, or even walking through the stations of the cross in a live setting, takes place entirely in the private thoughts of the viewers. The narrative structure itself—in this case, the stations—are not themselves changed by the viewer. In other words, to make the stations of the cross interactive in the same way a game is would require physically changing them—through a change in the digital code in a virtual form, or through decoration, defacement, or other alteration of the stained glass, stone, or paint that produced the material images.

Hypertext is thus a surprisingly suitable medium for telling the story of Jesus' suffering and death. In a hypertext experience, "The unimportance of the reader's proxy may be essential" to the success of the hypertext experience.[32] The reader inhabits a space on "the periphery of the action," interacting with the main characters, but not having the power to change the experience except, perhaps, to backtrack and to decide when to move forward again.[33] Hypertext, by providing only a fixed series of narrative nodes, suits the function of the stations of the cross by retaining much of the rigidity of the Christian story and of the real-life ritual of visiting the stations of the cross.

Bible Fight

A number of popular Jesus flash-games are available online that present Jesus as a character to be manipulated. For example, in *Running Jesus*, the player controls a Jesus avatar, clad in loincloth and bearing a large wooden cross. The setting is a racetrack, and the player must race against other "Jesuses" to the finish line by quickly pressing alternating keys. The intended interactivity is apparent in the game's tagline: "Take up the role [of] Jesus of Nazareth as you leg it down this 100m track. Come On You Saint!"[34] In *Jesus Dress-Up*, you do not play as Jesus, but instead you are presented with an image of Jesus on a cross, which you manipulate by placing different costume pieces on the crucified Jesus, much as one might manipulate the appearance of a paper doll. Both of these games have very stripped-down levels of interactivity, but do allow the player a sort of agency with the person of Jesus that many Christians would find offensive. In other words, the main problem is that you control Jesus and what happens to him.

In *Bible Fight*, players control any one of a number of predetermined religious avatars, one of which is a Jesus figure. When the game opens, the text reads in quasi-biblical script, "In the beginning there was a contest of strength amongst the most prominent figures in scripture to determine the mightiest. The tale of this great rivalry was thought lost forever. Until now. Let there be Bible Fight!" Each character has certain "powers" that can be used through particular manipulation of the keyboard; for Jesus, these powers include the "crown of thorns toss," which Jesus should use "as a deadly discus against opponents." Gamers playing as Jesus might also choose to "vent some frustration from that whole 'crucifixion' thing by smashing opponents with your old rugged cross."

For some game theorists, games may actually be defined by the presence of a contest. David Parlett asserts that "a formal game, by definition, has a winner; and winning is the 'end' of the game in both senses of the word."[35] Chris Crawford agrees that "conflict is an intrinsic element of all games."[36] So the transformation of the story of Jesus from the Bible into a game may bring with it a change in purpose; rather than simply accepting Jesus' death as a necessary event for the Christian's salvation, this game presents Jesus as angry about his fate and willing to take revenge on whomever gets in his way. His confrontation with Eve is particularly telling. As the player (as Jesus) is invited to brutally thump Eve with his cross and Eve responds with a snake as one of her weapons, it is hard to resist the sense that Jesus is attempting to punish Eve for her supposed acquiescence to the serpent's evil plot. Thus, the procedure of the game and its dualistic design actually encourage a classic misogynistic read on the fall.

Bible Fight may offend more Christians than *Running Jesus*, since it includes more remnants of the original biblical narrative. It uses the crown of thorns and even the cross as weapons of revenge for the crucifixion. A similar game, *Faith Fighter*, pits Jesus (or God) against world religious figures such as Buddha, Ganesh, or Muhammad. However, *Bible Fight*, with its more intense reference to the Bible via the script of the opening page and through the inclusion of other biblical characters as opponents, is a more direct transgression against the fidelity of the biblical story of the passion than *Faith Fighter* or *Running Jesus*.

If we return to the notion of "play," the reason for this offense becomes clear. Play, say Salen and Zimmerman, is "so powerful that it can change the structure itself."[37] That is, a game like *Bible Fight* presents us with a recognizable character, Jesus, but also disrupts the biblical narrative by placing Jesus in an anachronistic context with other biblical characters; creates a problematic sense of immersion by inviting us to play as Jesus; and "plays" with the Bible story in so radical a way that the only remnants of it are Jesus' weapons, the cross and crown of thorns. The player's response to such a game then depends tremendously on his or her intent, and whether he or she chooses to approach it as a game. A gamer therefore is free to play more radically with the system, a disruption to those who privilege the system of the Bible as a sacred text.

Roma Victor

Roma Victor is an MMORPG, a massively multiplayer online role-playing game, what Filiciak describes as "any computer network-mediated games in which at least one thousand players are role-playing simultaneously in a graphical environment."[38] On March 23, 2006, the following message appeared on *Roma Victor*'s official discussion board: "We're about to crucify one of the *Roma Victor* test team, Cynewulf, for ring-leading a gang of spawn killers in Corstopitum a month or so ago. It'll be the first of several crucifixions, which will be used as a banning and anti-griefing punishment tool. The crucified character will appear affixed to the cross on full public display for the duration of the ban. I'll drop by with a screenshot as soon as I get a chance."[39]Although some players exulted at this punishment, considering it an apt deterrent for griefing, others found it offensive. One poster complains that "they have [sunk] to this low of a level, in order to boost sales . . . Its [*sic*] wrong to make a mockery of the suffering of Christ."[40] *Roma Victor* CEO Kerry Fraser Robinson remarks,

> Although crucifixion is nowadays synonymous with persecution and religious symbolism, in 180 CE it was just one of many severe punishments used by the Romans to punish criminals and to send a clear message out to other potential wrong-doers. And since our online world is historically authentic, we feel that applying this punishment to cheats, hackers and other virtual wrongdoers is not only appropriate, but also adds to the gaming experience by resonating with classical history.[41]

The disagreement between those who approved of the crucifixion in *Roma Victor* and those who did not can be explained quite readily by Johan Huizinga's notion of the "magic circle" as articulated in his landmark study of play,

Homo Ludens. According to Huizinga, "All play moves and has its being within a play-ground marked off beforehand either materially or ideally, deliberately or as a matter of course." This can include, says Huizinga, an arena, a table, or even "the temple, the stage, the screen." In fact, he claims, all of these play spaces are "temporary worlds within the ordinary world, dedicated to the performance of an act apart."[42]

This case suggests, somewhat indirectly, that one's ability to immerse deeply in one's avatar depends in some sense upon to what extent one imports one's religious worldview into the online world. Those who choose to engage in a game will see that experience as distinct from their everyday lives, and may even see the field of play as a separate realm or world where different rules apply. Therefore, for those engaged in the magic circle of play and because that magic circle is the historical world of second-century Roman Britannia, the appropriate punishment for killing newly spawned avatars is crucifixion. Of course, for Christians who might stumble upon the game in the midst of this mock ritual activity, or who might hear about it in the news, the act seems blasphemous. Huizinga would agree with contemporary theorists Salen and Zimmerman that "the frame of a game is what communicates that those contained within it are 'playing' and that the space of play is separate in some way from that of the real world."[43] There's also the problem of immersion as avatar. Cynewulf, the "crucified" player in *Roma Victor*, certainly could feel no physical pain, and he must have realized that when the punishment period passed, he would regain freedom in the role-play world. Perhaps, one might suggest, Cynewulf's virtual experience of crucifixion is akin to docetic interpretations of the real crucifixion, especially the gnostic forms which imply that the "spirit" of wisdom left Jesus as he hung limply on the cross. In this view, the body of Jesus was a mere virtual or illusory avatar that had once hosted an entity that in fact cannot experience pain and certainly cannot die "in-world." So how intense could Cynewulf's own identification with the avatar have been if he could, in his embodied form, get up from his desk and go somewhere else?

Christ Killa

Christ Killa, an art project by Eric Medine, is a *Doom* mod in which the player moves about a virtual environment shooting loincloth-clad, gun-wielding Jesus bots. *Christ Killa* was first displayed in 2007 at Niche LA Video Art, a rentable gallery that is part of Los Angeles's popular Downtown Art Walk. The *Los Angeles City Beat* described the installation as "a video game linked to projectors and television monitors in which the player shoots hordes of homicidal Jesus Christs." Exhibit visitors were invited to play the game, a first-person shooter, which was displayed on television screens and by projector. The goal of the game is to kill as many "Christs" as you can, roaming through an environment filled with billboards, buildings, and fully armed, fatigue-clad Christs who pop up at any time ready to attack.

The game is loosely connected to the Christian narrative, but gives itself new narrative freedom by situating itself in the year 2099 after "the end of the world has come and gone." In an effort to save humanity for the earth, Medine explains, "a lone scientist" has cloned "Jesus H Christ from a piece of the Shroud of Turin in the hopes that he can repopulate the earth and create a new civilization." Unfortunately, says Stern, "something goes terribly wrong." The player must save the earth from Jesus—and not just from one Jesus figure, but from an ever-multiplying horde of Jesus figures who are bent not on peace but on murder.[44]

What's offensive in this game is easy to recognize, but the reasons for it may be harder to articulate. Most obvious is the notion of agency, which here is not reflected in playing *as* Jesus, but rather in playing *against* Jesus. Another reason is *Christ Killa*'s iconoclastic violence, intended to disrupt the reception of the image of Christ on the cross by presenting it within the game's rhetoric as a cause for violence. The player has the ability (and within the game's backstory, the moral obligation) to kill the cloned Jesus figures. Thus, within the fiction of the game, Jesus is the bad guy and the player is the good guy—one might even argue the messiah. The player's ability to immerse himself in the imagined avatar behind the gun invites a procedural violence against Jesus, justified by the assumption that he is just a clone. By so disrupting the biblical narrative and blending this disruption with agency as Jesus' enemy, the game invites a blasphemous procedural rhetoric.

Bible Champions: The Resurrection

Christian video games typically deal with the fate of the believer and his or her eschatological choices (as in *Left Behind: Eternal Forces*), or they focus on key moments in biblical history (*The Bible Game*), or they tell diluted forms of gospel stories in moralistic ways (the *Veggie Tales* games and the *Charlie Church Mouse* series). *Bible Champions* (Third Day Games, 2007) is an unusual exception to these rules, since it is a Christian-produced video game that teaches the story of the passion and resurrection to children. Players elect to play as either a young girl or young boy, clad in approximations of first-century robes, as they explore a crudely crafted digital model of ancient Jerusalem. If they follow directions properly (including following a digital arrow that tells them precisely where to go), players are rewarded with renditions of stories from the Gospels, primarily culled from the Gospel of John, the most theologically determinative in its presentation of the events in Jesus' life. Tellingly, when these narrations occur, viewers see a frozen image on the screen. The only movement comes from the female narrator, who reads from the New Testament.

Bible Champions: The Resurrection includes segments on Gospel events such as the trial before Pilate, the Last Supper, and Jesus with his disciples in the Garden of Gethsemane. As if the designers knew the dangerous interactive waters they were treading, segments of play skip from "The Last Supper" directly to "The Resurrection." In other words, although the designers were comfortable placing rigid readings of theologically laden events surrounding the crucifixion into the game as fixed narratives, they were not willing to present the crucifixion itself. Its omission starkly points out the implicit prohibition against Christian imagination of alternative trajectories of history and of story. This approach makes sense when we note that according to Henry Jenkins, "When we discuss games as stories, we are referring to games that either enable players to perform or witness narrative events."[45] For Christians, the former is theologically untenable. In the story of Jesus, God is the player-actor, not us. He makes the choices; we simply observe them.

This phenomenon explains quite clearly why the makers of *Bible Champions* choose to have the child avatars observing the story of Jesus. There is interactivity here, to be sure, but the rules of the game allow only certain things to be changed. Thus, the avatar can collect "faith" and "love" tokens, and locate objects. Once the preliminary tasks have been completed, the avatar touches a Bible icon, and the story resumes as told in the Gospels, primarily drawn from John's version of the passion. A new screen appears in which the avatar is not visible, and a narrator reads a Bible verse as the biblical story unfolds in fixed form before the viewer. The avatar recedes from view, and it is revealed that despite the interactivity allowed in the game, the player is really an observer.

The interactivity of the game is limited solely to exploratory activity on the fringes of the story. As Jenkins explains, narrative enters a game on two levels: "in terms of broadly defined goals or conflicts and on the level of localized incidents"[46] that players "witness." Clearly, the latter occurs in *Bible Champions*, offering the player agency only in the obedience in mustering the "faith" (tokens) that enable one to be rewarded with a click on the Bible to prompt the recitation of an unalterable story. This game demonstrates what we have seen already in other examples of religious games: the story of the crucifixion has little narrative plasticity for believers.

The Passion of the Christ: The Video Game?

Perhaps the best way to think about why there are no video games about the passion are to look at two powerful attempts to spoof that very possibility, both implicitly acknowledging the popularity of Mel Gibson's *The Passion of the Christ*. The first was an Italian ad campaign by Sony in 2005. The ad featured a poster with a young man with a crown of "thorns" and the text "Ten Years of Passion."

The crown of thorns is actually a collection of triangles, circles, and squares, a visual play on the controls for the Sony PlayStation system. The ad was obviously referencing Mel Gibson's *The Passion of the Christ*. Sony appears to be making what its marketers thought would be received as a joke, with a play on the word "passion," and perhaps a hidden marketing suggestion that players should be as willing to "sacrifice" themselves for gaming as Jesus was willing to die for humanity. With the control symbols embedded into the crown, the implication is also that the player is the "king" of gaming, perhaps suggesting another implicit message about the player's messiahship within the many first-person shooter games that Sony sponsors.

The ad was not well received by the Vatican, who seemed to grasp some of its troubling implications. Ninety-one-year-old Cardinal Ersilio Tonini remarked upon seeing the ad, "I often hear children say that heaven is the place where people drink coffee, which they remember from an advertisement." The media play such an enormous role in shaping youth culture, he says, that "now children can think that the Passion of Christ is a game."[47]

The second example is a homebrew YouTube imagining satirically what a *Passion of the Christ* video game for the Nintendo Wii would look like. In the video, teenage boys gleefully play the role of the soldiers in the scourging of Jesus, flinging their controllers as if they are controlling the whips. The YouTube video reverses the easy dualism of good and evil in Gibson's film and in the Gospels of the Roman soldiers as at best ignorant of who Jesus is and at worst maliciously rejecting the Son of God.

By depicting the boys playing as the soldiers, from their modern vantage point of supposed awareness of Jesus' true messianic identity, the video presents us with an ironic and somewhat disturbing invitation to imagine immersive identification with the enemies of Christ. The video also invites us to imagine the passion as a game, viewed as a contest between opponents, in this case Jesus and the Roman soldiers. To defeat Jesus, in this case, would be to win the game. If we imagine the "game" of salvation as the defeat of Jesus' enemies, then the reversal in the YouTube video is sinister, and for those who do not take it seriously, this is the source of its dark humor. The use of play here is effective in that the creators of the video take actual clips of Gibson's film and imagine them in a new interactive context, delineating through representation the profound implications of such a genre transformation.

CONCLUSION

This examination of retellings of the passion in different types of interactive media reveals quite plainly that the "game gaze" is not the same thing as the "cinema gaze."[48] The experiences of watching a film and playing a video game remain fundamentally different, marked most obviously by the film viewer's passive absorption of images on a screen and by the game player's kinetic engagement with images via hand controls, headsets, and perhaps even larger bodily movements. In video games, the pleasure is not "primarily visual" as in film, but rather it is "kinaesthetic, functional, and cognitive."[49] Games are not suitable for portrayal of the passion of Jesus precisely because they disrupt the linear view of sacred time, inject the possibility of other outcomes, invite immersion with the characters in a sacred story line, and stray far from the fixed narrative of the Bible. If the degree of play is what differentiates a film from a game, then it seems that the notion of interactivity really matters in the Jesus story, and the play is, in fact, the thing, and for Christians, the passion of the Christ is not a game—or if it is, it's the only game that matters.

4

Islamogaming

Digital Dignity via Alternative Storytelling

HEIDI CAMPBELL

In the past decade, religiously oriented video games have gained media and public attention. While the games are typically produced for a religious niche audience, many media outlets have become fascinated with the attempts of Christians, Jews, and Muslims to offer alternative narratives in the guise of traditional strategy or battle-based video games. For instance, evangelical Christians created *Left Behind: Eternal Forces*,[1] a video game based on a popular fiction series dramatizing the end of the world as told through Revelation, the last book of the Bible. In it players can join the last remaining righteous Christians in their Tribulation Force to battle an ungodly one-world government. To succeed they must remember to not let their "spirit ranking" run low by forgetting to pump the "prayer button," lest they be seduced or destroyed by the evil minions of the antichrist.

Judaism is not without its own video game superheroes, as seen in *The Shivah: A Rabbinical Adventure of Mourning and Mystery* (2006).[2] In this game, Rabbi Stone must solve the mystery behind a monetary gift made to his Lower East Side congregation in order to make sure that it has not been cursed. The story line behind the video game is marketed as its key feature and seems to trump the actual technical aspects of the game itself.[3] As the Web site for *The Shivah* states, "This game is not for everyone; no game is. But if you adore old-school adventure games; are willing to overlook antiquated graphics for the sake of a story with actual emotional impact . . . then downloading the demo is a mitzvah [religious commandment]."[4]

This trend toward producing video games that are religion-specific is creating a new genre of video games specifically for Muslims. The result is Islamogaming, which cultural critic Ed Halter describes as a "diverse field, ranging from amateur projects by students, unabashed anti-Zionist propaganda produced by an internationally recognized terrorist organization, religious games produced to teach Islam to kids and a set of more sober games designed to explore the complex realities of Middle Eastern history."[5]

This chapter explores the breadth and diversity of Islamogaming through highlighting three dominant classifications or subgenres. As Halter suggests, Islamogaming encompasses (1) games designed for religious education, (2) games that promote a political agenda or narrative about Islam and the Arab world, and (3) games offering new images of Muslims and the global Ummah, or worldwide Muslim community.[6] Then we investigate the ideological assumptions underlying the narratives in these games. What are the motivations and mind-sets of religious communities and game designers when they create religious video games? Through the window of Islamogaming, we see that religious gaming in general serves as a storytelling medium offering alternate social, political, or spiritual narratives that affirm particular ideological outlooks. Games can serve a specific function of promoting unique interpretations of religious life and faith. Alternatively, some games seek to counter dominant cultural narratives of their religious community that the media culture promotes.

RELIGIOUS EDUCATION VIA GAMING

One key focus within many religiously inspired video games is to entertain while teaching players about important aspects of religion and culture. I was first exposed to these types of games in 2004 while visiting the home of an Arab-Israeli friend when I saw her young daughter playing a video game that walked her through the different prayer positions for *salaat*. Many other games also serve as important teaching tools. The creators of Abu Isa games, which are produced in the United Kingdom, pitch their games as edutainment or "educational and fun based games enabling Muslims and non-Muslims to learn and grow their knowledge about Islamic Culture, Civilization and Science."[7] In *Abu Isa's A New Dawn*, players battle their way through space in a fighting-action game while learning the ninety-nine names of Allah. Another Abu Isa installment is *Abu Isa's Arabic Adventures*, a three-dimensional arcade game where players travel around a maze fighting enemies while learning basic Arabic. Most notable is *Abu Isa's Quest for Knowledge*, which presents a PC-based board game in which a player moves across a board maze covered with cloaked *ulema*, or Muslim legal scholars, who pose questions based on Islamic law. Players' success and ability to move up to higher levels depends upon their knowledge of the Shariah, or Islamic sacred law.

Other examples of religious education in the guise of entertainment can be seen in the work of the British software company Innovative Minds,[8] which seeks to produce multimedia games for "promoting a better understanding of Islam in the West." The company offers several games and teaching CDs for young children. *Islamic Thought*[9] aims to stimulate learning about Islam in today's world through articles and images on topics such as women in Islam, the global Muslim Ummah (community), or scientific teaching in the Qur'an. The creators suggest that stories and puzzles are "the best way to attract the youth to Islam."[10] This approach is also evident in their "Fun-Learn" Game Series, which promises to help children ages eight to sixteen acquire knowledge of Islam while they play. "Play" here can involve becoming familiar with *suras* (chapters) from the Qur'an in *The Book of Allah*, learning about the life and journey of the prophet in *Life of Muhammad*, or exploring the *Lion of Allah*, which teaches about the life and wisdom of Imam Ali ibn Abi Talib.

One of Innovative Minds' products receiving much Western media attention is the *Islamic Fun*[11] CD, which offers six games with colorful animation and sound effects to teach children ages five to eleven about Islam. Most are simple games such as *Building Blocks*, where players use digital blocks to create their own mosque, or several nonreligious-oriented games such as *Fishing Bear*, in which players help a bear use a pole to help him fulfill his hungry quest. However, one game on the CD is far more controversial. *The Resistance* has been flagged for allowing children to play the role of a farmer in South Lebanon who joins the Islamic Resistance to "defend your land and family from the invading Zionists."[12] The anti-Israel message communicated in this game is supported by the company's "Boycott Israel" page and campaign, which seek to raise awareness of the treatment of Palestinians in Israel.[13] Several press reports have cited a potential connection between Arab-focused warfare games—such as *The Resistance*—and reports that Al-Qaeda leaders have used similar video games to help train terrorists.[14] Innovative Minds responded to this criticism in a review of the game posted on the company's Web site:

> Some in the media have kicked up a fuss over this game. It seems that the media is silent when they, the zionists, use their tanks to slaughter our children but when our children play a shoot-em up game where they shoot zionist tanks in return for correct answers we are accused of training terrorists and instilling hatred towards Jews! On the contrary the questions in the game educate children not to fall for the zionist lie that zionism, jewishness and Judaism are synonymous but to understand that zionism, a racist ideology, has nothing to do with Judaism—one of the questions in the history/politics section asks "What is the difference between a Jew and a zionist?"[15]

The company argues that its main objective is to offer Muslim-inspired children's video games and other resources online in order to strengthen users' knowledge about Islam.

In general, religious education games are geared to a young audience, often to players as young as six years old. The games are often technically simple, revolving around an uncomplicated story line or goal with the primary function of educating players on basic tenets of religious faith and Muslim culture. While most of these games serve clear-cut goals of religious education, some of their backstories can be laced with ideas and ideology that may be problematic to other faith traditions or communities, as seen in *The Resistance*. These religious plotlines may be heavily laden with convictions that recast contemporary political relations and events within the Arab world from the perspective of a specific religious group's interpretation of Islam.

Using video games for religious education involves seeing media as a simple tool, a conduit[16] that can be easily adapted to transport religious messages. Video games as tools of religious education may serve different roles.[17] Some, such as *Abu Isa's Quest for Knowledge*, focus on practical subjects of religious education or encourage certain qualities such as patience or empathy among players. Others, such as those games featured on the *Islamic Fun* CD, serve as theoretical subjects of religious education, in which the act of play reinforces core religious values and offers participants a particular experience that can serve as a teachable moment. In both cases it is not the video game that serves as the primary subject but the narrative behind it that promotes a specific learning experience that reinforces the religious world. However, within the genre of Islamogaming there are those games that cross the boundary from religious teaching to ideological instruction as political narratives inform the

---

Gamers Speak

Daniel, seventeen years old, Mexican American, 3.15 GPA

- How much do you game each week? *14–15 hours*
- Why do you play? *It's fun, and I think of it as an anti-drug. Plus it helps me kill time.*
- What characters do you tend to assume? *Powerful characters, like Nazis.*
- If I asked your parents about the effects of video games on you and your relationships, what would they say? *It's a very bad habit, and it separates me. My parents don't like it.*
- How would your life be different without video games? *I think my grades would be a lot higher, and I'd just be better at school and socially.*
- What else would you want to say about video games? *They take up a lot of time and money, and they aren't really worth it once you've been playing for a long time.*

story line. While these games may seek to instruct users about Islam, they do so with a strong political agenda that creates very different outcomes for game design and play.

POLITICAL GAMES THAT REFRAME
THE ARAB-MUSLIM WORLD

The most highly criticized genre of Muslim video games is first-person shooter video games. These militaristic games seek to redress a perceived imbalance in the characterization of Muslims in many video games by reversing a common stereotype: they make Arabs the victors rather than the villains in combat. This subgenre of gaming is often informed by distinctly political views of Islam. Political Islam, often associated with fundamentalism or revivalism, is an ideological movement which strongly emphasizes that Islam possesses within it a theory of politics and an interconnection between religion and the state.[18] This is not a new idea, as the roots of political Islam can be traced back to discussions in the eighteenth and nineteenth centuries, yet political Islam as it has emerged in the twentieth century represents not simply a return to an earlier juridical tradition, but a new movement that seeks to transform the symbolic links between politics and religion into a more tangible, closely integrated bond.[19] This movement is marked by concrete ideological struggle against Western colonialism, secularism, corruption, and social injustice. More radical activists and groups go beyond these to "believing that theological doctrine and political realism necessitate violent revolution."[20] The values of political Islam are often highlighted in juxtaposition to perceived Western values of lust, greed, and excess.

Several poignant examples of political gaming exist. These include *Special Forces*,[21] a first-person shooter military game where players become armed members of the Islamic Resistance countering Israeli invasions of Lebanon and performing covert attacks on Israeli positions and politicians. The game was produced by the Hezbollah Internet Bureau with the intention of promoting a very clear pro-Islamic and anti-Israeli message. It is also seen by some as a tool for recruitment: "In this game the Israelis don't win—the resistance always wins."[22]

Another game offered as an online download is *The Stone Throwers*.[23] It was designed by Mohammad Hamza and strategically set on the Al-Aqsa Mosque, on the Dome of the Rock/Temple Mount in Jerusalem, one of the most contested religious sites in the world. The game was created at the beginning of the second Intifada (2000–2002), which started when the soon-to-be Israeli prime minister Ariel Sharon made a controversial visit to the site. In the game,

players take on the mission—armed only with rocks and their bare hands—
of confronting a group of "Israeli terrorists" who seek to infiltrate this holy
place. The game's Web site stresses that it "does not try to propagate hate
or violence against anybody or any people" but rather seeks to support the
Palestinian cause, "proving that Arabs are able to respond against Israeli and
western-made computer games that convey a distorted image about Arabs."[24]
Yet this image of peaceful protest is challenged as players choose from three
game levels: (1) the Stone Child, (2) I Fear No Enemy, or (3) I Fear Not
Death. This last in particular sends a clear message, punctuated by the final
message that appears on the screen at the end of the game.

> Game Over: Well maybe you have killed some Israeli soldiers . . . in
> the Computer world . . . But THIS IS THE REAL WORLD. [*insert image
> of a crowd carrying a young man in a casket, draped with the Palestinian
> flag*] . . . Stop the killing of the Innocents in Palestine . . . Before the
> game is really over.

According to the game designer, *Stone Throwers* is meant to highlight the
struggle of Palestinians living in Israel and to offer an alternative image of
Arabs. Through the game he hopes to raise awareness of the tense situation
and provide a narrative that "responds against Israeli and western-made computer games that convey a distorted image about Arabs."[25]

Another company known for creating politically inspired games is Afkar
Media, a Syrian software company. Several of the video games they have
developed are criticized for the way they retell historical events and empower
Arab characters by representing them as freedom fighters rather than aggres-
sors. Its first game, *Under Ash*,[26] was developed between 1999 and 2001, and
according to Afkar Media's Web site was the first commercially successful
Arabic video game. It is described as a "shooting based on true stories of a
Palestinian youngster from Jerusalem, and how the burning situation in the
occupied territories forced him to grip a stone and defend himself during the
first intifada uprising from 1989 to 1995."[27] Its sequel, *Under Siege* (2005), is
another three-dimensional single-player shooter game where players take on
the perspective of a Palestinian to do battle with Israeli military personnel.
The game is meant to reflect the lives and stories of Palestinian families during the second Intifada. While it avoids suicide bombing and terrorist simulations, players are given an arsenal of weapons, including grenades, rocket
launchers, and sniper rifles, to do battle with the Israeli army from Jenin to
Hebron. Due to graphic violence, both of these games are rated for players
ages thirteen and above. Yet Afkar Media feels the games are important as
they offer an alternative story of Arab conflicts. As stated on the official *Under
Siege* Web site:

> When you live in middle-east you can't avoid being part of the image[. A]s a development company we believe that we had to do our share of responsibility in telling the story behind this conflict and targeting youngsters who depend on video games and movies (which always tell the counter side) to build their acknowledgement about the world.[28]

Because they often simply replace caricatures of Muslims with extremist caricatures of Jews, these games are often seen as being blatantly anti-Semitic and anti-Israeli. These themes are continued in *Under Siege: Golden Edition*, which also focuses on graphic violence. Players shoot at military personnel as they act out the plight of specific Palestinians during the second Intifada, though the creators stress the game "does not include shooting at civilians or abusing them."[29] Afkar Media also developed a sequel with similar underlying narratives, *Under Siege: The Remnants of Human*,[30] though the company has not formally released the game. All of these games represent an attempt by Afkar Media to use real-world Middle East events to tell another story of the Arab experience, a story of struggle and survival in suffering. In an interview with Omand3D.com, a Middle Eastern online graphic arts publication, the company stresses that its work is meant to inspire:

> We have been motivated to engage into this genre due to the natural need in our community for new sources of digital media that reflect our own needs to express our own identity and our ability to create and innovate just like any other modern culture in the world. The lack of products that reflect our Islamic and Arabic culture is clear and we are in a serious need of professionals that could supply our markets with products that could reflect our identity and yet be appealing to the youth.[31]

Yet there are reasons for the controversy over these first-person shooter games, which focus on enacting violence on the enemy. In many respects, these examples show a distinctive understanding of the Arab-Israeli situation in the Middle East, and they may be a response to the objectification of Muslims as villains in other video games. Here the game creators seek to offer alternative images of Arabs as freedom fighters, people of conviction who have possibly been framed falsely by the Western media. Indeed the games' creation may seem justified in light of such games as *Muslim Massacre*, which gained international criticism in 2008 for inviting players to take on the role of an American "hero" armed with "an arsenal of the world's most destructive weapons" to kill as many Muslims as possible.[32] Critics viewed the game as highly inflammatory, as it directed players to hunt down and kill not only the terrorist Osama bin Laden, but also the prophet Muhammad and even Allah. Such incendiary virtual acts led its creator, an American computer programmer based in Australia, to be charged under Queensland's Anti-discrimination Act.[33]

Such hostile framing of Islam provides a basis for understanding why some Muslim game designers feel justified in creating violent games that seek to reverse these roles and stereotyping. Yet the Muslim community has not wholly embraced such characterizations and games, and groups such as the Muslim Council of Britain have condemned some of these games.[34] Other critics of these games have further claimed that creators "are paying so much attention to the political and religious part; they are not concentrating on the technical parts of the game."[35]

Motivated by a political agenda, these games focus on social-political narratives rather than religious instruction. The rise of political gaming described above can be explained as a response to Orientalist tendencies found in mainstream gaming. Sisler and others have argued that Arabs are often portrayed in roles that highlight either romantic representations of Arab females as exotics in need of rescue or of Arab males as evil villains. Thus the " 'orientalist' mode of representation can be perceived as an exclusion from modern constructive discursive, overshadowing the represented contribution to contemporary reality."[36] Games such as *Special Forces*, *Stone Throwers*, and *Under Siege* seek to break traditional "other-ing" patterns by reconstructing Arabs as heroes and overemphasizing the role of freedom fighters. However, Sisler says that self-presentations of Arabs and Muslims often stray into "blatantly ideological and propagandistic construction"[37] that may reinforce problematic stereotypes of Arabs as martyrs and terrorists. In response, some Arab-oriented video games have sought to counter these Orientalist characterizations by offering new images of Muslims as heroes, but doing so in ways that avoid strongly political narratives.

ALTERNATIVE IMAGES OF ISLAM AND MUSLIMS

Another key subgenre within Islamogaming is games that offer alternative accounts of the world told through a Muslim-centered perspective. Similar to first-person shooter games, these games seek to tell a particular story about Arab culture and history. Yet here attention is placed on presenting a creative mythic narrative that highlights either the past or the future of Islamic civilization. While these stories still deal with plots of conflict, they focus less on vilifying Israel and the West, emphasizing rather a positive image of Islam and Muslims.

One example is *Maze of Destiny*, whose elaborate backstory involves a perfect Islamic world turned dark and desolate. Darlak the Deceiver has hidden the Qur'an and imprisoned all religious teachers. Players must dare to enter Darlak's dungeon for the quest, which is described at the Muslim e-store SimplyIslam.com as the ultimate challenge: "Can you recover the missing letters of Surah Fatiha, rescue the teachers of the Quran, and re-establish the true worship of Allah on Earth?"[38] The graphics are basic and the gaming is primitive, but form follows function here as gamers are instructed in Islamic teachings along their journey to restore Islamic truth to the world. Included on the game CD are two other games (*Ummah Defense 1 & 2*) that offer players a world united under the banner of Islam in the year 2114. As a member of the Intergalactic Muslim Council, the player must battle the Flying Evil Robot Armada led by Abu Lahab XVIII, the last unbeliever left on earth, who has constructed this force in an attempt to destroy the world's Muslims.

Some media accounts have argued that *Ummah Defense* is a thinly veiled metaphor for the encroachment of the West on the Muslim world, and that the robots represent an allegory for the predator drones used by the U.S. military.[39] However, most suspect that this concern is due to some of the games mentioned above which consciously malign the West and Israel. For the most part these action-adventure games simply provide an idealized world (in this case, one in which Islam is central) and highlight a good vs. evil conflict where predators, be they evil wizards or robots, must be battled. Another example is *The Adventures of Ahmed*, an Islamic action adventure game produced in 2003 where players take on the role of a medieval Muslim warrior to do battle with an evil king. In its online trailer, the company claims this engaging adventure will "teach your child hadiths [sayings of the prophet, *pbuh*] whilst playing the game, your child plays the role of a Muslim hero."[40] Games such as this seek to not only present an alternative view of Muslims, who become heroes rather than villains or victims, but also highlight that one gains success in life through living out religious principles.

A further example that illustrates the remixing of Muslim heroes is Afkar Media's project *Quraish*,[41] an Arabic-language three-dimensional real-time strategy game. *Quraish* is a notable change from the company's previous games, which were set in contemporary Palestine. This game's story line begins in the Arabian desert in 590 CE and tracks the development of the first century of Islam in the Middle East from the perspective of four groups in the region: Bedouins, Arabs, Persians, and Romans. Named after the Prophet Muhammad's tribe, Al-Quraysh, the game attempts to present different views on the historic development of Islam by offering players the opportunity to see events from the perspective of the group they choose to lead. The game's Web site highlights this multiple-perspective telling of history, stating, "Was it 'Al Jihad' the holy war that makes them conquer? Was it the tolerance of this spiritual religion? Or is it the willingness of their gifted leaders? Well . . .

you will have the chance to choose it. . . . You will have the chance to choose it by your self!" While based on a political narrative, *Quraish* takes seriously the representation of the prophet Muhammad, his followers, and his sayings in ways that evoke what Afkar Media executive Radwan Kasmiya calls "Digital Dignity."[42] By this he means the emotions that arise when a game "offers a true perspective" to the Arab player community, so that they can relate to the story line as being authentic or reflecting their own background and culture in positive ways.[43] Here, historic reality and religious values are taken with equal seriousness and brought to bear together in a fantasy action game. Muslims are characterized not only as warriors but as people of faith and tradition.

A final example in this subgenre is *Faaris*, billed as a role-playing game where players take on the role of a fifteen-year-old Muslim horseman who must embark on a perilous journey when his village is attacked and his grand-parents are taken by the king of darkness Yabulon. Along the way, players learn about *salaat* (prayer), *wudu* (ritual washing), and the Qur'an and hadith through many of the characters they meet along the journey. While an under-lying narrative seems to be to teach children to fight, this is couched in the fact that through absorbing religious instruction they truly become conquer-ors. The alternative narratives within this subgenre of Islamogaming promote a very different image to the Orientalist framings of Arabs; here, to be a hero means to speak Arabic and fight evil.[44]

These games play an interesting role, serving as public relations tools for the Muslim community by stressing positive images of Islamic culture, values, and history. By focusing on mythical historic or futuristic narratives, they separate themselves from political gaming by placing emphasis on the moral actions of the player over the unfolding of the plotline. Muslim characters are portrayed as victors and champions, and their religious devotion is the central part of what makes them heroic. These images still affirm problematic stereotypes of Muslims primarily as warriors as they reinforce ideas of battle and conflict. However, the conflict narrative is such a central part of many video games that it can be argued that most video games contribute to such stereotyping in many different categories. Of particular importance here is the underlying symbolic and ideological framing that is taking place and the attempts of Muslim game designers to offer counternarratives to the domi-nant stories promoted within gaming.

REFLECTIONS ON ISLAMOGAMING

Online video games have been described as virtual "third places" that cre-ate "spaces for social interaction and relationships beyond the workplace and home . . . that typically function to expose the individual to a diversity of worldviews."[45] This exploration illustrates how religious video games can serve as important and unique storytelling media for a given religious community. Religious gaming plays the role of storyteller by affirming specific religious, social, or even political narratives central to a religious tradition or community. While they may be marketed as games seeking to have a mass appeal, they primarily serve as internal tools to affirm the specific beliefs and stories of a given group. These games create "third places" that expose religious gamers to stories that guide, teach, socialize, or even indoctrinate them toward specific beliefs and outlooks.

In recent work, I have argued that religious groups and users often undergo a complex negotiation and decision-making process in their determination about whether they will incorporate new media technologies into the life of their community.[46] This negotiation process involves evaluating new media in light of past community precedents of media engagement and situating it within the current needs and goals of the community. Negotiation can lead in one of three directions—acceptance and appropriation, rejection and resistance, or reconstruction and innovation—or a combination of these strategies. In acceptance and appropriation, media is embraced as a neutral tool to be used for religious purposes or to enhance the life of the community. In rejection and resistance, media is approached with caution due to problematic features or the results that it generates, so some aspects of the technology may be rejected and some uses or outcomes resisted. In both reconstruction and innovation, the decision is made to reshape the technology in some way in order to enhance the community. A community of religious groups thus becomes empowered as users restructure the technology in ways that may differ from the initial intent of that technology's designers, because the values, desires, and needs of the religious audience may require a different response to technology than that of the general population. Perhaps designers infuse the technology with a new narrative that complements the story of the religious community or they alter the technology's platform or features so that its use supports religious practices. In some cases, innovation may even lead to new religious practices as the technology extends possibilities for religious engagement in the contemporary world.

Within the phenomenon of Islamogaming we see a trend toward the acceptance and appropriation of gaming technology as religious narratives and goals are easily projected onto various gaming genres. We also see movement toward innovation in gaming as designers create new narratives to suit particular religious or sociopolitical intentions. Video games with pronounced religious narratives or motivation do more than project religious values and stories onto a technological platform; these games play specific roles for the beliefs of the designers and the religious community they represent. Such games provide positive and problematic images of Islam, although many of the more violent games can be seen as reactionary responses to negative stereotyping of Muslims and Arabs within other popular video games.

These games also raise many interesting questions, especially in relation to the geopolitics of gaming for religious communities. Do first-person shooter games with strong sociopolitical narratives encourage ideological and actual warfare? Might putting a religious person into the role of warrior run counter to certain religious values and ideals? What should our ethical response be to the act of scapegoating or demonization of different religious groups within gaming? Do religious gamers and designers have a certain ethical responsibility to counter the promotion of such narratives and typologies? These areas in need of further exploration are important, especially when we consider the powerful role religious games can play in offering alternative stories and promoting different values in the world of gaming.

5

Wii Are In*spirit*ed

The Transformation of Home Video Gaming Consoles (and Us)

KUTTER CALLAWAY

In October 1977, just over a year before I was born, Atari released the VCS (later renamed the "2600"), one of the first in-home video computer systems capable of operating a wide array of games on a singular console. Although considered by many an ephemeral conceit akin to Pet Rocks and eight-track stereos, this apparently innocuous technology has indelibly altered not only the contemporary cultural landscape but also an entire generation's fundamental awareness of the world. Consequently, a number of the most distinct memories from my formative years involve the lusting after, acquisition of, or rapt participation in some form of video games. When a neighborhood friend was the first on our block to acquire a Nintendo Entertainment System (NES), I immediately descended into his basement to feast on what I believed to be nothing less than a crystallized form of digital beauty. Much to our chagrin, we emerged twelve hours later to find police combing our streets, searching for the "missing" children our parents had duly reported. After my brothers and I upgraded our Atari 2600 with an NES, which we subsequently replaced with a Sega Genesis, a Super Nintendo, a PlayStation, a Nintendo 64, and a Sega Dreamcast, I began to measure the very passage of time in terms of which generation of consoles we were playing. Accordingly, video games have served as an ever-present backdrop in the narrative of my life. As one of five children, I investigated the delicate nuances of sportsmanship while playing *Tetris* and *Madden NFL* with my siblings. As a college student, I watched friends drop out of school because of their *GoldenEye* obsession. As a husband, I and my wife entertained other couples by hosting *Mario Party* nights. And as a pastor working in various ecclesial contexts, I constructed ministry events in which entire evenings were dedicated to playing *Halo*. Even now, one of my brothers works as a character artist for Sony's *God of War III*, and I occasionally serve as a play tester for the same game. In short, I have never known a world without video games.

In the following analysis, I operate with the base assumption that, rather than an anomalous phenomena, my particular experience is representative of a broader, more ubiquitous reality. That is, video games are a pervasive cultural form that both reflects and constructs the contemporary cultural imagination, serving as a primary locus of meaning making and identity formation for those born in the post-Atari era.[1] Put simply, video games matter. Yet the question I want to press in this investigation is more than simply anthropological or sociological; it is explicitly theological. Namely, how might we speak theologically concerning video games, not simply as cultural products, but as concrete forms of life that are intrinsically related to the deep-lived passions and desires of contemporary persons? Ultimately, how might we understand video games in relation to the presence and work of God in the contemporary situation?[2]

More specifically, though, I would like to consider the evolution of in-home video gaming consoles. In particular, as the investigation offers a salient example of how broader cultural impulses provoke individuals to pursue particular goods, I want to focus on the recent proliferation of the paradigm-shifting Nintendo Wii as reflective of the desires and passions around which contemporary persons orient their lives. Ultimately, I want to advance the thesis that, rather than decrying the contemporary urge to find meaning in the decidedly embodied experience offered by gaming consoles such as the Wii, we might best understand this impulse by locating it within a larger theological framework, conceiving of it in terms of the energizing presence of God's Spirit in the world; the significance we derive from these concrete engagements with the virtual world is indeed related to our embodied existence. However, we are not simply embodied; Wii are inspirited.

Thus, in this chapter, we not only address the key developments that have punctuated the historical progression of home gaming consoles but also the manners in which the Wii experience, in contradistinction to other gaming experiences, is accepted and understood as an expressly embodied experience. Moreover, in order to locate this discussion within a larger theological framework, we press the question of how the contemporary cultural passion for the Wii relates to the larger movement of the Spirit in the world, and how this passion offers a pointed challenge to theology.

A BRIEF HISTORY OF (VIDEO GAME CONSOLE) TIME

In their introductions to the two editions of *The Video Game Theory Reader*, Mark Wolf and Bernard Perron offer two insights that prove instructive for our analysis. The first concerns the importance of attending to historical developments in our analyses of the video gaming experience. Wolf and Perron state,

> Knowledge of older games provides a historical context and background from which more recent games have evolved and on which their own forms, genres, and conventions rely. More attention should be paid to older games . . . developed over time, rather than merely on the latest incarnations of these things as though they have no past or predecessors.[3]

Second, drawing on a wide array of video game theories, they offer a helpful definition of "video games" that we employ for the rest of our discussion: "Of all the various approaches that have been taken in defining the video game, a few elements seem to appear persistently. . . . The most fundamental of these elements are: an *algorithm*, *player activity*, *interface*, and *graphics*."[4]

Therefore, in this first section, we briefly take into consideration the historical context from which the Wii has evolved, fully recognizing that the manner in which we divide up video gaming history is largely a product of our particular interests. Additionally, though, we allow Wolf and Perron's definition of "video game" to guide and limit our analysis of the various iterations of home video gaming consoles. Consequently, we consider each console's distinct contributions to the video gaming experience in terms of its graphics, interface, and player activity.[5] In so doing, we assume a ludological rather than a narrative approach to video game analysis. As Gonzalo Frasca points out, "Unlike traditional media, video games are not just based on representation but on an alternative semiotical structure known as simulation. Even if simulations and narrative share some common elements—character, settings, events—their mechanics are essentially different. More importantly, they also offer distinct rhetorical possibilities."[6] In other words, in our analysis of video gaming as a meaningful cultural practice, *how* a game is played is equally as important as what the game is about.

Atari 2600

The story I want to tell begins in 1977 with the Atari 2600, the first commercially successful video game console that supported myriad games through the use of individual game cartridges.[7] Owing to a combination of the console's technological capabilities (a processor containing 128 bytes of internal RAM) along with the ingenuity of Atari's programmers, the 2600 offered consumers a graphically mesmerizing experience, which included "high-resolution objects, colors, and low-resolution backgrounds."[8] While the user interface, which included both paddle and joystick controllers, was unaccommodating by contemporary standards, it too was an improvement on the simple, two-directional knobs that accompanied the various *Pong* consoles released prior to 1976. Most significant, though, by making a home video game console that was technologically advanced and relatively affordable, Atari shifted the primary location of player activity. Users were able to engage in the video gaming experience without pumping quarters into a machine and without leaving the comfort of their own home. As a result, the Atari 2600 became one of the best-selling consoles in history, totaling more than 25 million units sold worldwide.

Nintendo Entertainment System

Debuting in the United States in 1985, the Nintendo Entertainment System (NES) not only resuscitated a dying industry,[9] but it effectively charted the course that console development would follow for the next twenty years. Chief among the NES's contributions was the marked advancement in graphics from the Atari 2600, made possible by an 8-bit central processor that "would finally give way to the distinctive, cartoonish look of third- and fourth-generation consoles."[10] Additionally, the interface for the NES, which replaced the joystick controllers of earlier consoles with game controllers that utilized a cross-shaped directional pad and two round buttons, set the standard for all user interfaces that would follow. Thus, player activity was condensed to the sequential depression and release of a series of buttons. Ultimately, though, what resulted from Nintendo's success with the NES (over 60 million units sold) was the codification of the technological advances that enabled Nintendo to attain commercial viability and to reenergize an enervated industry. Consequently, every home video gaming system that emerged after the NES offered a gaming experience oriented around two primary developments: the enhancement of graphics over prior consoles and the increasing complexity of an essentially standardized user interface. One's share of the market, it was believed, was directly correlated with a console's increasingly breathtaking visuals and an ever more sophisticated interface.

Sony PlayStation

The release of Sony's PlayStation in 1994 further solidified the notion that advanced graphical capabilities and an equally complex interface were the keys to a console's commercial success. Initially developed as a CD-ROM add-on for the Super Nintendo, the PlayStation was the first 32-bit "3D-centric console,"[11] which allowed Sony to develop games with unparalleled speed and quality of graphics. Additionally, in order to manipulate effectively the PlayStation's visually stunning, three-dimensional worlds, Sony increased the complexity of its user interface, mounting additional buttons on the top of the controllers. Thus, while users were treated to previously unimaginable graphical capabilities, the PlayStation's interface required a markedly higher level of technical sophistication and manual dexterity in order for individuals to engage in the gaming experience. Nonetheless, the PlayStation has become one of the single best-selling consoles in history, amassing more than 100 million units sold since its debut.

Consoles of the Twenty-First Century

In the years following the PlayStation's success, the gaming industry has rarely deviated from its formulaic conception of what consumers desire in the gaming experience. While we might chart the development of other console designers (e.g., Sega or 3DO), or recount the individual consoles produced by Nintendo (e.g., N64 and GameCube), Sony (e.g., PlayStation 2 and 3), and Microsoft (e.g., Xbox and Xbox 360), the basic narrative remains the same: gaming companies have historically developed their systems to meet the apparent consumer desire for more sophisticated graphics and more complex user interfaces. Thus, each successive generation of consoles has featured more powerful processors, larger hard drives, greater memory capacity, and technologically superior video capabilities—all with the express intent of producing more visually vibrant, fluid, and pleasing (i.e., "real") gaming experiences.[12] However, perhaps equally significant, player activity, while certainly more complex, has remained virtually identical for the last twenty years. Yet, with the overwhelming proliferation of home consoles, there seemed to be little need for tinkering with such a successful modus operandi. That is, of course, until the advent of the Wii.

WII WOULD LIKE TO SHIFT THE PARADIGM

Released in 2006, the Nintendo Wii represents a monumental shift in the development of home gaming consoles. As indicated above, the historical context from which the Wii emerged was marked by a general consensus that consumers wanted more powerful systems that could unleash the visual potential of a game's virtual worlds. This fundamental conception has been expressed most fully with the development of the Xbox 360 and the PlayStation 3, both of which allow for unparalleled visual beauty in the gaming experience. Yet, as a response to their decreasing market share since the inception of the PlayStation, and in light of the ever-shrinking base of consumers whose technical mastery attracted them to a complex interface and whose economic freedom allowed them to purchase a four-hundred- to six-hundred-dollar system, Nintendo reconceived its entire approach toward home gaming consoles. Rather than contend for the hard-core gaming market, which would require a more powerful and, thereby, more expensive machine, Nintendo targeted a broader audience, hoping to involve the non-gamer, younger children, and entire families in the gaming experience. To achieve this goal, however, Nintendo had to defy more than two decades of the gaming industry's conventional wisdom. As one of the Wii's lead developers, Shigeru Miyamoto, recalls, "The consensus [at Nintendo] was that power isn't everything for a console. Too many powerful consoles can't coexist. It's like having only ferocious dinosaurs. They might fight and hasten their own extinction."[13]

At the risk of understatement, Nintendo's unconventional gamble has paid off. While the PlayStation 3 and the Xbox 360 have consistently failed to meet the commercial expectations established by their highly successful predecessors, the Wii has become the fastest-selling home console of all time. Since November 2006, it has sold over 50 million units worldwide, which is nearly double the sales of the Xbox 360 and more than twice that of the PlayStation 3.[14] Even amid a downturn in the economy, in 2008 consumers in the United States purchased over five hundred thousand Wii's on "Black Friday" alone and 10.17 million over the course of the year. If not a legitimate cultural phenomenon, the Wii has, at the very least, captured the hearts and minds of contemporary culture. The question "why?" is most significant for the present discussion. Why are individuals and families so passionately pursuing this type of good—a toy—during a global economic recession? Why, rather than just hard-core gamers, are non-gamers, young children, and adults attracted to the Wii? What about the Wii imbues it with such mass appeal? And what changes within the cultural imagination have allowed individuals to construe the Wii experience as a valuable form of contemporary life? It would seem that, in light of the overwhelming consumption of the Wii over and against other home gaming consoles, contemporary persons are in fact seeking a particular type of experience—an experience that they perceive, at least initially and in some manner, that the Wii provides. Yet, what about the Wii, specifically, causes contemporary persons to associate the experience that it provides with the broader passions and desires around which they orient their lives? To answer this question, I want to identify three themes that emerge in the Wii experience that directly relate to the elements of a video game we identified earlier.

Interface

The paradigm shift that Nintendo initiated is primarily the result of a full reimagining of the user interface. Although a few exceptions do exist, from the time of the original NES, home console controllers have remained largely unchanged. While gamers had become comfortable with the classic controller, in many ways, the old user interface was not only dictating player activity but also "the way graphics were made, the way battles were fought in role-playing games, [and] the arc of in-game stories. They were all being made to fit one standard."[15] Thus, Nintendo introduced the Wii remote, a wireless motion-sensor device shaped like a television remote control that allows gamers to manipulate on-screen activity through a full range of bodily movements. Rather than simply pressing buttons, the intuitive controller allows players to mimic actual physical activity such as swinging a golf club, conducting an orchestra, or performing meticulous surgical operations. In some cases, the physical intensity engendered by Nintendo's newly conceived interface was such that users were prone to inadvertently release their controllers during game play, thereby threatening the livelihood of other users and risking damage to expensive television screens.[16] Consequently, the gaming experience that the Wii offers is not one that simply involves the rapid movement of one's thumbs in response to visual stimuli. Rather, a player's entire physical structure is implicated in the gaming experience through a unique user interface. Thus, as a fully embodied engagement with the virtual world, the Wii experience is an expressly *somatic* experience.[17] It follows, then, that contemporary persons might perceive the Wii as a meaningful form of life, not simply because of its novelty, but because, in some way, the embodied experience it provides is related to our deep-lived passion for a somatic engagement with the world.[18]

Graphics

Issuing directly from the desire to create a home gaming experience based upon a player's embodied interaction, Nintendo developed a console that elevated the Wii's revolutionary user interface over powerful graphic technology. Herein lies the fundamental paradigm shift, for the Wii is by no means a powerful system in relation to its contemporaries. Whereas the Xbox 360 and the PlayStation 3 each offer a 3.2GHz processor, 512 Megabytes of RAM, upward of 160GB of hard-drive space, and high-definition outputs, the Wii is equipped with a 729MHz processor, 88 Megabytes of RAM, 512MB of flash memory, and features no actual HDTV graphics.[19] Needless to say, the graphic capabilities of the Wii are simply dwarfed by its competitors.[20]

Gamers Speak

Sebastian, seventeen years old, Mexican American, 3.8 GPA, Honor Roll

- What games do you tend to play? *Violent games.*
- Why do you play? *Because I'm bored and have nothing else to do.*
- What characters do you tend to assume? *The cool-looking ones.*
- How would your life be different without video games? *I probably would have been athletic and had friends.*
- What else would you want to say about video games? *They are expensive.*

However, whereas the consoles of the older paradigm provide a primarily cognitive experience in which one responds to increasingly lifelike visual stimuli, the Wii offers a gaming experience that involves one's tactile, aural, vestibular, and kinesthetic senses. The Wii's multisensory nature, however, is not isolated to the Wii remote. The Wii balance board is a wireless device that looks like a bathroom scale and allows users not only to engage in exercises that contribute to physical fitness, but also to participate in snowboarding or skateboarding games by emulating the sports' actual movements. Additionally, Electronic Arts recently released *EA Sports: Active Trainer*, a game that comes equipped with resistance bands and a leg strap that holds the Wii remote in order to track a player's lower-body movements. However, even with these expressly embodied games and input devices, the Wii experience is not purely sensual. It is, after all, still a gaming console, which necessarily involves a requisite level of cognitive stimulation, yet by emphasizing its somatic, multisensory interface over purely graphical requirements, the Wii experience firmly locates the mind within the body. In other words, playing the Wii is a holistic experience. As such, the Wii not only offers a unique gaming experience in relation to every other home console currently available, it reflects a contemporary impulse toward holism that drives individuals to pursue the experience the Wii provides as well as construe it as meaningful.[21]

Player Activity

Ultimately, the combination of the Wii's revolutionary user interface with its unconventional graphical power has most directly affected player activity. Thus, as we intimated above, its primary significance is ludological. That is, the activity involved in the Wii's gaming experience is demonstrably different than any other home console past or present and has played a key role in its commercial appeal. There is no need to master a sophisticated sequence of commands to manipulate on-screen activity. Rather, anyone who can swing a tennis racket or turn the steering wheel of a car can effectively play tennis or participate in a NASCAR race. Accordingly, the ease and simplicity with which players participate in the Wii's gaming experience has played a significant role in attracting younger children and non-gamers, and it appeals to this much broader demographic in part because of how the Wii makes people feel. In contrast to other systems, the simplicity of the Wii's player activity does not leave users feeling incapable or obtuse, but engaged and, at times, accomplished. Thus, there is an affective or emotional dimension to the Wii experience. As Miyamoto suggests, "Nowadays, software makers want games to be so realistic, but first and foremost games should evoke emotions. . . . The Japanese word *itoshii* is used when you think fondly of someone. You wouldn't normally feel that when playing games, but that's what I was striving for."[22]

The Wii's affective appeal, though, is not isolated to non-gamers. Using its new Virtual Console technology, players are able to purchase and download any game Nintendo has ever made, along with a number of games from other platforms such as the Commodore 64, NEOGEO, and Sega Genesis. This feature is especially significant in light of the growing interest in retro-gaming among many hard-core gamers, for it offers a nostalgic experience—one that is often highly emotional. As gamer Chelly Green recalls, "I have all these warm memories of playing over at friends' [houses] at 3 a.m. when I was younger with a little TV hidden in the bed . . . [and] of the first time we found the ice beam in *Metroid*."[23] Consequently, as Beck and Wade have suggested, the emotions that video games evoke, especially among the gamer generation, function as the interpretive lens through which not only the gaming experience, but life as a whole is interpreted and understood.[24] In other words, our emotions are central to the power and meaning of the video game experience, and insofar as the Wii provides an occasion in which players are engaged affectively, contemporary persons are able to construe both the Wii experience and the whole of their lives in terms of their deeply felt passions and desires—those highly emotional impulses around which they orient their lives.[25]

THE BODY, THE SPIRIT, AND THE WII

So we have identified bodies, holism, and emotions as central to the Wii's mass appeal—all themes that, perhaps not surprisingly, the Christian tradition appears to be either ill equipped to address or simply unwilling to engage. Owing in large part to its Augustinian, and therefore Platonic and Neoplatonic heritage, the Western theological tradition has often treated the somatic, holistic, and affective dimensions of human life with suspicion. Consequently, theological considerations of embodied experiences are often beholden to a Platonic conception of humanity's "imprisonment" in the world of "visible" but "less than real" material forms.[26] Moreover, as with Augustine's distinctly Neoplatonic thought, emotionally laden forms of life are construed in terms of the "misleading" and "disorienting" effects of affections and sensual pleasures.[27] This basic uncertainty concerning our bodies and emotions—an uncertainty deeply embedded in the Western theological imagination—serves as one of the core problems in our ability to understand the theological significance of the video gaming experience. Therefore, the question I want to pursue in this final section is as follows: how might we speak theologically concerning the contemporary drive to find meaning in the Wii's gaming experience from our perspective within a tradition that has been historically ambivalent toward somatic, holistic, and affective experiences? In answering this question—and thereby in challenging the traditional conceptions we have inherited—I want to suggest that we might best understand these impulses by conceiving of them in terms of the energizing presence of God's Spirit in the world.[28]

Wii Are Somatic

In the preceding section, we outlined three themes concerning the manner in which contemporary persons associate their passionate pursuit of the Wii with their deep-lived desires. The first theme we identified was the somatic nature of the Wii gaming experience. Due to its unique interface, the Wii offers a necessarily physical, embodied, and sensual experience. Although many in the Western theological tradition have remained suspicious about this physicality and sensuality, the work of Friedrich Schleiermacher proves instructive for reflecting theologically on the relationship between the presence of the Spirit and the somatic nature of the gaming experience. Schleiermacher conceived of "feeling"—one's embodied, sensual experience of "absolute dependence"—as the constitutive element in all genuinely "religious" experiences. Therefore, in developing Schleiermacher's thought, we might say that human beings are fundamentally sensual creatures.[29] And while our sensuality might certainly be misdirected or disoriented, thereby marring our relational constitution, conceiving of our sensual nature as the source of the human malady denies the movement of the Spirit in our embodied lives, for the Spirit affirms us as somatic, sensual creatures by taking up residence in our bodies: "Your body is a temple of the Holy Spirit within you" (1 Cor. 6:19). Thus, by speaking of the physicality of the Wii gaming experience in terms of the Spirit's embodied presence, our sensual engagement with video games is seen, not as meretricious, but as an essential part of what makes our life in the world beautiful and good.[30] Moreover, as it is made manifest in the unrivaled consumption of the Wii, these yearnings for a bodily, sensual encounter in contemporary culture reflect the pervasive presence of the Spirit who is constantly orienting somatic creatures toward other bodies and, ultimately, toward an embodied relatedness with God.[31] The theological question, then, is not how we might move beyond the sensuality inherent in the gaming experience, but how we might value and affirm this sensuality as an essential component in our ability to "glorify God in [our bodies]" (1 Cor. 6:20).[32]

Wii Are Holistic

Following closely from the first theme, we determined that the Wii experience is not purely physical, but holistic. Along with the somatic dimensions of the Wii's user interface, the cognitive elements of the gaming experience are recognized as integral components in the unification of the individual's mind and body. And, at least initially, individuals within contemporary culture seem to associate the holistic experience afforded by the Wii with a more general desire for experiences that locate the mind *within* the body. Yet how might we speak of this holistic drive within contemporary culture in terms of the presence and movement of the Spirit? Perhaps, as with Jürgen Moltmann, we might recognize that the reunification of presently fragmented human beings is central to the presence and movement of the Spirit of God. According to Moltmann, in light of modern theology's hostility toward the body, which is the result of the "continuing Platonizing of Christianity," the development of a "holistic doctrine of God the Holy Spirit" is "literally essential" for theological reflection:

> It [a holistic doctrine of the Spirit] must be holistic in at least two ways. On the one hand, it must comprehend human beings *in their total being*, soul and body, consciousness and the unconscious, person and sociality, society and social institutions. On the other hand it must also embrace the wholeness of the community of creation, which is shared by human beings, the earth, and all other created beings and things.[33]

For Moltmann, the Spirit we encounter through our concrete engagement with the world is an energizing presence, breathing creative life into whole persons—both minds and bodies. In a similar vein the Psalmist sings, "Create in me a clean heart [i.e., the 'inner person' or 'mind']), O God, and put a new and right spirit [i.e., the embodied 'seat of emotions'] within me. Do not cast me away from your presence, and do not take your holy spirit from me" (Psalm 51:10–11). Thus, the presence of the Spirit that is made manifest in the gaming experience—the life-giving breath of God—engenders a holistic engagement with both the cognitive and somatic dimensions of our life in the world. We might conclude, then, that the holistic impulse driving individuals to consume the Wii and to participate in the experience it provides is more than a simple desire for novelty; it is rather an inchoate "in-spirited-ness," provoked by the presence and movement of the Spirit in contemporary life.

Wii Are Affective

The final theme we addressed had to do with the affective dimensions of the Wii experience and the manners in which these emotions often serve to orient contemporary persons' general "awareness of the world." As we noted above, the Western theological tradition has historically exhibited a great deal of trepidation regarding the affective dimensions of human life. Yet, if the primary interpretive lens through which the majority of the gaming generation imagines their life-in-the-world is affective, then it has to do with how cultural forms and practices—from a piece of art, to a personal relationship, to a virtual world—make us "feel." Thus, it is imperative that we refrain from speaking of these emotional orientations as encumbrances to the Trinitarian God's project in the world, for, rather than impediments to the Spirit's work, they are the Spirit's very milieu.[34] Rather than directing us away from a fundamental component of the human experience, the Spirit's presence enables us to construe and construct the world in, with, and through our emotions. At Pentecost, Peter sought not to deny the emotional fervor that consumed those quickened by the Spirit's presence. Neither did he balk at his compatriots' behavior, which was ecstatic enough to be misconstrued as drunkenness (Acts 2:13–16). Instead, he spoke of their emotional exuberance in terms of the larger work of the Spirit and affirmed their emotionality as an integral part of God's project in the world, which culminated in the resurrected Christ. The prophesying, the envisioning, and the dreaming—all highly emotional manners of construing the world—were explicitly related to the presence of the Spirit as the manifestation of God's redemptive plan (Acts 2:17–33). Thus, like Peter, rather than decrying the contemporary impulse toward forming an essentially affective awareness of the world, we might do well to recognize it as the movement of the Spirit, who ceaselessly works to reclaim our affective conceptions of the world by reorienting us to the One in whom all our emotions find their ultimate fulfillment.

WII ARE IN*SPIRIT*ED

From the time I was eleven years old, I spent the weeks leading up to every Christmas and birthday constructing a series of near-flawless arguments designed to convince my parents that my very life depended upon the possession of a Nintendo Game Boy. In spite of my well-crafted rhetoric, however, I never received one. I can still hear the echo of my mother's words: "You play video games enough at home as it is. I don't want you playing them *everywhere*." While I was unwilling to admit it at the time, she was, as mothers often are, absolutely correct. Besides being a somewhat portly adolescent, myriad other factors suggested that I would greatly benefit from a few moments away from the virtual world. And to this day, I remain thankful for my parents' fundamental apprehension toward a life consumed by video games. I recount this story to emphasize what I am, in fact, not saying. In no way am I intending to suggest here that a Christian approach toward video games involves any sort of wholesale embrace of the virtual world and all that it entails. Wisdom and discernment are surely necessary components of any faithful construal of cultural products and their attendant forms of life, especially when those products function formatively.

Yet this discussion takes place within a cultural context in which the Christian community's traditional forms of life are increasingly—if not entirely—treated with suspicion, forced to the periphery, and disregarded as insignificant. And in their place, innumerable cultural practices have arisen that serve as the primary location for meaning making and identity formation in our postmodern world. These practices are, for lack of a better word, "religious" in character. Therefore, in the present analysis, rather than judging these practices under the rubric of a culturally abstracted Christian "truth," and then offering a critique and condemnation of their apparent insufficiency, we have simply been pressing the question of how we might understand the manners in which God is already present, moving, and at work in the contemporary cultural experience. Specifically, I have asserted that, rather than decrying the urge to find meaning in the decidedly embodied experiences offered by gaming consoles such as the Wii, we might best understand this contemporary impulse by locating it within a larger theological framework, conceiving of it in terms of God's inspiriting presence in the world.

However, I do want to stress the incipient state of this project and suggest two specific areas in which it might be further developed. First, as we have focused our discussion on the particularities of the Wii as a home gaming console, we have necessarily limited ourselves to the singular and historically isolated experience it offers. That the Wii has affected a significant shift in the conventions of home gaming is not in question. However, given the rate of technological change in the world of video games, by the time this essay is in print, the advances made by the Wii may have already been shown to be a passé blip in the history of video gaming. Thus, more needs to be said concerning the sensual, holistic, and affective dimensions of the practice of video gaming as a whole. While the Wii is certainly dominating the market at the time of this writing, how might we speak of the Spirit's movement in the gaming experiences offered by more conventional consoles or even other gaming media, especially as they appeal more often to hard-core gamers? Second, though, we might develop more fully our approach to the video game experience as a contemporary cultural practice. More specifically, given the ritualized nature of gaming experiences, along with the passion with which individuals and communities both pursue them, we might develop our theological understanding of these experiences as devotional practices. Are we to consider the essentially secular devotional practice of video gaming as a mere intimation or precursor to an alternative and intrinsically more satisfying practice—one that assumes the form of traditional Christian worship? Or, in light of our consideration of the work of the Spirit in creation, might we consider these practices as potentially (trans)formative acts of worship that are simply in need of a new orientation—one that finds all our somatic, holistic, and affective desires ultimately fulfilled in God's "in-Spirit-ing" presence? While, in many cases, I would certainly argue the former, I am unable to reject the latter out of hand; it seems that, ultimately, the construction and development of these cultural practices reflects, not a longing for a particular ritual form, but a fundamental yearning for the presence of God—an incomparably beautiful presence that ceaselessly inspirits us, breathing life even into the virtual worlds Wii inhabit.

SECTION 2

Halos

6

Myst and *Halo*

A Conversation with Rand Miller and Marty O'Donnell

LISA SWAIN

In the summer of 2009, I sat down with my former colleague at Biola University, Craig Detweiler, to interview two powerhouses in the gaming industry. On our conference call was Rand Miller of Cyan Worlds, who along with his brother, Robyn, designed, created, and starred in *Myst*. Not only hailed as the most commercially successful computer game of the twentieth century, critics also universally agreed that *Myst* elevated gaming from adolescent pastime to artful expression. *Wired* magazine raved, "*Myst* was better than anything anyone had ever seen. *Myst* was beautiful, complicated, emotional, dark, intelligent, absorbing. It was the only thing like itself; it had invented its own category."[1] Rand continued to innovate through multiple sequels, including *Riven* and, most recently, the massively multiplayer online game *Uru*.

We were also joined by award-winning composer Marty O'Donnell of Bungie Studios. His many memorable soundtracks include *Myth*, *Oni*, and the revered *Halo* trilogy (created with Michael Salvatori). In 2001, *Rolling Stone* hailed *Halo: Combat Evolved* as "Best Original Soundtrack." *Halo 2* became North America's best-selling soundtrack of all time. For *Halo 3*, O'Donnell and Salvatori composed for a twenty-four-voice choir and a sixty-piece orchestra. Critics and fans have pronounced, "As John Williams is to movies, so Marty O'Donnell is to video games."

While much of the faith community seems oblivious to the power and influence of the gaming industry, this interview stands as a testament that Christians have been enthusiastically involved from its earliest years, creating some of its biggest hits and revolutionizing the field. Rand Miller and Marty O'Donnell talked to us from their homes in the verdant surroundings of Washington State. What follows is an excerpt of that conversation.

PIONEERS

Craig Detweiler: *I wonder if we might be living in the golden age of video games. It seems like every few years we've had a* major *leap forward in technology. Did you ever imagine that you'd be pioneers in the world of video games and interactive entertainment?*

Rand Miller: I don't think you know you're a pioneer until you turn around and find the arrows in your back. [General laughter]

Lisa Swain: *Ouch.*

Rand: I didn't realize any of that. Parts of it I wouldn't wish on anyone. It's a tough, tough industry to be in. It has its moments. But, it's a whole different animal to a certain extent.

Marty O'Donnell: Well, I can say that I was in a different industry. I was doing film and commercials and stuff out of Chicago. But I always played games. In [19]93, Rand's young friend, eighteen-year-old Josh Staub, came to my house and showed me *Myst*. I started playing the beta version of that game and just fell in love with what those guys had done. They truly were pioneers and . . . this is not blowing smoke, by the way, Rand. But, really Cyan took the video game business as an art form and just jumped it forward leaps and bounds. That's what actually drew me in. It's like finally I could feel there was a place for somebody that did the kind of work I did *in* this business. So, I thank Robyn and Rand for that.

Rand: Thank you for that, Marty.

Marty: Well, it's true.

Craig: *You guys met on* Riven. *How did that come about?*

Rand: It was Josh Staub and his dad Dick. Marty was a friend of theirs, and they were friends of ours. We met Marty. I don't even remember what the trip was. But we came to your studio there in Chicago.

Marty: I pretty much hijacked you guys. You thought I was just going to be a driver to take you to some interview. Dick said, "Hey, Marty, I shouldn't do this, but I'm going to let you pick those guys up." So that's what I did.

Rand: And we had a blast. Marty's sensibilities and background and faith as well . . . we had a lot in common. So, it was cool. And the interesting part was we were just getting started in the sound work in these games and Marty was coming from a whole different direction. He was so intrigued and motivated to apply all the stuff he knew, which was a lot more than we knew, into the video game arena. Don't get me wrong; this was an education for all of us as we went along. Every game we got, we felt like we were just learning as we went. It was never a science. We failed as much as we succeeded at every turn. So Marty got to learn along with us as we were upping the bar for *Riven*. And I think it was a great adventure.

Marty: Yeah, it really was. I think we really pushed the quality part way forward, especially on the audio side. And the graphics too were incredible for the time. Everything else. It was a really nice step forward. The fun thing about meeting Robyn and Rand though was for me . . . since I had played through *Myst* . . . just like a lot of people out there . . . you play *Myst* and you actually get to know Robyn and Rand in some warped degree because they are present in the game and their influence is all over it. So I knew more about them than they knew about me. But the fun thing was as we were comparing notes about our faith and our upbringing is they had both seen a film my dad did in the early '60s called *The Gospel Blimp*.

Rand: I was going to mention that, Marty.

Marty: I just thought it was so fun because it's like we immediately had this other connection. Probably at some high school retreat for YFC or whatever you guys were in, you were forced to watch *The Gospel Blimp*. I thought that was great.

Rand: It still holds up really well. You know it's time for a remake of that, Marty.

Marty: Hey, Rand, let's talk about that. That's a great idea.

PLAYFUL ROOTS

Craig: *What do you think your parents hoped you would do? Were they sort of embarrassed . . . didn't know how to talk about it . . . didn't know how to describe what their kids were doing . . . that type of thing?*

Rand: My dad's a pastor, so I actually have never asked him what he hoped I would do. I think they saw I was always gung-ho in whatever I was looking into. I was straying closer to sciences and more geeky areas, so they weren't too worried. They figured that was pretty safe. And I guess they felt it was safe as long as I was a programmer at a bank, which lasted about ten years. Then when I told them I was going to quit and do games for a living, they probably had their questions at that point.

Marty: Yeah, my father was an actor and a director. And my mom was a musician and a piano teacher. So, I think they were just happy that I found some sort of work that was able to put food on the table. So they had nothing to say . . . like, "I should be a lawyer like them." They were pretty crazy anyway.

Lisa: *Rand, since you brought up your dad being a pastor and you moving into this area of play, I just want to know what role do you think play has in a Christian's life? Would your father answer that question differently than you would, Rand?*

Rand: I grew up playing in ways that my dad really enjoyed—which was exploring. No matter where we lived, we were out on jeep trails or exploring old Indian ruins or going to canoe on rivers. We were exploring the world and that felt a lot like play, but it wasn't exactly football or blackjack or Monopoly. So play has got a really wide gamut there that you can do.

But as far as the games we did (like *Myst*), I think my parents are pretty happy with at least the angle we took. You know they've had questions through the years. But I don't think they question play from a Christian point of view.

Marty: There was actually something we used to do when I was a little kid, which has for the first time dawned on me. And my dad was the one who started it. We would turn all the lights off in the house, and my dad and my sister and myself would get cap guns and shoot each other. And I still remember those evenings where we'd do that in pitch black and hide and then shoot each other when we found each other with cap guns. . . . That was some of the most fun I ever had. I'm realizing that was probably more of an influence than I was thinking. My dad loved to play, both my folks loved to play. We played games all the time. We went exploring. We did all sorts of stuff. But it never seemed like it was ever a conflict with any sort of Christian theology or any sort of morality, so it was always encouraged.

Lisa: *I'm glad both of you had very fun fathers.*

Rand: It's funny, the playing that I grew up with was more oriented around relationships, now that I think back. We were always exploring in a group and laughing. And we'd sit down around the table after dinner and play board games or card games as a group, and it was always fun. So, there was an aspect of community that was always involved as well growing up. Whether or not I've carried that on well with the video game thing . . . that can be a question we get to later.

Lisa: *Different kind of community anyway. Excellent.*

Craig: *I think one thing that set both* Myst *and* Halo *apart is that you actually rewarded your players' intelligence. You expected more of your audience. Was that a conscious choice to make games in a sense smarter rather than dumbing them down as some might have suggested?*

Rand: Yeah, I think the fact is that there are only so many ways you can innovate, and at some point as the games get more sophisticated you're trying to express more in them. Frankly, you can pack more in by dumbing them down and going to that level. Or you can express more by adding more story in, like the *Halo* guys did with a pretty thick story line that wove through those games. I think the story element is fascinating and difficult in video games. I think the easy route is to dumb them down and blow things away and just throw in a story as a side effect.

Marty: There is a famous quote by one of the guys who worked on *Doom*. I think John Carmack said, "Story in games is like articles in *Playboy*." [Laughter] I'm actually cleaning that up slightly. That is something that we [at Bungie] completely disagree with. But because I think we're somewhat in the pioneering stage . . . what it means to actually tell a compelling story or to engage people's minds in a way that potentially can make them have a change of mind or thought or heart or something after they've played the game as before they've played the game. That's something that a lot of us, especially here [at Bungie], we try to do that. I think Robyn and Rand [at Cyan] always felt that. There are select game developers that think that's something to explore. How successful any of us are yet, I think still remains to be seen.

SETTING PRECEDENTS

Craig: *What you did, I think, was counterprogramming. You kind of broke the rules of how a game should look, how it should come at you. Even in the score, Marty, right, you broke the rules of what a score should be?*

Marty: Well, actually I'm not really positive. That's the other good thing about being early into stuff is that there really *are* no rules. That was probably the thing that attracted me to get into the [gaming] industry. When I listened to *Myst* I had played tons of Nintendo games. Well, I mean I should say I watched my children play those games.

There were some traditions that were starting. There was really innocuous "beep beep bupee" kind of electronic music that just looped in the background and had no relationship to anything else. And then there were a few games that started to stretch with that a little bit. The thing I loved about *Myst* was [the music]. . . . I think your publisher said, "Look, we really need to have music." And Robyn did a very film-score kind of approach to it . . . very ambient. There wasn't always music playing. And sometimes when music did play it was hard to distinguish it from an ambient background. It was very compelling and just opened up things so you could have silence. You could have sound effects. You could have dialogue. You could have music scores. It just elevated what is possible in games. Technically, I just don't think it's as constrained as it was. Not so much about breaking rules as it is just expanding what's available.

Rand: Yeah, I don't think we felt like we were breaking rules as much as trying to mimic life or the real world a bit better. The tools got better. The computers were more sophisticated. And I don't know that we even considered we were making games as much as we like to explore, so we thought, *We'll build a world to explore in the computer.*

The story Marty brought up was true. We weren't going to put music in because you don't usually hear music in the real world other than elevators. So we left it out and just put this weird ambience in. And the publisher said, "Try putting music in." It was kind of our ignorance that we left it out, because when Robyn did create some music—and he's a great musician so it was some really unique music—we were intrigued by the amount of emotion it brought into this real world we were trying to build. And so it just became a tool to further contribute to the reality of the world.

Craig: *Rand, with* Myst *there are all of these beautiful, incredibly vivid environments. Is that a reflection of your appreciation for the natural world? Are you creating a hyper-world? A little of both? What do you think?*

Rand: Yeah, I think it's the natural and the unnatural. Honestly, *Myst* felt like it was simply taking us back to some childhood desire to explore. Don't get me wrong, there was a lot of work and a lot of hard design put into it. But in actuality we were building a place we'd like to go to. And when you don't have a lot of limits as far as what you're starting with, when your premise is that there are these books that can take you anywhere, it's a nice blank slate to be able to build the places you'd like to go.

Marty: You know, Rand, I don't know if I ever told you this, but when Josh Staub first showed me *Myst* I was playing through it all night. I was sort of astounded at how beautiful some of those [scenes were] . . . especially on the island. . . . I'm looking at these giant pine trees. And of course I'm from Chicago in the Midwest, which is somewhat bleak from a natural perspective. And then I came out to visit you guys and that's the way it looks out here in the Northwest. I just didn't even know that. I saw all these trees. You guys were just making what you had in your back yard! And the follow-up on that is that when all the Bungie guys who started in Chicago were moved out here to Seattle, immediately *Halo* had giant pine trees and a waterfall that looks a lot like Snoqualmie Falls. Whatever is around you, the artists just can't help it, if they're loving the place, it's going to show up in the game.

THE CREATIVE PROCESS

Craig: *There was no way you could have anticipated such massive-size hits with both the* Myst *series and the* Halo *series. I mean you've got these incredible fans. Broke all kinds of sales records. Novelizations. Graphic novels, all this stuff. What happened there? How did you achieve such crazy success?*

Marty: Come on, Rand, just do it over and over again. You've got the formula now. [General laughter]

Rand: You know you can only do what's predestined, Marty. [More laughter] I'd like to say that we planned all that out well. But . . . timing . . . where

> I believe that the creative aspect of nature, of how we reflect God . . . that's the eternal thing. Not what we actually create, but the act of creating itself. I know that sounds really pompous and high-handed because we're just making games but . . . in the process of making anything, there's some sort of reflection of God in there someplace. We were made to do that.
>
> —Marty O'Donnell

you are and what you're doing and how you do it and what equipment is available and any number of other quantum related random events contribute to the success of anything in this world.

Marty: I think one of the potentially common elements between Cyan in the early days and Bungie in its early days of game development is there was just a passion for doing something that hadn't been done before. It was never about "Let's plan for success" or "Let's plan for massive critical acclaim or worldwide crazy fans" or anything. That was never part of the plan. It was, "Let's just do this thing we're really passionate about and basically get surprised by how the public reacts."

Rand: Yep.

Marty: Yeah. The thing I said about, "Hey, Rand, you've figured out the formula, just keep doing it." That's actually something that really happened to me. We had a guy at Microsoft I was trying to talk to about this passionate group of guys that wanted to make new, innovative things. We'd already had this massive success with *Halo*. And he was like, "Well, gosh, why do you guys want to do that? You have the formula. Just keep repeating it. And that's all you need to do." No, the formula was that we were passionate. If you make us continue to do the thing that we've been doing, we will eventually lose the passion and we'll no longer be making something that's valuable.

Lisa: *Is that where your faith has had the greatest influence on your work? You had to trust that you were following truth instead of just simply duplicating a formula?*

Rand: It'd be great to tell you that in an ideal world—yeah, my faith is strong enough that I'm only going to follow those passionate things that are divine and are full of truth. But unfortunately, it would be a lie. There is always this tug of faith in the back, but the cares of actually doing a project and getting it done and the logistics . . . all those things pull away in the opposite direction of passion. So you try and make some thread of passion. And in the first projects it's a lot easier because the page is blank and the pure adrenaline that you're running on gives you the energy.

But as you progress you're fighting more with the passionate side of things and the tug of how this relates to your life and what this has to do with God at all. Is this just a job? Or, I've got to make a living anyway? How much do I push at some point? And those are all real-world struggles that everybody probably fights with the same as we do.

Marty: It makes me think a little bit about C. S. Lewis's sermon "The Weight of Glory," where he talks about [how] we are all immortal. It's not the things or the buildings or the creations that we have that are eternal. It's the people. It's the snoring man behind you in church. It's the annoying lady. These are all the eternal people.

God has made us creative, and there is something just amazing about the fact that as his creation we have some tiny reflection of creativity. I believe that the creative aspect of nature, of how we reflect God . . . that's the eternal thing. Not what we actually create, but the act of creating itself. I know that sounds really pompous and high-handed because we're just making games but . . . in the process of making anything, there's some sort of reflection of God in there someplace. We were made to do that.

Rand: I totally agree with Marty. There's this weird aspect of creating . . . especially if you believe in a Creator. It's either allegorical or egotistical depending on where you take it. But there's this feeling sometimes when you're building a thing. It makes you get in God's head a little bit . . . like, what was God thinking when he made this? What was *he* going for? The same questions that you ask anybody who's doing creative work. Why did you do this? What were you trying to accomplish? Were you proud of your work? I want to ask God those things. What *exactly* were you trying to accomplish with this?

GAMES AND FREE WILL

Lisa: *Rand, I am so glad you said that. I'm actually going to pull a quote from another interview of yours because I think it's pretty potent. You were talking about story and the challenges of writing a story where you introduce free will and your quote was, "Without getting too philosophical, choice is an amazingly complicated gift. The selfish choice comes naturally. And power is simply a choice effect amplifier."*

I thought that was amazing. When I read that my thought immediately went to God's challenge of showing us truth when he had created a world that has free will. And I thought that was really profound and in a lot of ways what you're saying about the act of creating—it is indeed imago Dei. *You're definitely reflecting God's image in the very act of creating a game.*

Marty: I love that quote.

Lisa: *Isn't it powerful?*

Marty: Oh, yeah.

Rand: Who said that? [General laughter]

Lisa: You *said it.* [More laughter] *You were talking to Jennifer Miller from Just Adventure.*

Rand: Yeah . . . This could get real deep 'cause the whole game design thing has taken me on some amazing paths. But the one path that impresses me more than others is the lengths that God went to achieve free will. And I know there's huge debate about what free will is and everything. But the point is that idea of us having choice, I think, is *everything* that drove God into building this creation. It's the masterstroke of what he was going for. And I just can't *wait* to sit down and ask him a few questions from the sub-creator game designer kind of point of view.

Marty: But what's fun for me is that I've actually talked to a lot of the guys in the game business about Arminianism and Calvinism, which is hilarious 'cause almost nobody knows what I'm talking about. But the way that applies to what we do in games is that as game creators, we really are like small "g" god in the sense that we are in control of everything. If we want to, we can know everything that the player is doing and essentially there is no free will in a game. You do this or you're not going to make any progress.

But one of the things I think we enjoy doing is figuring out ways to create environments and worlds and stories and pathways that give the illusion of free will, even though we're in control of the final outcomes. And when you start actually thinking about that as you're designing games, all of the sudden you go, "Hey, that kind of sounds like the way it feels to be a human on earth and be a creation of God that knows the beginning from the end and knows all things. That's pretty cool 'cause it feels like we have free will even though maybe we don't exactly." But I don't know how that all fits. Like Rand says, it will be fun to find out at some point how that all comes together.

Craig: *It seems that both the games* Myst *and* Halo *are basically about civilizations that blow that choice though, aren't they? They begin with the fallen civilization, whether it's the D'Ni or the Forerunners. They've each had a taste of that and didn't quite pull it off. Is that fair to say?*

Marty: Hmm.

Rand: Yeah. Yeah.

Marty: I think we're creating stuff that's a reflection of fallen man, even though I don't think the majority of the guys here who work at Bungie think that way. But it is a reflection of what they see and what feels heroic and what feels tragic. It's those classic stories basically . . . archetypes.

Craig: *What about these* Halo *nights that churches are sponsoring where they lock the kids in and play the game around the clock?*

Marty: Obviously that's blasphemous. [General laughter]

Rand: They should be watching *Gospel Blimp*. [More laughter]

Marty: Yes, exactly. Well, to be serious about it, I think some of that is a reflection of the modern evangelical church desire to [say], "Hey, we gotta reach the kids where they are. Let's bring them into our physical space. What are they into?" If *Halo* happens to be the popular thing at the moment, then that's something that youth pastors might realize is a good hook to get the kids into the church.

Craig: *Well, the part that seems odd to me is that . . . doesn't* Halo *inherently question religions? It has all these false prophets and this blind allegiance to the gods, and it sort of questions. What do you think? In its core, is it antireligious?*

Marty: Well, it sounds to me like you're talking about the Bible, too, so . . .

Craig: *Whoa . . .*

Marty: [There] sure are a lot of stories in the Bible where they question organized religion or the religion of the day. On Mars Hill [in Acts 17], I think there's a whole lot of questioning of false gods and prophets there. But, trust me—nobody other than those of us within Bungie who are Christian are in any way trying to sneak in some sort of pro-Christian evangelical kind of message. At the same time, nobody here is trying to overtly make or even subtly trying to be against religion or

Christianity or anything else. I think it's a reflection of—once again, it's a reflection of the world as we see it.

Lisa: *I actually find it interesting that Christians are willing to entertain in their games things that they wouldn't necessarily entertain in a straight film. That's hopeful to me in a way because it does get them to engage a world in a more descriptive manner instead of prescriptive manner. That can be a healthy thing.*

> Anything we create that has some sort of ulterior motive like we're only creating this art in order to win people to the kingdom—that's just never rung true for me.
>
> —Marty O'Donnell

Marty: Yeah, anything we create that has some sort of ulterior motive like we're only creating this art in order to win people to the kingdom—that's just never rung true for me. So, I agree with you basically. But I don't even think "prescriptive" art or film or books or any of that stuff is really very legitimate, frankly. I know that sounds pretty harsh. But somebody once said, "There are no Christian books, there are only books by Christian people." The idea that I'm going to go write a Christian book rather than I'm just going to write the best book I can and out of my own personal belief and faith . . . that's going to come through. But if you're telling a story that has anything to do with reality, there's going to be some bad stuff because that's what's around us. And if you leave all that out, it seems pretty false.

BEYOND AN AGENDA

Rand: "Agenda" has a foul stench. Unless of course you're part of the agenda and then you can't smell it, I guess. [General laughter]

Lisa: *Another great quote.*

Rand: Mostly, it's not a good way to love people, frankly. So, the discussion we've had here [at Cyan] is whether there's anything that's valid to have an agenda? Is it okay to preach a sermon with an agenda? Is it okay to paint a picture with an agenda? At what point is it okay to have an agenda? It's an interesting line that you can start to discuss. But I know *one* place you shouldn't have an agenda, and that's with relationships with people. That's where to me it has its foulest stench.

But I don't know where video games fall in that actually, to be honest with you. There are parts of me that feel like Art with a capital "A." What differentiates craftsmanship and Art with a capital "A" is some kind of desire to communicate truth. And I don't know if that's always an agenda if what I'm trying to do is communicate some truth. I don't know if that always has to be an agenda.

Marty: Yeah, it's interesting. It's always been my philosophy [that] we are creating culture, we're not copying culture. And that sounds like another big pompous statement. But it always seems to me that as soon as you copy something else that's successful, you've lost your legitimacy basically. So if you're always trying to create something that isn't a copy of something else, then I think truth will sneak in there.

Rand: Probably like a lot of people who've done one creative thing and think about another, there's a couple of stories that gel around in my head that I'd love to write about at some point. The interesting element of that is there is a message in those stories. They're simple stories. I think there are really fun stories. But they also have a deeper meaning, something behind the scenes. I struggle with how much am I allowed to have an agenda there. It feels like a story without a message at *all* is like a *waste* somehow. I guess what I'm defining "truth" is, if something tells me something real about myself or the world around me. Something true. And if a story doesn't do that, I feel like, well, that was kind of a waste or it was a roller-coaster ride. And so I wonder if you're trying to infuse something with truth, is it always an agenda? I don't know.

Marty: I don't know how to define those words all that well, but my feeling is that agenda has something more to do with trying to manipulate people into something they're not expecting or to behave in a way that they are not currently behaving. You have some sort of manipulative motive in the agenda. But if you think about any of Christ's parables . . . it was just amazing to me how many times somebody would ask him a direct question and he would say, "Well, let me tell you a story." I don't think his stories had an agenda in the way that Rand is talking about, but they certainly had amazingly deep truths.

Lisa: *Yeah, I agree with you, Marty.*

Rand: Well, I would think the Pharisees look at that and go, "Well, of course he has an agenda." People are going to look at those stories and depending on their point of view [they'll] say, "He's trying to subvert us. He's trying to change people's minds. He's trying to preach something different from what we know is true." So, they see the subtlety in what they assume is his agenda and I guess I'm defining it that way, which doesn't seem like a bad thing on his part. Yeah, he kind of did have an agenda, but in his relationships with people it didn't come through as much.

COMMUNITY

Craig: *You started getting into the idea of community . . . gaming and how it's affected relationships. Rand, Myst felt a little like an isolated world. And you've now moved toward this live online community with Uru. And Marty, I think* Halo's *ability for live interaction is what elevated it to this totally different level of fan base, the* Halo *nation. Is gaming a solitary pursuit? Can it be a community pursuit? What do you think are the effects of it?*

> At some point the doctrine starts to sound a lot like noise and the relationships start to sound like music.
>
> —Rand Miller

Rand: I think once we looked back at it [*Myst*], it was less solitary than what we had thought. I think we found that people were playing it with other people whether we planned it that way or not. They were either sitting with friends in front of the screen and saying, "Oh, go down that path or click on that thing." Or they were talking about it with what they had done the night before at school or work. Because it felt like you were exploring; you felt like you had to share a story with someone. You were the storyteller and everybody was the storyteller. It wasn't a prescribed story. You were just explaining what you had discovered the night before.

Marty: Hey, Rand, let me interject something, if you don't mind.

Rand: Sure.

Marty: It has to do with *Myst* and *Riven* and community. I had a client—I was still doing commercials when I worked with Cyan on *Riven*—he was so excited. He loved *Myst* and he got *Riven* and he and his wife played it together exactly the way Rand describes, where he basically drove—which means he clicked the mouse—but she was the one taking notes, telling him where to go and what to do. And they got so into it. They turned all the lights off. They'd crank up the speakers. They were totally into it. And he came to me and he said that when the two of them got toward the end of the game, when they were about to go up the elevator that takes them to Kathryn's prison and just before he pushed the button to have the elevator go up, his wife grabbed his arm and she said, "Do you think it will hold both of us?" And what's really cool is he said, "I'm not sure." And so, when I heard him tell that story I almost got chills because I thought, *Holy mackerel, these guys really accomplished what we were all hoping would be accomplished. They created a world that became so real to this couple that they both thought they were getting on an elevator together.* And I thought, *Wow, for whatever else, that's pretty cool.*

Rand: That's very cool. Those are the stories I love because I think in the end something about relationship and community is the important part. I think that's true from all my years as a Christian pastor's son. It's like at some point the doctrine starts to sound a lot like noise and the relationships start to sound like music.

Marty: Yeah, good quote.

Lisa: *Yeah, we're going to have to make Rand T-shirts or something.*

Rand: The cool thing is this little side effect of all the community. You know we had fans of *Myst* that got into it, like the husband and wife and other people who really got into it. From my point of view those people are awesome. Some of them are way into it like the Trekkies and Mysties or whatever. But getting to meet those people and realizing, man, these people . . . some of them are hurting. . . . We know people who have died of various diseases and have been handicapped and have been married because they met each other [through gaming]. Real life intrudes on the game life, and that to me is the amazing part. That's the real part.

Marty: The fan community comes together in so many different ways and so many different places. When we were first trying to get an online Xbox live thing, we talked about the "virtual couch" because we found out that there were so many people playing *Halo* together on a couch. There would be four-player co-ops and two-player co-ops from the very beginning. And people really got into this habit of having *Halo* nights and communities around playing this game.

Lisa: *That's very good. I think a lot of the criticisms that have been launched against games come from the fact that it's a different kind of community than yours, Rand, what you grew up in with your parents, with your dad and brother going through caves or exploring. It's a different kind of community now, and I guess it can be threatening to some until we adjust to it.*

Rand: Yeah, people are pretty simple, and to a certain extent, I think that people just want to matter. That's what drives us in a lot of ways to play games and to get married. If I can matter to one person because we have something in common or because that person loves me for some unknown reason, it satisfies something deep inside. And so I think there's natural community forming with shared interests. *Myst*, in particular, just because there was a group of people who had that in common and began to care for each other and they mattered to each other. In some ways, it's disconcerting because it seems like the issues that we struggle with in this world are [with] people who don't matter to anybody. That's who criminals are. At some point they go to jail and really nobody cares about them. That's who the kids are who grow up to be criminals. They don't matter at all, and they're *screaming* to matter somehow and they don't. That's a failure of Christianity because that's who we're supposed to be. Not "supposed to." "Supposed to" is such an agenda word. If I really believed what Jesus was saying, it would change me, where those are the people I would love with everything I've got. I just couldn't stop it. And as I grow, I find myself loving those people more. But, boy, it takes a long time to do that. Everybody needs to matter, and it needs to not be video games that do it. It needs to be people who do it.

PARTING CONCLUSIONS

Craig: *One [more] question I didn't ask that might just be helpful to some of our readers. The actual physical production process: is there a simple* *way to describe the process to people? Or is there no simple way to describe the process?*

Rand: I'll give you the simple way to describe it to people—it's HELL. [Laughter]

Marty: I'll tell ya, this is the way my father described writing: "It's like giving birth to barbed wire." [Laughter]

Lisa: *Ow.*

Rand: I hope we're painting a picture for you. [Laughter]

Lisa: *I think we've got it.*

Rand: I don't want it to come across that somehow I have got all these answers together. I fight with things like everyone. I struggle with things like everyone. I go back and forth in struggles with everyday life, the way I think everybody does, trying to figure out what Jesus' words are. I read them and it goes through some kind of filter in my brain and it says, "Man, that's true, and man, I've got to figure out how to live that better and connect with God better and do all those things. Oh, and by the way I make video games, too. I have relationships with other people. And I've got to take out my trash tomorrow." It's all similar except that what we make gets put out there, much like people who make any kind of media. So, it's a little more visible, but we fight the same battles.

Marty: The thing that I'm actually happy about . . . [is] when I think about the fact that Robyn and Rand were so influential in the early part of gaming. And I know there are guys here at Bungie and scattered throughout the game business that are Christians. There are people all over that are working on this stuff that have deep spiritual journeys. It's not like we're doing anything other than possibly just being salt without agendas. For some reason we're in these positions where this is something we get to do for a living and we get to have a passion about doing it, and it so happens that we're also Christian. It would be really kind of rotten if somehow our faith prevented us from being able to do this stuff, because then it would be only people without faith that would be doing these things. That to me is really unacceptable.

Lisa: *Well, you both have inspired me because it's very clear that your passion for faith equals or surpasses your passion for your art. It does inform it, but it's an imperfect journey. But, thank God there are people like you out there that are struggling with it.*

7

Madden Rules

Sports and the Future of Competitive Video Games

MATTHEW KITCHEN

I have never worked a day in my life. I went from player to coach to a broadcaster, and I am the luckiest guy in the world.
John Madden at his NFL Hall of Fame induction speech[1]

Although I'm only in my twenties, my recollection of the first sports video games is similar to my parents'. When they played *Pong* with their friends in the seventies, it was like seeing *Star Wars* for the first time. Following a single blip was sufficiently diverting, yet *Pong* was a giant leap forward from its awkward predecessor, *Tennis for Two*. Years later, I sat with a black joystick in hand, my thumb on a single red button, playing a generic Atari sports game simply titled "Baseball." The teams consisted of red and blue two-dimensional stick figures. To my friends and me, this was the cutting edge of technology. Sure, the joystick was awkward and the controls were confusing at best, but the fact that this game of baseball required seventeen fewer people than a live game was all right by me. Little did I know at the time that only a couple years later, the Atari would go into the closet for good, replaced by the 8-bit Nintendo Entertainment System. Now I was no longer batter number 7 on the blue team. Instead I was Bo Jackson of the Los Angeles Raiders, zigzagging my way up and down the field for my fourth touchdown of the game.

Bo Jackson and Nintendo's *Tecmo Super Bowl* made me use a phrase for the first time that I thought I would never use again. On the contrary, I've uttered it approximately every four years since 1992: "This is the best video games will ever be!" Soon we went from eight plays to thirty-two playbooks. From clunky basketball titles like *Double Dribble* and *Arch Rivals* to the high-flying

108

acrobatics of *NBA JAM* and the pure simulation of the *NBA Live* series. In 1995, I used *World Series Baseball* to play a part in the success of my Atlanta Braves, and in 1997, I used *NCAA College Football* to right the wrongs of Arizona State's Rose Bowl loss.

Then in late 2000, the world of sports video games changed. John Madden had been a fixture in the football world for almost four decades, from playing with the Eagles to coaching the Super Bowl XI Champion Raiders. As a TV commentator, Madden became the voice of pro football for a generation. Although remarkably successful as a coach and commentator, Madden's "loan" of his name to a 1988 Apple II football simulator might mark his most significant contribution. He recalls, "Well, I started the videogame before there were videogames. When we first started, we were going to make a computer game. . . . I figured it would be a good teaching tool, a good coaching tool."[2] Thanks to Madden's hands-on help and audio commentary, the *Madden NFL* franchise has exceeded limits, expectations, and profit margins. Electronic Arts has consistently celebrated $100 million in opening-week sales, making *Madden NFL* the highest-revenue-generating series in North America. (ESPN's resident "Sports Guy" Bill Simmons is still lobbying to have its annual August release date turned into a national holiday.) Over the past twenty years, it has evolved with (and even outlasted) technologies like the Sega Dreamcast and 3DO.[3] While licensed games like *NFL Blitz*, *Quarterback Club*, and *Game Day* were popular among a small sect of devotees, when *Madden 2001* hit the shelves, the competition was over. If *Pong* was *Star Wars*, then *Madden* was *The Matrix*. Not only were the graphics and textures better than we could have possibly imagined fifteen years earlier, but the movement of the players, the precision of the game play, and the simulation of the sport were well above our collective heads. The *Madden* video game enshrined John Madden as an icon of the electronic sports era.

Madden NFL brought real-time strategy and adjustments similar to genuine NFL games. The 2003 edition introduced online play for consoles like the Xbox and PlayStation 2. The Playmaker tool allowed players to make audibles at the line of scrimmage just like Peyton Manning. In subsequent editions, the joystick became a "hitstick" on defense or a "truckstick" for big, burly running backs to break a tackle. Smart routes were introduced, allowing players to adjust their wide receivers' preestablished patterns. Such dynamic, split-second decision making made each edition of *Madden NFL* that much closer to the on-field experience. As people began to play *Madden NFL* more seriously, online competitions began to spring up. Video games were suddenly becoming their own professional sport, with sponsored "athletes" and prime-time slots on ESPN's networks and platforms. *Madden Nation* piled the best players onto a cross-country bus trip, turning video games into a competitive reality show. A game intended to simulate professional football has become an e-sports league of its own.

How did we get here? In just twenty years, we've replaced a black joystick and single red button with the Wii remote and the Xbox controller. We've exchanged stick figures for recognizable three-dimensional athletes. Now we're replacing our favorite athletes with ourselves. As video games continue to evolve, we have to wonder whether a ceiling exists for the innovation and relevance of video games in our lives. Where are professional video games heading? Will they ever be considered a legitimate sport? What does our obsession with competition and competitive video games suggest about us as the video game generation? As individuals? As people of faith? Can we reconcile our seemingly insatiable desire to win with Jesus' assertion that the first shall be last?

OUR COMPETITIVE NATURE

It is pretty easy to be a fan these days. Sports used to occupy the last five minutes of the local newscast. Now, dozens of cable channels and millions of Web sites broadcast all sports, all the time. Web 2.0 allows us to watch nearly any game in the world, read rumors, play fantasy sports, post our thoughts, and get instant stats, analyses, and box scores. We can even interact with our favorite athletes on social networking sites. My friend Don recently showed me how he listens to Vin Scully call the Dodgers' baseball games on his cell phone. This is a dream come true for people who still remember the UHF dial on their black-and-white television.

Working at ESPN has given me an even deeper understanding of what sports can mean in our culture. Jesse Owens's victories at the 1936 Berlin Olympics undermined Hitler's attempts to claim racial superiority. Jackie Robinson broke the color barrier in baseball well before Rosa Parks challenged racist policies on an Alabama bus. Nations wept at the murder of Israeli athletes at the 1972 Munich Olympics. USA Hockey's 1980 Olympic "Miracle on Ice" became a source of national pride. Eras are often defined by their sports. When NFL safety Pat Tillman was shot by friendly fire in Afghanistan, it called the entire war on terror into question. Baseball's steroid scandal raises uncomfortable questions about what measures athletes adopt to win. Such flagrant cutting of corners may reflect the winner-take-all philosophy that also undermined Wall Street and precipitated a global financial crisis.

While complaints ring out against the desensitizing effects of *Grand Theft Auto* or *Resident Evil*, our obsession with competition goes almost unnoticed. Competition drives us to be better at everything, from work and education to politics and safety. It results in greener lawns, smarter cars, and whiter teeth. We keep score as a social lubricant. We pit our favorite teams against our friends', claiming superiority based on the jersey we wear. Everything has become a horse race, with oddsmakers and pundits reducing politics, the stock market, or the box office to a competition. Thanks to video games, we no longer have to wait for Friday night football games or Sunday golf to challenge someone. Games offer new ways to compare ourselves more directly every day. That competitive nature can sometimes take us over the edge.

My own competitive spirit brought me dangerously close to a fistfight once in college. What started as a harmless *Madden 2004* marathon turned into Eric, a guy on my hall, running an offense that consisted of exactly zero pass attempts and over four hundred yards of Michael Vick pulling the ball in and scrambling for touchdowns. My beloved Arizona Cardinals were no match, and I ended up saying things about his mother for which I would later apologize. At this point or some time prior, I had stopped "playing" video games and started taking them a little too seriously. My roommates would agree, as they were forced to witness me throw controllers, kick pieces of furniture, and complain endlessly about how the computer on EA's *NFL Street* had "cheated." My behavior was abhorrent, but unfortunately it also wasn't uncommon. As I've grown older it's become clear to me that there are two kinds of competitors in this world: those who can actually have fun playing a game and those whose only drive is to win. I'll admit to being part of the latter.

Do you remember the first time you won or lost? That pride (or lack thereof) becomes permanently attached to our feelings. However immature, those feelings can remain a key driver throughout the rest of our lives. I can still replay the final moments when my sixth-grade basketball team won the city championship. I can see my friend Donnie streaking the length of the court for the game-winning layup. I can still remember the pride I felt as I defended the inbounds pass, denying the other team any attempt at a last-second miracle. What I can't remember is any time since then that I've felt that completely content (something I'll no doubt have to share with a shrink in the future). Those of us with a serious competitive streak take everything—our intelligence and our relationships, our religion, our leisure time, and our addictions—and attempt to determine the "winner." Winner of what? We have no idea.

KEEPING SCORE

If it doesn't matter who wins or loses, then why do they keep score?

Vince Lombardi[4]

It is tough to measure victory in life. Is it based on income? Friendship? Family? In sports, success is not a matter of opinion. There are rules in place, agreed upon by all sides, to determine winners and losers. In *The Joy of Sports*, theologian Michael Novak suggests that we "observe toddlers at play, how they establish rules. 'This is water. This is land. You can't step on those. . . .' The spirit of play is the invention of rules. . . . The description of a fixed universe is the first and indispensable step of every free act."[5] The same objectivity applies to video games, where predetermined goals are of paramount importance to the perception of victory. The end is justified by the means, and the end is always clear. There are rules and goals, winners and losers. Theologian Robert K. Johnston implies that only after "having surrendered oneself to the rules and form of the game, one experiences, paradoxically, the full flush of freedom."[6] Only when we know the boundaries of what Johan Huizinga described as "the magic circle" can we freely enter into the spirit of play.

Video games also offer a unique opportunity to author our own competitive experience. They allow us to be the coach *and* the athlete. They give us the chance to be the hero or the goat with the simple push of a button. Video games are also unique in that they offer different types of competition. We can jump from boxing to bowling to golf in the span of fifteen minutes. They can be quite communal. But much of the time, we compete in isolation against either the computer or our previous performances. We establish our own standards of excellence. How we compete in those situations speaks volumes about how we choose to live in the digital age. Are we satisfied with modest gains? Do we push ourselves to be better every day? Are we easily exasperated? Do we quickly push reset? Or can we approach competitive gaming with a childlike sense of wonder and joy?

Sports and video games have always been intertwined. With the help of an analog computer, an oscilloscope, and a couple of transistor switches for controllers, *Tennis for Two* debuted at Visitor's Day of the Brookhaven National Laboratory in 1958. As the first video game, it used a gravity simulator to imitate the back-and-forth of a tennis game. *Pong* followed in its wake and helped launch video games into the lives and homes of the 1970s, making them an early staple of American youth culture.

The programmers of the 1970s hoped to individualize the gaming experience by incorporating artificial intelligence. While *Space Invaders* technically relied on AI, the competition between man and computer was more about the CPU's ability to throw stored patterns of attack at its human opponent. The lack of sophistication in the patterns, along with our ability to quickly adapt, made the games less challenging over time. Since they were also extremely addictive, though, no one seemed to care.

Eventually, artificial intelligence changed the way we play and how we keep score. With the rise of single-player arcade cabinets, competitive programmers and gamers alike felt the need to compare their performances against one another. Taking a cue from their pinball brethren, programmers adapted the high score for video games in the submarine adventure game *SeaWolf* (1976). The personalized high score followed a couple years later in 1979 with *Star Fire*. We've been chasing the elusive "AAA" ever since. Midway's *Pac-Man* (1980) became the most addictive (and profitable) form of man versus computer competition to date. *Pac-Man* was followed by survival-style games like *Donkey Kong, Tetris,* and *Geometry Wars*.

Sports games of the 1990s abandoned the pattern-based AI of *Mike Tyson's Punch-Out*, exchanging it for more sophisticated strategy. With *Madden NFL,* the quirks of professional coaches and athletes were hardwired into the gaming software. Games could be adapted to players' actions, choices, and movements. First-person shooters, including *GoldenEye 007* and *Half-Life,* developed enemies that could recognize attacks, hide, and respond tactically and intelligently. Still, while the challenge grew ever more impressive, the computer could never mimic the thrill of challenging one another in live competition. With the arrival of real-time strategy, we discovered that our greatest opponent might be the person sitting next to us. Tournaments and online gaming exploded with the opportunity to play live, sophisticated competition against anyone, anytime, anywhere, worldwide. Video games became a global contest.

BY THE NUMBERS

> An argument arose among [Jesus' disciples] as to which one of them was the greatest.
>
> *Luke 9:46*

Comparison is an ancient temptation. Alexander wasn't content to be merely good. Jesus' disciples were establishing a pecking order even in his midst. While beating the game is satisfying, the competition we crave most is against one another. We want to challenge our limitations and prove our worth against our peers. High scores are a thinly veiled attempt to establish a hierarchy, to outrank one another. The same validation never comes from beating a computer, no matter how sophisticated. Our desire to win may involve hours of memorizing and practicing the tracks of *Mario Kart* or throwing our controller when we lose a game of *Halo*.

A growing number of people choose to find pride and validation in the controllable world of video games. Psychologist Richard M. Ryan of the

University of Rochester studies the motivational aspects of gaming. Ryan and his research team are testing the idea that games can satisfy the psychological needs for control, mastery, and connection. Ryan suggests, "People can feel a lot of autonomy and competence during play, and also it can be a place to relate with others, albeit in a virtual context."[7] Like athletes, gamers want their performance to be quantified by the numbers.

Athletes' accomplishments are often branded by their numbers. Babe Ruth hit 714 home runs. Wilt Chamberlain scored a hundred points in a single NBA game. Jack Nicklaus won eighteen major golf victories. Joe DiMaggio will forever be remembered for his 56-game hitting streak. We grant the athletes who achieve these milestones eternal sports immortality. While Ruth's long-standing record was finally broken, the lore that accompanies his accomplishments remains. Pundits may say the numbers don't matter, but statistics often become *the* story when an athlete passes on. Tiger Woods will one day be the gamer generation's Babe Ruth, the most enduring icon of his era and sport. But what happens if those numbers are artificially inflated, achieved by amoral or immoral means? Despite his home run records, a shamed Barry Bonds will serve as our Shoeless Joe Jackson, disgraced forever by history.

Those who dominate video games also live on in the record books. More specifically, they endure in the records kept on file by Walter Day at Twin Galaxies. The small-town coin-op in Ottumwa, Iowa, has risen to be the self-proclaimed "worldwide authority on player rankings, gaming statistics, and championship tournaments."[8] It has been at been at the center of competitive gaming, from the first video game tournament in 1983 to the first American video game team and the advent of the "official" player rankings. Twin Gal-

---

Gamers Speak

Christopher, fourteen years old, Caucasian, on Honor Roll

- What's your favorite competitive video game? Why do you like it so much? Starcraft: Brood Wars, *because I enjoy strategic games that challenge my thinking.*
- Who do you like to fight against? Why? *I like to fight against computers because I take pleasure in the thought that I can strategize better than a computing machine.*
- Do you like to compete with a team or on your own? Why? *I like to compete with a team because then I am not the only person being relied upon to win.*

Nathan, fifteen years old, Chinese American

- What's your favorite competitive video game? Why do you like it so much? Halo 3, *because I get to beat my brother.*

axies' current record book reaches almost fifteen hundred pages and includes gamers from more than thirty countries.

One number has recently been singled out as the benchmark for gamers, yet like baseball's tainted home-run record, that gaming record faces similar allegations of performance enhancement. Steve Wiebe and Billy Mitchell's battle for Donkey Kong supremacy, officiated by Twin Galaxies in the cult documentary *The King of Kong: A Fistful of Quarters* (2007), is the stuff of legend. After being laid off by Boeing, Steve Wiebe decided his legacy would be as the world's greatest Donkey Kong player. He won the title (and lost) on multiple occasions. The dramatic saga of the rivalry between Wiebe and Mitchell includes backstabbing, attempted psych-outs, breaking and entering, enhanced motherboards, juvenile smack talk, and a doctored performance tape. It demonstrates the lengths to which people go in order to be recognized as the world's greatest something. Anything.

Jesus addressed similar grandstanding among his disciples. He subverted their understanding of greatness, lifting up a little child instead. His measurement of victory? "Whoever welcomes this child in my name welcomes me, and whoever welcomes me welcomes the one who sent me; for the least among all of you is the greatest" (Luke 9:48–50). The ethics of Jesus challenge the competitive nature of sports, the desire to determine a winner. While boxers slug it out or gamers record the most frags, Jesus suggests we turn the other cheek (Matt. 5:39–41). A strategy of nonretaliation in the face of attack would result in much shorter video games. Players would face a painfully quick defeat.

So how have so many Christians willingly donned football uniforms and boxing gloves? Organizations like the YMCA (Young Men's Christian Association) linked body and spirit, even spawning new sports like basketball and volleyball. The Fellowship of Christian Athletes celebrates the character-building aspects of sports. Star athletes like Reggie White and Kurt Warner shared their Christian testimony with thousands of adoring fans. These "muscular" Christians draw upon the writings of Paul.[9] They cite his challenges to "boast on the day of Christ that I did not run in vain" (Phil. 2:16) and to "press on toward the goal for the prize" (Phil. 3:14). Paul draws upon Greek athletic competitions for spiritual analogies: "Do you not know that in a race the runners all compete, but only one receives the prize? Run in such a way that you may win it" (1 Cor. 9:24). Annual Super Bowl Sunday sermons help to define such competitive challenges in a spiritual context. Similarly, Paul appeals to those instincts, urging us to practice a rigorous discipleship. Can our obsessive drives be harnessed for divine purposes? And if so, can the focus of the gamer generation be turned toward goodwill?

VIDEO GAMES: THE NEXT SPORT?

> For the new millennium comes a new sportsman, the e-sportsman.
> So, he is the first cyber athlete, so to speak. . . .You know, you look
> back fifty years from now and there had to be someone at the turn
> of the century that played baseball. There had to be a Babe Ruth
> and a Ty Cobb. There has to be a Johnathan "Fatal1ty" Wendel.
> *Marketing guru Mark Walden on* 60 Minutes[10]

During my time at ESPN I've ended up in more than one debate over what
constitutes an athlete. ESPN's intense coverage of the World Series of Poker
has had us in the newsroom questioning whether a poker player's endurance
takes a certain amount of athleticism. Can the strain that Phil Ivey's mind and
body go through during a marathon poker session put him in the category
of "athlete"? To most spectators, calling Ivey an athlete would be ridiculous,
but there's no question that elite poker requires stamina. Now, the argument
continues: "Could playing a video game ever be considered a sport?" To those
outside the gaming world, the easy answer is no. As with poker, any game
you can do while sitting in a chair (aside from *Murderball*) is an activity at
best, not a sport. Professional athletes want to believe that there exists a strict
pyramid of athleticism with NBA forwards and NFL cornerbacks likely at the
top; swimmers, sprinters, and hockey players somewhere in the middle; and
golfers (along with NFL kickers, high school cheerleaders, and Marko Jarić)
on the bottom rung.

So what does it take to become a legitimate sport? Tournaments and teams?
Major League Gaming, the world's largest professional video gaming league,
was founded in 2002.[11] Do your games have to be seen on ESPN? *Madden
Nation* solves that problem. It already completed its fifth season. Do you need
agents, contracts, and big paydays? *Halo 3*'s 2008 national champions netted
one hundred thousand dollars for a single tournament. Do you need teammates and coaches? Playbooks, strategies, and practice? Major League Gaming includes those as well. Champion Johnathan "Fatal1ty" Wendel spends
eight to twelve hours a day in front of a screen. But he emphasizes the athletic side of professional video games, "It's all about hand-eye coordination,
reflexes, timing, strategy, being quick on your feet, being able to think fast. . . .
You got to be doing everything."[12] He draws upon his background as a star
high school tennis player. "I work out a lot—you know, being physically fit
and making sure your neurotransmitters are working properly and making sure
that you're on beat and you're ready to go," says Wendel. As pro gaming gets
more popular and as the Wii makes it more active, the argument that video
games will never be a legitimate sport weakens. The only things keeping it out

of the lexicon now are sportswriters (old) and professional athletes (scared), neither of whom will be able to hold off the revolution for very long.

The video gaming culture has a unique opportunity to use gamers' skills to question the professional power structure. If a Wii bowler beats a professional bowler on the Wii, then who's better at the sport? Could a *Madden NFL* guru ever use his skills and get a job as an offensive coordinator? Hopefully. I once played Pebble Beach, and am about thirty strokes better on the Wii's digital replica. Even with an open window on a nice day, a virtual round of golf with *Tiger Woods* on the Wii can't really compare to the overall experience. But I can save four hundred dollars by playing in my living room. Is it okay for me to compare myself to a scratch golfer? In the digital age the answer is yes, because the activities are no longer mutually exclusive. One takes more skill and the other costs less money, but at the end of the day everyone is playing golf. As technology gets more sophisticated, the digital world has the opportunity to be what John Madden envisioned: a training ground and a teaching tool.

Major League Gaming has slowly found its culture, athletes, and audience. What it still hasn't had is a universal cultural moment, the instant when something seemingly unknown becomes altogether global. The NBA had it (with the arrival of Michael Jordan), poker had it (via Chris Moneymaker), and the NFL had it twice (the 1958 and 1969 NFL championships). Professional boxing had it (the Rumble in the Jungle) and then lost it (Tyson versus Holyfield II).

For pro gamers, that moment is still to be determined. DirecTV's Championship Gaming Series did not survive the global economic meltdown.[13] The Cyberathlete Professional League was dogged by accusations that players were being exploited and winnings not being paid.[14] Professional gaming in Europe initially centered around the Electronic Sports League (ESL). South Korea has emerged as the largest market for pro gamers. Three Korean cable TV channels broadcast matches around the clock. Samsung sponsored the first five editions of the World Cyber Games (WCG). With almost five hundred thousand dollars in prize money, the World Cyber Games have expanded beyond South Korea to Singapore, Italy, Germany, and China. As a two-time WCG champion, Lim Yo-Hwan earns more than three hundred thousand dollars annually from purses and endorsements. One of Lim's primary competitors, Hing Jin-Ho, has insured his fingers for sixty thousand dollars.[15] Such are the unique gifts and skills associated with professional video gaming.

In North America, Major League Gaming emerged as the industry's best shot at legitimacy when it signed a broadcast deal with the ESPN360 Web site. Their tour borrows from NASCAR, with sixteen teams competing at six events spread over an eight-month season. Competition currently centers around four Xbox 360 games—*Halo 3, Gears of War 2, Call of Duty 4*, and *Rainbox Six: Vegas 2*—and *World of Warcraft* (for the PC). The most accomplished teams, such as "Carbon," "Str8 Rippin'," and "Final Boss," have their own Web sites and dedicated fans. They even have coaches, like twenty-two-year-old Andrew Poor of Final Boss. Their team captain, Dave "Walshy" Walsh, has patented "the Claw" hold for the game controller, keeping his right thumb on the right stick while still pressing buttons. Competitors study "his *Halo 2* strategies the way chess aficionados study Kasparov."[16] Even though *60 Minutes* profiled Johnathan "Fatal1ty" Wendel as "the best video game player in America,"[17] pro gaming still remains relatively underground. Whether it's the first million-dollar contract, the first celebrity gamer, or the first well-televised event, pro gaming has an opportunity to become a recognized worldwide sport.

With legitimacy will come other challenges. As in all sports where money makes its way to the table, pro gamers will soon face the issue of motivation. Tom Ryan of Final Boss reflects on his profession: "I think I could do it for another five years. It's not like a real job. But it feels like a real job sometimes." His mother, Anne Ryan, suggests, "It's a little hard to say that my kids dropped out of school for video games. . . . But it's like an athlete deciding to go pro: do it now before you break a leg or someone younger and stronger comes along."[18] Unfortunately, an adolescent joy may become a professional chore. World Cyber Game champ Lim Yo-Hwan admits, "It's work, not fun" training at the game *Starcraft* for ten hours a day with his teammates and coach.[19] MLG player Tom Taylor practices a vampire lifestyle, rising late in the afternoon, playing all night, and going to bed at sunrise. ESPN reported, "The week before an event, he'll practice up to 14 hours a day; the week *after* an event, he'll sleep up to 18 hours a day, fending off the nagging cough, blurry vision and overall malaise that pros call 'tournament death.' "[20] Stanford psychologists Mark Lepper and David Greene found that even preschool children will lose their love of play once it is tied to rewards.[21] Joyful play must come as its own reward, without goals or inducements. Has the next generation already lost the playfulness that John Madden celebrated at his Hall of Fame induction—that remarkable sense of freedom that he never worked a day in his life?

A THEOLOGY OF PLAY

> There are still people in America who do not take videogames seriously. These are the same people who question the relevance of hip-hop and assume newspapers will exist in twenty-five years.
> *Chuck Klosterman*[22]

With pro gaming on the rise, we have to ask ourselves why we play video games. Why do games exist? What will the culture look like when, at a young age, people begin to play with a professional future (read: money) to motivate them? How will this mentality shape the landscape of the industry as a whole? Will games be created based on the appeal they might have for a competitive gaming market? Absolutely. Will we continue to play for the sheer, exhilarating joy? For a generation raised on scorekeeping, we must develop a theology of play.

Unfortunately, the Protestant work ethic has been placed in opposition to the apparent frivolity of play. But the rise of leisure time and the explosion of video games demand a serious reflection on play. Theologian Robert K. Johnston wonders, "Is there an alternative both to the traditional work ethic that has dominated Christian thought and to the hedonism and narcissism that characterizes much contemporary discussion of play?"[23] Johnston suggests that our ambivalence may arise from the different biblical rationales attached to keeping the Sabbath. In Deuteronomy 5, the Israelites are commanded to rest so they can remember that the Lord brought them out of bondage, out of Egypt. We break from our work in order to celebrate the exodus. But Exodus 20 ties the Sabbath to creation. If the Creator God rested after six days of world making, then surely we also need to take a break, to set aside at least one day of the week to play.[24] While Protestants may see Sundays as preparation for the six workdays to follow, we must also consider the possibility that the Sabbath was intended to remind us that life itself is a gift, an opportunity to play. The breaking of our routine offers us some perspective—a shocking and restful reminder that life cannot be mastered or controlled no matter how hard we work. Now, with gamers turning their play into work, perhaps we need to take a break from our games as a way to reacquire a similar sense of perspective. Life is not a game to be mastered, but an opportunity to play all manner of games within God's glorious creation.

A robust theology of play also sets aside time for feasts and festivals.[25] The Hebrews commemorated sacred occasions with dancing and food. A festival like Purim celebrates the reversal that came through Esther and Mordecai's quick thinking. The lot (*pur* in Hebrew) that Haman had intended to destroy Israel actually brought death and judgment to him. The month had "turned for them from sorrow into gladness and from mourning into a holiday" (Esth. 9:22). When Ezra reopened the forgotten laws of God, the Israelites were aggrieved by their shortcomings. But Nehemiah chided the Israelites for not celebrating enough. He said to them, "Go your way, eat the fat and drink sweet wine and send portions of them to those for whom nothing is prepared, for this day is holy to our LORD; and do not be grieved, for the joy of the LORD is your strength" (Neh. 8:10). Perhaps the rise of annual or quarterly professional gaming tournaments corresponds to similar shortcomings in our ecclesial settings. We have celebrated too rarely, causing our teenagers to find joy and community within massive LAN parties instead. A local area network of ten thousand computer gamers converged in Jonkoping, Sweden, for DreamHack Winter 2007.[26] A wide range of ages and countries were included. Like the ancient biblical festivals, work stopped, the parties went all night, and participants lost all sense of time. One significant difference: the players were united by a shared love of gaming rather than God.

Before we distance ourselves from such gatherings, we must remember Jesus had a bad reputation as "a glutton and a drunkard, a friend of tax collectors and sinners" (Luke 7:34). When the Pharisees questioned his association with tax collectors in Luke 15, Jesus responded with the powerful story of the Prodigal Son. He demonstrated the father's proclivity for welcoming the outsider, making room for those who have wasted their time, talent, and money on frivolous things. When the prodigal came running back to the father, it was an occasion for celebration, an extravagant feast, yet the most faithful older brother disdained such excess. Jesus offended his contemporaries not necessarily via feasting, but from a questionable guest list. He made room for those deemed unclean or other. Gamers are often (unfairly) seen as those on the fringe of society. People who don't understand their passion assign them unfair labels of being nerdy, or fat, or living in their mothers' basements. While gamers are made to feel like they exist in the margins, Jesus seeks solidarity with those whom others see as lost, including New Testament characters like Zacchaeus, a prostitute, and the Samaritan woman at the well. Christ gave us a passion for a reason and if he were here now, he might grab a controller and throw down in a healthy game of *Halo 3*. He wouldn't even need cheat codes. God gave us sports, video games, and a competitive spirit because he loves us and wants us to challenge ourselves and be happy doing so every day. He gave his Son for much the same reason. When Jesus ultimately lost, we won. How's that for God's perfect ending to the game of life?

8

Poets, Posers, and Guitar Heroes

Virtual Art for a Virtual Age

ANDREW MCALPINE

What would the world be, once bereft of wet and wildness? Let them be left. O let them be left, wildness and wet; Long live the weeds and the wilderness yet.

Gerard Manley Hopkins

No TV party tonight!
Black Flag

The lights dim, and the stillness in the room is electric. The first sound to break the silence is a thunderous kick drum, counting out a grim death march, one two three four. Then, the cacophonous squeal of an electric guitar introduces an inhuman voice: "*I AM IRON MAN!*" The band kicks into full gear—the low rumble of the bass and the shrill ringing of the crash drive the song into a frenzy. And finally, Ozzy's banshee shriek swoops in from the rafters. The crowd goes wild.

All this isn't happening in some pitch-black, smoke-filled Black Sabbath show in 1970. In fact, the surroundings are startlingly familiar: a couple of ratty couches, family pictures on the wall, the smell of Mom's tuna casserole coming from the next room. The sound is leaking from the TV speakers, and the crowd and the band are just pixels on the family's old Magnavox. The instrument spewing those mind-melting classic riffs? A cheap plastic guitar, with five multicolored buttons where strings ought to be. The blissed-out rock star making magic with his fingers? A twelve-year-old kid in his pajamas. Welcome to the incredible, strange, and totally illusory world of *Guitar Hero.*

121

Guitar Hero has become many things: a cultural phenomenon, a business smash, and a mandatory experience for any human being with that burning, secret desire to be a rock star (and, judging by the numbers, there are millions coming out of that particular closet every year). It has revolutionized the way music commerce works in the twenty-first century and has spawned scores of imitators and sequels that have created a multibillion-dollar market. But *Guitar Hero* is more than the latest fad sucking the sweet marrow of our disposable income; it's our collective desire for fame made manifest, a way to live out the rock-and-roll fantasy in a nice, neat package. And like anything else that desires to make art nice, neat, and marketable, it's thrust into conflict with the real thing: something that is messy, complex, human, and ultimately a way to commune with each other and God. Scott Cairns, a poet, essayist, and teacher, has this to say about the place and purpose of art:

> I want [my students] to see themselves, and what they create, as part of an ongoing, vital tradition. I want them to turn away from the modernist, personal mode and its taste for ennui. I want them to find in poetry a means of consoling their losses, a way of witnessing grace, and an access to living, even now, in what we still might call the Kingdom of God. I want us all to be free of petty passions, and freed into serving enormous passions.[1]

The escapism found in *Guitar Hero* stands in stark relief to the creative potential and responsibility that we possess. We are buried in a mountain of diversions, but as people called to a different sort of reality, we shouldn't settle for anything less than authentic creation.

DAYDREAM (IMAGI)NATION

Before *Guitar Hero* became a household name, it was just another video game released in the holiday season of 2005 for the PlayStation 2 video game console by Harmonix Music Systems. To the uninitiated, *Guitar Hero* is a rhythm-based game that uses a specialized, guitar-shaped controller to allow the player to "play" the guitar parts of a wide variety of rock songs, from classic barnburners to more recent offerings from brand-new bands. The interface is surprisingly simple: the screen displays a scrolling fretboard with five columns corresponding to the five buttons on the guitar controller. As the song progresses, notes will descend onto the screen, and the player has to press the correct button and "strum" (with an ingenious hingelike lever on the body of the guitar) at the correct time to get a high score and make it through the song. If the player makes too many mistakes, then the game is over and he or she has to try again. In the game's sequels and in competitors' games, various elements have been added and subtracted—for example, special moves, more buttons, different game modes, and even more instruments—but the core game play remains the same. If you hit the right buttons at the right time, you can do no wrong.

Guitar Hero was not the first game to simulate the experience of rock-and-roll guitar. Japanese publisher Konami has been releasing a series of guitar-based rhythm games called *GuitarFreaks* for arcades and home consoles since the late 1990s. What made *Guitar Hero* different from these games, however, and what allowed it to explode music games from a niche market to a world-wide industry were two unique (and absolutely essential) qualities. The first is that the game has a roster of beloved, well-known songs that make up the bedrock of its game play. The second, in a true testament to the talent of the developers, is that playing the game feels eerily accurate and real. When you're mashing those buttons it feels less like you're following along with the song than that you are actually playing the song, making those noises yourself. It's a bizarre and strangely fulfilling exercise, and I have to imagine that I'm not alone when I say that when I played the game for the first time, it was all I could do to keep from jumping around and headbanging along with the music.

These qualities add up to one potent and potentially problematic experience: total wish fulfillment. By making the experience realistic-feeling and allowing players to jam along with familiar songs, Harmonix did more than just offer a new experience to a hard-core gaming culture; it tapped into a larger (and, though the game has been successful worldwide, a uniquely American) narrative of rock-and-roll mythology, escapism, and the desire to rise above the pack and be a star. While not everyone can profess the digital desire to pump gangsters full of holes or fight off an alien invasion, the jaw-dropping sales of *Guitar Hero* and its offspring like *The Beatles: Rock Band* show that the desire to (as the MC5 so gloriously put it) "kick out the jams" is something that your average Joe and Jane have been waiting for, whether they knew or not, the entirety of their radio-listening lives. Exit the listener, enter the performer.

Since its original iteration, later games have only added to the rock-and-roll fantasy. *Guitar Hero* lets you become the axeman, the focal point of the show. *Rock Band*, another Harmonix project released in 2007, went a step further and allowed you and your friends to start a virtual band, complete with guitar, bass, vocals, and drums.[2] Despite the move toward a more communal environment, the experience still tends to be a narcissistic one, whether in success ("Did you see how I pulled off that solo?") or in failure ("Dude, you have *got* to lock down that drum part!"). This is perfectly illustrated in a TV advertisement for *Rock Band 2* in which dozens of vaguely attractive people all play along with the same song, each jamming away with intense conviction on their chosen *Rock Band* instrument, each totally oblivious to the people surrounding him or her. That's because, even if you happen to be playing simultaneously with a friend or three, *Rock Band* is not a truly cooperative endeavor. Instead, your bandmates function more like props, in the same vein as the plastic replica controllers—just another element to deepen the illusion of superstardom, an experience that, by definition, cannot be shared. However, *The Beatles: Rock Band* went to great lengths to increase the interactivity, to put players amidst the Fab Four and their most famous venues. With *DJ Hero*, games crossed into hip-hop, a sample of a sample.

Of course, music alone isn't enough to deliver the perfect home rock-star experience. Our real-life rock stars are more complicated beasts, and American mythology demands more than just sound. It requires a look (preferably of the edgy variety), a story (preferably of the rags-to-riches variety), and the ephemeral, hard-to-qualify-but-easy-to-recognize, most important ingredient in this alchemic equation: *attitude*. Attitude! The perennial favorite of marketing departments around the world, the glue that holds youth culture together, that indefinable *zing!* that turns an ordinary product into a sensation. Make no mistake: Like the rock and roll it aspires to emulate, *Guitar Hero* and its ilk have attitude in spades.

MEET THE NEW YOU

This is where the other elements of *Guitar Hero* and *Rock Band* come into play. Game play, no matter how technically sound or innovative, can only take you so far. It's the art design, the sound, and the story that push a video game across the line from diversion to obsession. Again, the designers do not disappoint. The first *Guitar Hero* games offer a selection of virtual avatars to choose from, to act as your onscreen stand-in and replicate your performance in the virtual arena. Their premade creations act as a who's who of rock-and-roll archetypes: you have the dirty, leather-clad bar rock guy; you have the Jimi Hendrix look-alike armed with headband and psychedelic apparel; you have the slinky riot-grrl (the most obviously sexualized of the bunch); and you have my personal favorite, the mohawked punk dude, girded in spikes and a righteous sneer. While this can lead to some funny moments (I have never met a single punk who would be caught dead playing a Boston song, much less with the enthusiasm "Johnny Napalm" devotes to the tune), the overall effect is clever and convincing—choose your character, choose your guitar, live the fantasy.

Starting with *Rock Band* and continuing to the more recent games, you are no longer limited to the imaginations of the game developers: a fully fledged character creator allows you to customize your own avatar down to the smallest details, encouraging you to craft whatever counterpart you desire to act out your rock-and-roll road trip. Once you sculpt your virtual visage, you can outfit yourself with an impressive array of accoutrements from several rock subcultures: grab a pair of tattered punk jeans, put on a goth fishnet shirt, throw on some glam makeup, and get ready to thrash. When the game came out, I spent a good thirty minutes trying to re-create myself as accurately as possible, down to the clothes I was wearing at the time. The virtual me was remarkably similar to the real me: glasses, sideburns, torn-up jeans, and a military shirt. There were a few differences, however. No matter how hard I tried, the game would not allow the virtual me to have the same, uh, gamer's physique that I have in real life, and I could certainly never afford the designer duds that most closely matched my own thrifty attire. So, I was stuck in a nicer body, with nicer clothes, and a complexion clearer than freshly wiped glass. Poor me, right? The line between reality and fiction was rapidly blurring, with only a rose-tinted lens and remarkable speed-picking skills separating flesh-and-blood from pixels-and-animation.

Of course, the genius of the game is that my self-invention didn't stop there. As you progress through the game, you earn "money" with which you can buy new instruments and new clothing, unlocking more outlandish equipment and looks. Bored with the me-approximation I had created, I started replacing my relatively conservative clothes, hair, and accessories with increasingly elaborate costumes, so that by the end of the game my character was clad in a Sgt. Pepper–like suit with a gigantic beard and more piercings than any ordinary human can safely obtain.

The question arises: is this some alternate vision of myself, a playful construct enabled by this new technology, or is this the idealized me, my true vision of myself in a perfect world? The answer is probably some mix of the two, and therein lies the seductive power of the character creator. We get to be people we don't have the guts (or the money, or the social wherewithal) to be in real life. Escapism, long the provenance of media in general and video games in particular, has just been personalized. Welcome to the brave new world.

BUSY BEING BORN

As residents of the wireless kingdom of the twenty-first century, most of us are no strangers to the constant process of remaking and revising our avatars. The desire to forge a new person for ourselves is not a new one. Our history and literature are littered with forgeries, fakes, and self-creations (think of the disguises of *Twelfth Night*, the journey from Cassius Clay to Muhammad Ali, and—perhaps most importantly—the bestowal of the surname of "Ramone" on a band of New York punk rockers). The Christian faith likewise begins with a name change, an act of remaking: from Abram to Abraham and Saul to Paul, we stand in a holy tradition of abandoning one's old self and reforming into a new person with a new identity and purpose.

For the vast majority of recorded history, going up to my parents' generation, an act of remaking was not an easy one. It required the dissolution of old ties and the assumption of a new identity. After all, if you are to be a new person, you can't be constantly reminded of the person you once were. However, with the advent of Web 2.0, everything changed. With the explosion of the blogosphere, social networking sites, and new and more powerful interactive electronic entertainments, we were given all the tools we needed to create and sustain multiple versions of ourselves and the anonymity to express these avatars without having to compromise our everyday lives. Getting bullied at school? Remake yourself into a badass warrior in the virtual arena. Bored with your friends? Take some sexy pictures of yourself and make some new ones on MySpace. For every interest and hobby there is a built-in group of peers, for every dissatisfaction there is a remedy, and for every real-life disappointment there is a virtual simulation of success. An identity rooted in community or our divine heritage seems downright archaic.

Guitar Hero fills an important niche in our new World 2.0.[3] The Western world may be largely secular, but we all need our gods and goddesses, and in the absence of a shared faith system and community deities, rock stars do the job nicely. Music is a sort of magic to begin with, and when you magnify the music makers and constantly project their dalliances, squabbles, and kingly lifestyles onto our screens, they form their own pantheons of sorcerers and sorceresses, new idols for hungry worshipers. Skeptical? Step into a dorm room and look at the posters of Bob Marley and Kurt Cobain, icons for a new breed of modern martyr. Or step into the bedroom of a randomly chosen junior high student and check out the newest curios from the Miley Cyrus merchandising machine. Again, this is nothing new in itself. What's new, full of potential, and potentially destructive, is the appropriation of the rock-and-roll mythos into the defining paradigm of World 2.0. Being watchers, consumers, or even worshipers is not enough; we must all become creators— authors of ourselves and the world around us.

In an interview with *Wired* magazine in September 2006, Beck—the rock-and-roll pioneer known for his gleeful disregard for the limitations of genre— gave the following quotation regarding the dynamic multimedia release of his most recent album, *Guero*:

> There are so many dimensions to what a record can be these days. Artists can and should approach making an album as an opportunity to do a series of releases—one that's visual, one that has alternate versions, and one that's something the listener can participate in or arrange and change. It's time for the album to embrace the technology.[4]

The album in question was released in a standard form, in a deluxe CD/DVD edition with interactive art to accompany every song, in various unauthorized mash-ups created and distributed on the Internet, and remixed by various artists as *Guerolito*. For his follow-up album, *The Information* (2006), Beck went even further, distributing a blank physical record with a packaged create-your-own-cover-art sticker set and including a DVD with his homemade "video version" of the album. If given the opportunity, he would continue to stretch the boundaries of the rock-and-roll album as we know it:

> Even though the mashup sensibility has become something of a cliché, I'd love to put out an album that you could edit and mix and layer directly in iTunes. We did a remix project on a Web site a few years back where we put up the tracks to a song and let people make their own versions. There was something really inspiring about the variety and quality of the music that people gave back. In an ideal world, I'd find a way to let people truly interact with the records I put out—not just remix the songs, but maybe play them like a video game.[5]

We've reached a watershed moment in the marriage between art and technology, a sort of redefine-the-relationship conversation where we have to redraw the boundaries and take account of where the plates have shifted beneath us. Traditionally, technology has acted as a restrictive agent toward all our forms of electronic entertainment. Our recording consoles only have eight tracks, so that's how many instruments we get to play. Our computers can only process so many pixels, so we get two paddles and a ball.

We're accustomed to our technology advancing at an exponential rate, so I doubt it was much of a surprise to anyone that video games, music technology, and computerized communication became increasingly complex and powerful as the last half-century ticked away. We've seen beautifully rendered virtual worlds replace pixilated paddles, laptop studios replace tape-and-reel monstrosities, and the Internet transform from a curio for the technocracy to the lingua franca of the developed world. What was more difficult to predict, however, is that technology did more than simply enhance and refine the way we experience play, art, and communication. Technology shook the established foundations of what was possible, and the giants who traditionally acted as gatekeepers (who drew the lines, minded the bottom line, and walked the wall that separated producers and consumers) began to crumble and fall.

We find ourselves at a strange, important time. Former cultural giants, though doomed, are still clutching for whatever they can grasp, and even as they are gasping for breath they struggle to regain their footing and stay on top. Newspapers, once the unchallenged disseminators of information and opinion, are dying off one by one, unable to compete with the new (free!) multiplicity of voices given a speakerphone by the easy creation, maintenance, and publicity of a blog. The major record companies are slowly going bankrupt, their monopoly on pop music vanishing with the advent of peer-to-peer piracy, cheap and simple digital recording, and the community that Web sites like MySpace can foster. It's only a matter of time before video game companies, though they continue to stay a slight step ahead of their more old-fashioned brethren, find their profit margins and market superiority impugned by advancing Internet speeds, cheaper hard drive space, and creative independent developers. All our old barriers that once separated producer from consumer, artist from audience, and programmer from player are crashing to the ground around us. We've been given the keys to the kingdom. The question is, what will we choose to build there?

ANALOG ART IN A DIGITAL WORLD

If World 2.0 were to have a single word assigned to best define it, it would be "interactivity." As Beck predicted with *Guero*, we seem to be outgrowing (or at least desire to outgrow) the traditional model of media, art, and entertainment, in which we are given a product by the artist (who has been bankrolled, produced, and distributed as a business enterprise). By purchasing their product, we fund the companies that fund the artists, and the cycle continues. But now we have the toolbox to involve ourselves at just about every stage of production. We can make our own music, tamper with other people's art, publish our thoughts, comment upon other people's thoughts, and construct just about any edifice imaginable in our virtual sandbox. So what do we do now that the cycle as we know it is broken?

Well, it turns out we do more of the same. We have yet to develop a vision of what art and entertainment look like in our new, democratized marketplace, so we continue to adhere to an old system, which—though feigning interactivity—leaves us as passive as a kid in a movie theater. The runaway success of *Guitar Hero* and its offspring is not fully explained by its ingenious marketing and game play. It is symptomatic of a larger cultural indecision, a fence sitting between art and entertainment, passivity and creativity, isolation and community. In World 2.0, we know we have the power (and even the right) to be rock stars. *Guitar Hero* taps perfectly into that desire to remake ourselves into the images we see on television and record sleeves and become the heroes of our own rock-and-roll narrative. However, a curious thing happens when we are handed a simulacrum of superstardom: we take on all the trappings of our music culture while ignoring the most basic element at the foundation of all the hoopla: *art*.

I'm going to hold my breath and make a big leap here. Ready? Video games are not art.

I am not referring to the quality of video games in relation to, say, music or paintings, but to the nature of game playing itself. I have had some marvelous experiences playing video games. I remember in great detail and with fondness fighting through the last level of the *X-Men* arcade game, furiously pumping quarters into the machine with three of my similarly excited prepubescent friends. I remember being moved almost to tears in high school when I was watching the ending cinema of *Final Fantasy VII* and saw the culmination of over thirty hours of my life invested in that massive game.

Similarly, I have had unremarkable experiences with canonized Great Art—seeing the *Mona Lisa* in person, for example, or reading *Beowulf*. My judgment of games as separate from art has nothing to do with the goodness or badness of either, but on the fact that the experience of playing a game is entirely separate from the aesthetic experience of interacting with art.

Video games are, by design, infused with a number of artistic elements. At the very least, as a visual medium they must have some sort of onscreen iconography. As the technology for games has evolved, we've seen an incredible continual movement from the primitive pixels of the 1970s and 1980s to breathtaking, fully realized virtual worlds that can either closely approximate reality or create their own stylized universes. In addition, many games have moved closer and closer to the realm traditionally occupied by Hollywood by using state-of-the-art sound design, stirring musical scores, and story lines that approach the sophistication of great films and novels. The net effect of this art design is to more fully immerse the player in the virtual world, to stimulate visual, auditory, and emotional investment into the game. However, no matter what level of artistry has gone into the design of the game, it doesn't change the fundamental experience of game playing, in the same way that a beautifully carved set of chess pieces doesn't make the essential experience of playing chess any different.

In their book *Game Design Workshop*, noted video game developers and scholars Tracy Fullerton, Christopher Swain, and Steven Hoffman address this phenomenon. "We already have said that games are formal systems; that they are defined as games, and not some other type of interaction, by their formal elements." They posit that a game is defined first as one of these formal systems of rules and goals, and second by the dramatic and artistic elements (graphics, character, story) that help to engage the player. If a game were to emphasize these artistic elements at the expense of basic competitive forms, "A game would lose its 'gameness' and become some other activity."[6]

It would be reasonable to ask at this point, "So if you don't think that art is necessarily better than game playing, why does this distinction even matter?" When you have a game like *Guitar Hero*, which takes something that traditionally belongs in the realm of art—music—and appropriates it into the entirely different conceptual framework of game playing, it makes for an interesting (and mostly unprecedented) situation.

A game employs an arbitrary set of rules that revolve around a goal (or set of goals), creating an arena for play to take place that can express itself in simple and incredibly complex ways. The simplest sort of game might be a competition like a footrace, with simple parameters (a starting place and a finish line), a single objective (reach the finish line first), and very few methods with which to achieve the goal (run faster than everyone else). Chess is an example of a more complex game. Its parameters and objective are still relatively simple (use your pieces on a defined board space to trap or eliminate your opponent's king), but the methodology with which you can achieve the goal is vastly sophisticated and varied. An even more complex game might have parameters and objectives that change as the game progresses. Video games run the gamut from the simple (*Pong*, *Asteroids*) to the complex (*Halo*, *Civilization*, *Grand Theft Auto*), but the sophistication of the machinery doesn't change the nature of what's taking place. As a player you determine the goal and manipulate the rules of the game world to accomplish that goal.

Art, however, works in very different ways than a game. First, art is not something you can win (elementary school blue ribbons aside), at least not in the same way you can win a game. Artists may have certain goals and ideas of what their work is and how it operates, but the artistic experience is a subjective one, and any parameters or "goals" imposed upon the aesthetic experience are bound to be insufficient.

Second, while games can evoke any number of emotions, they are all subsumed in the competitive experience that is taking place. So while you may be moved by the story and music and visual direction that are present in a game, that doesn't change the "point" of the experience—to achieve your objective through manipulation of the game world. The aesthetic experience, however, is an exploratory one; there is no point to it other than the experience itself. Leo Tolstoy attempts a definition of this experience in his book *What is Art?* "Art is a human activity consisting in this, that one man consciously by means of certain signs, hands on to others feelings he has lived through, and that others are infected by those feelings and experience them."[7] Games are competitive, while art is communicative. For this reason, no matter how sophisticated or sublime the trappings of a video game become, the experience will never be an aesthetic one.

Back to *Guitar Hero*. How do you take a rock-and-roll song, a piece of music with no point other than just to be experienced, and turn it into something quantifiable, measurable, and playable? How do you *win* "Iron Man"? The answer is by turning the subjective experience into an objective one, assigning buttons to the musical notes, making a guitar-shaped controller to put those buttons on, and then selling over $2 billion worth of the franchise to customers hungry for the rock-and-roll experience.[8] How do we reconcile the different ways in which art and games work? It might be helpful to consult the great rock critic Lester Bangs:

> To make the crucial distinction, trained fingers might as well be trained seals unless there's a mind flexing behind them. But that's beside the point, finally. Because this success saga has nothing to do with reality. None of this ever had anything to do with music, either, and even less now than ever before, as the emphasis shifts with subtle firmness from "show" to "spectacle."[9]

Even though Bangs is referring to Emerson, Lake, and Palmer's conceptually grandiose and artistically sterile live show, it's easy to imagine the same thing being said about *Guitar Hero*'s precision-as-performance rhythm police game play. A gamer could potentially spend hours nailing the "expert" level notation of "Freebird" without having actually listened to the song a single time. To see this in action all you have to do is look up any one of the homemade hundreds of *Guitar Hero* videos on the Internet, in which average men and women perform truly remarkable feats of memorization and digital dexterity. Their fingers are seemingly disconnected from any sort of cerebral processes (a cynical onlooker could argue that this is, in fact, a tenable link from *Guitar Hero* to its rock-and-roll forebears, but let's ignore them for a moment) and their eyes are stuck to the screen where neon rhythmic indicators flash by at a seizure-inducing pace. Art is, of course, totally irrelevant to this (admittedly impressive) display of hand-eye coordination. A comparable activity would be if you memorized a Shakespearean monologue with the intent of reciting it with the greatest speed and syllabic accuracy possible. Art is involved, I suppose, but only as window dressing, a frame for the main event.

FILLING THE SILENCE

Now we get down to the million-dollar question: *so what?* What does it matter if a popular video game apes rock-and-roll music to deliver a fun, competitive experience? Surely it couldn't be more damaging to the youth of America than a game that lets you gun down virtual civilians or massacre aliens. And surely there's enough gunning down of real civilians in this world that it seems petty and insignificant to waste time and energy talking about the dangers of a game. We are constantly beset by a surplus of local problems and global crises. Why should anyone listen to a self-righteous audiophile whine about the state of popular entertainment?

Because at its best, art can transcend our oversaturated markets of diversion and entertainment and become something greater than itself. Whether it's in the gritty utterances of Tom Waits or the rage-filled guitars of the Stooges or somewhere a million hairstyles in between, even a thing (and I say this with utter, absolute, unconditional love) as hackneyed and banal as a pop group can communicate something meaningful in its sha-la-las and programmed beats. Philosophy can teach us and politics can inform us, but rock and roll has the potential to move us in a way that speaks to our guts as deeply as our heads.

Nick Cave is an artist familiar with the holy interaction between guts and groove. Whether found in the black-as-night gothic garage rock of his early career or in his more recent metamorphosis into raving rock-and-roll philosopher, Cave's music lives in that strange crossroads where careening, sexual physicality meets the still meditations of the soul. In other words, these are the kinds of songs that could make you weep in seconds, but that don't have a chance in hell of weaseling their way onto a video game playlist. In a lecture on the love song that he delivered in Vienna in 1998, Nick Cave ruminates on the connection between music and the mysterious, borrowing the concept of *duende*[10] from Spanish poet Federico García Lorca:

> All in all it would appear that *duende* is too fragile to survive the brutality of technology and the ever increasing acceleration of the music industry. Perhaps there is just no money in sadness, no dollars in *duende*. Sadness or *duende* needs space to breathe. Melancholy hates haste and floats in silence. It must be handled with care.

Later in the lecture, Nick Cave delves to the bottom of what makes a love song (and, I suggest, any meaningful piece of art) work:

> The love song must be born into the realm of the irrational, absurd, the distracted, the melancholic, the obsessive, the insane, for the love song is the noise of love itself and love is, of course, a form of madness. Whether it be the love of God, or romantic, erotic love—these are manifestations of our need to be torn away from the rational, to take leave of our senses, so to speak. Love songs come in many guises and are seemingly written for many reasons—as declarations or to wound—I have written songs for all of these reasons—but ultimately

the love songs exist to fill, with language, the silence between our-selves and God, to decrease the distance between the temporal and the divine.[11]

So maybe there is more at stake here than a bit of turf in the culture wars. It's hard to see how the kind of strange, unexplainable noises that Cave is talking about have any comfortable place in the neon arcade of *Guitar Hero*. Look at Cave himself: yes, there are electric guitars. Yes, there are hip-shaking beats. Yes, there are weirdo hairstyles and bitchin' facial hair. But in a strange mathematics, these elements add up to something more powerfully human than the most hyperentertaining experience technology can provide.

We are all part of an ongoing, sacred conversation. As (hopeful?) people of faith we cross our wires and listen closely and hope we can make out the voice of God in the static. And God knows we are enveloped in static. We are beset by a multiplicity of voices—pundits, governments, blogs, and commentators, all churning twenty-four hours a day and all wanting something from us. They want our allegiance, our resources, and our love. In our constant quest to form ourselves into our ideal avatars, perfectly suited for our new virtual landscape, reality becomes less and less fixed, until we lose sight of what this technology is for in the first place. As (aspiring?) people of faith we claim to believe that that which seems foolish at first can hold truth, and that which makes sense at first can be a force for evil. In this kind of reality, a kindly old man quoting Scripture and wearing a tie just might be another dehumanizing force. In this kind of reality, a lipsticked dude in drag telling us to hang onto ourselves might just be gospel truth. And truth, whether it comes from the pen of Augustine or the jangly guitars of Alex Chilton, is the only currency it takes to get in on the conversation. If we listen to each other carefully enough, we might just hear the voice of God.

The antidote to the hermeneutically sealed virtual worlds we've been marketed might just be found in (you guessed it) a video game. Nintendo's *Wii Music* is strange, unpolished, uncool, and only barely qualifies as a game at all. The game play consists of virtually performing and arranging renditions of mostly public domain songs. The graphics are laughable, the song selection is limited, and there is no real way to progress in the game world. Sounds like a recipe for fun, right? I mean, who hasn't fantasized about playing bassoon on a rocking rendition of "Twinkle, Twinkle, Little Star"? However, despite its shortcomings, *Wii Music* has the ability to deliver something the blaring, neon-gilded giants of *Guitar Hero* and *Rock Band* cannot—a truly creative experience, where you can explore new sounds and put them together in different ways. When you bring other friends to the game, it is not as props for your rock-and-roll fantasy. You must listen to each other and play together, or the song will sound terrible. There is no reward for sounding good together, no way of comparing stats or earning bragging rights. But even if the instruments aren't real, the creative experience you share together is—something a million *Guitar Hero* sessions can't provide. I don't know how well *Wii Music* will sell (I suspect not well), but it might just offer a template for music games of the future, a way toward something approximating truth.

Disclaimer: I like video games a lot. I probably play them more than I should. And *Guitar Hero* is fun. Really, really fun. I've played it before, and I will happily play it again. But ultimately, it has nothing to offer but diversion, a way to forget who we are for a little while and play pretend. We have to remember that we've been offered so much more; our World 2.0 is wired for communication and expression. The forces that once dictated what we could listen to, what we could read, and what we could create are falling down around us and we've been given the tools to build something new in their place. Will we choose illusion and wish fulfillment, or will we wrestle with pricklier, more potent things?

9

BioShock to the System

Smart Choices in Video Games

KEVIN NEWGREN

I recently spent several hours exploring the destruction that ensues when people stop working toward the good of their community and pursue their own rational self-interest. I found that when everyone looks out only for their own good, there are certain responsibilities that no one wants to take up, breeding neglect and resentment. I learned that when the bonds of moral limitations are removed, great evil can be done. I learned all these lessons while dodging bullets and shooting lightning bolts from my fingertips. I learned them while playing a video game.

Released in 2007, *BioShock* is not only a fun and successful video game; it is a deliberate attack on the philosophy of Ayn Rand. In this game, players explore the ruins of an underwater society created by an idealist by the name of Andrew Ryan, an obvious reference to the Objectivist philosopher and writer. Above the fallen city of Rapture, a scarlet banner reads, "No gods or kings—only man." On its surface, the game is an engaging first-person shooter with great sound and visuals. However, the story and setting of *Bio-Shock* teach a powerful lesson about utilitarianism. The game depicts what happens to a world without God, where individuals serve as their own ultimate arbiters of truth. *BioShock* is also a vibrant ethical exploration of stem cell research, of the dangers of turning our bodies into mere biology.

These messages come in an unconventional package, however. For the past forty years, the video game industry has frequently been targeted as the reason for various undesirable behaviors in our children. It has been blamed for rising obesity rates, illiteracy, violence, and adolescent apathy. Like many other games, *BioShock* has come under scrutiny for its content; for example, some reviewers have criticized it for offering material rewards for the killing of "little sisters" within the game, a moral controversy discussed in greater detail below. Scrutiny of video game content is an important issue, but isn't something more going on within these games? As a psychologist, I wonder, *Have video games simply become a convenient scapegoat?* Can we go beyond the question of harm, and ask if video games are helping players? Is it possible that interactive entertainment can actually sharpen our ethics and benefit our souls?

INTERACTIVITY, FOR BETTER AND FOR WORSE

Would you kindly?
Atlas, BioShock

For game developers, the interactivity of games presents opportunities to engage the participant in a way that other forms of media cannot. Games like *BioShock* allow players to see the consequences of their own actions, be they positive or negative, and also encourage a vigorous and deeply personal interaction with the material. Some people view this interactivity as a blessing and an opportunity, others as a curse. Let's start with the much-hyped concerns. Following a stream of criticism that started with movies, music, and comic books, video games have come to be regarded as the current medium that is damaging our youth. The fear has always been that violent images in media of any form will corrupt children and turn them into violent deviants. When it comes to video games, the medium's greatest strength may also be its greatest reason for concern. Interactivity offers unique benefits, but also has its Achilles' heel. A number of studies link video games with behaviors or physiological changes that may lead to violence.[1] These studies have analyzed, among other things, frequency of violent games use and delinquent behavior, increases in aggressive thoughts and behaviors, and desensitization to violent images following video game play. While these concerns should be taken seriously, such studies risk missing a greater point: if games are strong enough to do harm, they can also do good. They have great potential for creating a meaningful and moving experience for participants.

Taking seriously the role of personal and parental responsibility in making wise choices about video games, I would posit that the benefits of video games by far outweigh the downsides. Many children and teens today play video games, and instead of violence rates escalating, it appears that in the past two decades youth violence in the United States has been decreasing.[2] According to the Department of Health and Human Services, arrest records, victimization data, and hospital emergency room records—all of which have been used to track acts of youth violence—hit their peak in 1993 and have since been in steady decline.[3] In this case, we do not appear to be going in a handbasket directly en route to warmer climates beneath us. In fact, some evidence exists that video games have positive effects on youth. Despite initial concerns about video games sapping attention spans, the opposite appears to be true. Playing action-based video games may actually increase some aspects of visual attention.[4] It could be argued that moderate video game use could actually be good for the brain.

It's even possible that the interactivity of video games may improve intelligence. In a 2005 article for *Wired* magazine, Steven Johnson spoke with philosophy professor James Flynn about recent trends in children's IQ scores.[5] Flynn discovered in 1984 that IQ scores as a whole had been improving over the previous half century. He found a fourteen-point gain in scores between 1932 and 1978. Since IQ scores are obtained by comparing a person's score on various intelligence tasks against the general public, this gain in fourteen points suggests that the general public was getting better at completing the tasks included within IQ tests.

However, in the 1980s, Flynn discovered that the annual gain in IQ scores was increasing. Between 1947 and 1972, the annual rate of IQ increase was 0.31 point, but in the 1990s this jumped to 0.36 point. Why did we have a sudden boom in intelligence scores? What changed in the 1980s to make people "smarter"?

Johnson proposes that this increase is due to the presence of electronic gadgets, stating that the type of thinking we do when we attempt to program a VCR is good exercise for the type of brain activity that IQ tests measure. Johnson then states specifically that video games are a good example of this

Gamers Speak

Nathan, fifteen years old, Chinese American

- How, if at all, are your parents involved in video games? *They buy the games and sometimes play.*
- What do you like about playing video games with your parents? *Spending time with them and being able to tell them what to do.*
- How, if at all, have you tried to get around the rules your parents have set for your gaming? *Play when they are not at home.*

Christopher, fourteen years old, Caucasian, on Honor Roll

- If I asked your parents about the effects of video games on you and your relationships, what would they say? *I think they would say there isn't really an effect on the relationship from the games. With friends and with my brother, it is a form of bonding because I do play with them and I think it brings us closer.*

type of brain activity through the visual puzzles and reasoning challenges that they pose. Johnson explores these ideas further in his book *Everything Bad Is Good for You: How Today's Popular Culture Is Actually Making Us Smarter*.[6] In it, he explains the bias that is involved in cultural criticism of video games. Well-intentioned individuals bemoan the use of video games as replacing the book, fearing the impact such a shift will have on children. However, Johnson points out that rather than replacing the book and making zombies of children, video games challenge the mind and in many ways can be seen as an asset.

THE HERO MYTH

Whether it be a blessing or a curse, video games' potential impact lend the medium an opportunity to tell stories that both stimulate and move the participant. Though not all games invest in story, the appeal for many games resides in their ability to envelop players in new worlds, complete with sophisticated backstories and complex plots. This fits well with the postmodern era. In *A Matrix of Meanings*, Craig Detweiler and Barry Taylor suggest the response to the postliteral is to encourage the mythological.[7] As we move past a fixation upon facts, we crave larger metanarratives. The medium of the video game reflects this shift, but it also answers it in the themes of the games themselves.

In their book on game design, Andrew Rollings and Ernest Adams give prospective video game designers advice on writing the story of the game. They recommend creating stories around a concept titled the "mono-myth," an idea they attribute to Joseph Campbell's 1949 book, *The Hero with a Thousand Faces*.[8] They describe twelve stages of the mono-myth. The hero exists in an ordinary world, where he or she receives a call to adventure. At first the hero refuses the call, and then meets with a mentor, leading him or her to cross the first threshold into the adventure. The hero will experience tests, face enemies, and gain allies. The hero will then approach the "innermost cave" or the place where the final ordeal will occur. There is the ordeal, which is followed by a reward. The hero will then begin the road back home, and will experience a resurrection of sorts. The hero then returns home with the reward.

This model recurs in video games because it caters to an internal narrative that strikes a chord with most people. This type of story draws us in. Game designers are encouraged to use this format because it helps players identify with the hero, entering into the game narrative and immersing them in the game. This immersion makes the game more enjoyable.

If you play a few video games, you quickly learn how often Campbell's twelve stages are incorporated. The settings may change from a fantasy world to a futuristic one, or the reward may range from finding a device to saving your town to rescuing a princess. However, the basic outline remains very recognizable. It is actually a challenge to find a story-driven game that does not cater to this mono-myth.

For Christians, this mono-myth may sound especially familiar. Jesus was an extraordinary hero born into an ordinary world. He first was encouraged to answer the call to adventure when he was asked to turn the water into wine. At first he declined, stating that it was not yet his time, but at the urging of his mother, he performed his first public miracle. He was tempted by the devil and gained allies through his disciples. He performed many miraculous signs before he approached the "innermost cave" of Jerusalem. His greatest ordeal began in the hours leading up to his crucifixion. Jesus' torment in the garden of Gethsemane was followed by betrayal and arrest and trial. On the cross, Jesus confronted evil, sin, and separation from God. The reward for his sacrifice was the forgiveness of sins. He was resurrected after three days and returned to his disciples with the reward of the Holy Spirit.

This mono-myth appears to have been written on our hearts. Our souls, whether we know it or not, appear to want to commune with a hero of this type. Video games can reclaim this mythology. They have the potential not only to communicate the story of the ultimate hero but also to invite us into that story in engaging ways. Moreover, they provide the opportunity to participate in games with redemption as subject matter. These general themes provide a range of opportunities to open up conversations centered on how Christ may be reflected in, or differ from, the protagonists in these games.

This possibility can be revealed by once again returning to the game *BioShock*. Players take on the role of a plane crash survivor named Jack. Marooned and alone, he explores the underwater utopia, Rapture, battling mutants and mechanical drones. (Beware: spoilers ahead.) Jack discovers that he has returned to his roots to destroy the creator of Rapture, Andrew Ryan. But Jack's actions could give an evil tyrant, Fontaine, control of the land. Players can make the choice to turn away from this tyrant, and free the inhabitants from his rule, rather than perpetuate some of the evils being carried out. But three different endings are programmed into the game, dependent upon the players' actions.[9] *BioShock* offers an opportunity to consider and feel the consequences of redeeming a fallen place.

BAD THEOLOGY, INFERIOR GAMES: *CATECHUMEN* AND *LEFT BEHIND*

While *BioShock* and other games rely upon narrative complexity and imagination to create compelling worlds for players, leading participants toward thoughtful rumination on issues like sin, redemption, and utopia, they are not designed to be "Christian" entertainment. When researching for this chapter, I ran across a Web site that sold explicitly Christian video games. I downloaded demos of an assortment of these games and played them. I found that most of these games had one thing in common: they were horrible.

Casting aside problems such as glitches in the programs, or mediocre graphics and interface, there were blatant problems with the theology behind the games. One game, titled *Catechumen*, puts players in the place of Christians in Rome during the great persecutions. An angel appears and tells the player that the devil has possessed the Romans, and urges the player to do something about it. The angel provides a "sword of the spirit" that can be used to shoot blasts of blue light at Roman soldiers. Three to four blasts of light cause the soldiers to fall on their knees and start praying while a chorus sings "hallelujah."

This game appears to be a Christian response to "violent" video games, so in place of bullets the gamer shoots blasts of the Holy Spirit. But this contrivance simply does not make for a successful game. The reason that the game does not work is that it claims to preach truth, while it lies. No Christian ever ran around with a "sword of the spirit" zapping Roman soldiers into religious submission. If we construct a false world, how could we ever hope to become relevant and present truth to others? Even when taken as an allegory, the message communicated does not reflect any competent notion of how a person's faith is actually shared.

In 2007, a new Christian-themed game titled *Left Behind: Eternal Forces*, based on the *Left Behind* book series by Jerry Jenkins and Tim LaHaye, was released to the public. The *Left Behind* game had a bigger budget and higher production values than previous Christian games. It offered full-motion video cut scenes, and graphics that were at least in the same ballpark as mainstream offerings. However, critics did not warm to the game, which received a composite score of only 3.4 out of 10 among all of the reviews canvassed by Gamespot.com.[10] *Left Behind: Eternal Forces* represented an improvement in many areas, but still lacked in the same glaring places as previous Christian games. The place in which, ironically, this Christian game fell short was in its theology.

Initially it generated some backlash in the designer's decisions regarding gender roles, which may at first glance appear to be a social issue but is also a theological one. In this game, players send "Disciplers" out to share their faith with neutral civilians. These Disciplers recruit neutral characters to the Christian side. Players can then send these new converts to different buildings in the city to gain various professions, such as Soldiers, Builders, Healers, or Musicians. These professions allow individuals to carry out important tasks in the game. In the initial version of the game, male converts could become any available profession, while female converts could only become Healers or Musicians. Furthermore, though women were allowed to progress further in the Musician profession than men, no significant special skills or benefits set them apart from the male converts. This inequality affected game play substantially in that players were rewarded for converting as many men as they possibly could and avoiding the female civilians unless as a last resort.

The decision to prevent women from becoming Disciplers could have been initially made to avoid offending Christians who disapprove of women doing anything that could appear as preaching. The decision to prevent women from becoming Soldiers could be a result of not wishing to offend those who feel women should not be allowed in the military. Although no church denominations officially oppose women building things, the game prevents women from becoming Builders. Interestingly enough, a patch later offered for the game by the developers allowed women to become Disciplers, but did not change their other limitations.

What ends up being most offensive about this theological decision is the simple fact that there is not much women can do in this game that men cannot do better or equally. With the mentioned limitations in place, women become inferior persons in this game, a game design that reflects poor theology. While *Left Behind* attempts to offer good morals, it ultimately demeans women no differently than games like *Grand Theft Auto*, which allow players to beat up prostitutes.

In addition to its problematic theological views of women, this game offers an embarrassingly simplistic view of the world. In order to reflect the spiritual warfare presented in the *Left Behind* books, characters have a spirituality meter in addition to their health meter. Players' spirituality meters increase when they pray or stand near a worship singer while they sing praise songs. The spirituality meter decreases when they stand near rock musicians while they play. In contrast to Christian characters gaining spirituality by praying, evil characters decrease their spirituality meter by swearing, as if foul language can neutralize prayers. Overall, the game offers an oversimplified, black-and-white view of the Christian life.

Left Behind: Eternal Forces also falls into another common trap I have seen in Christian video games. Between levels, players are faced with a screen filled with text describing arguments for creationism and other apologetics while they listen to a recent song by a Christian artist (complete with a link to buy the song if desired). This comes across as an attempt to stuff as much Christianity in a game as possible, in order to justify the label "Christian video game." In many of the other Christian games I tried there was often a point during play in which the game paused in order to force players to read some stretch of Scripture before continuing. As in *Eternal Forces*, these other references had no direct connection to the plot of the game, but existed merely to force players to read something Christian. It is certainly troubling when Scripture or theology is presented in the same manner as advertisements between television shows. A good game should have theology integrated into the structure and story, not merely thrown at players while loading screens between levels.

Problems arise from misguided attempts to baptize a medium with Christianity and sell it. These games are not popular for a reason, and it has nothing to do with the presence of Christian themes. Games like *Catechumen* and *Left Behind* present a false vision of Christianity, one in which moral choices are always obvious and progress can be easily charted.

The best games, by contrast, use interactivity to allow for conscious moral choices, even when—as we shall see—those choices involve navigating shades of gray. The most innovative games draw upon narrative structure and story to invite players into a new world. They embrace subtlety and use the hallmark benefit of the medium—interactivity—to allow gamers to come to their own conclusions.

ETHICS, CHOICE, AND FREE WILL

A man chooses, a slave obeys.
Andrew Ryan, BioShock

As mentioned previously, the setting and story of *BioShock* clearly sets up an argument against the Objectivist philosophy of Ayn Rand, who espoused the belief that the purpose of life is to rationally seek out one's own interests. In the game, players are guided by a character named "Atlas," a reference to Rand's book *Atlas Shrugged*, in which she describes her philosophy in the form of a narrative story.

In the course of the game, pieces of the story behind Rapture's downfall are revealed through journal entries the player runs across while exploring the ruins. You learn that many denizens of the dystopian society arrived at Rapture with expectations that they would be kings and queens of this underwater land. However, with everyone looking out for their own self-interest to the detriment of the community, those who found themselves relegated to menial work felt deep bitterness. When everyone looked first to their own rational interests, the community of Rapture experienced unrest and constant revolution.

An essay could present rational arguments against Objectivism. However, just as Rand attempted to display Objectivism in the format of literature through *Atlas Shrugged, BioShock* uses a new medium to display an ethical counterargument. *BioShock* allows one to experience the game designer's objection to this philosophy through sights and sounds that reveal the consequences of human selfishness. It also allows the participant an opportunity to actively redeem the consequences of such evil.

Greater horrors are unleashed, however, when the researchers of Rapture uncover the means to manipulate biology, without the constraints of moral objection. Within this fallen underwater utopia are characters that look like young girls, called "little sisters." Some characters within the game describe these little sisters as monsters, while others consider them human children who have been trapped. As a player you are faced with a choice: should you harvest the monstrous sisters or set the captives free? If you release them, the sisters' appearance changes and they transform into little girls again. If you harvest them, you gain their "genetic material" (known as ADAM), which can empower you to shoot flames, electricity, and telekinetic waves from your fingers—all abilities that prolong your own survival in the game.

In the game, additional drugs called EVE can also enhance your powers. Not coincidentally, these stem cells share the name of the first humans, ADAM and EVE. *BioShock* tempts players to acquire as much ADAM as possible to grow in stature and rewrite the human genome. But what happens if you overdose on ADAM and EVE? Insanity! As you progress in *BioShock*, it becomes apparent that freeing the "little sisters" is the "good" path, whereas harvesting them is the "evil" path. Yet the evil path is the one that garners an immediate reward, increasing the temptation to gain at another's expense. A player who wants to complete the game as a "good" character may face difficult struggles since he or she cannot benefit as much from releasing as from harvesting.

This aspect of *BioShock* makes an interesting contribution to the dialogue of bioethics. Is this creature before me considered "human"? Is it morally permissible to benefit from harvesting this creature? Does this game give me something to think about when I consider possible stances to stem-cell research? These subtle additions speak louder than the blatant messages seen in other games. The potential exists for some very powerful conversations stemming from this video game, among both adults and teenagers.

BioShock also addresses the issue of free will versus predestination. In the game you play a character who is initially unnamed and unknown. As the player of the game, you direct the character with a joystick, or mouse and keyboard, in order to direct him to solve problems and reach goals. You appear to have a number of choices as to how you will complete these goals. As mentioned above, you can either harvest or free the "little sisters." After completing a task collecting photos for a madman, you have the choice to let him go free or to kill him. The choices appear to be relatively open-ended. *BioShock* game designer Ken Levine acknowledges the complexities inherent in the game, saying, "You do have to make a leap of faith. And I like that notion because in life, the moral path is quite often a little less clear on the upside."[11]

However, midway through the game (again, plot spoilers ahead) you learn that you are not an independently thinking character. You realize that you have been following commands without your knowledge. The main character has been created to respond to the phrase "would you kindly" with complete obedience to any command given. During game play you may not have noticed this, but you learn at this point that any time an objective was given in the game, this phrase preceded it. Despite the freedom you appeared to have in solving puzzles, the goals were chosen for you, and you had no choice but to obey them or stand staring at the wall.

While playing this game, I felt an eerie sense of being tricked and manipulated. Although players have choices and some degree of control, the game designers have paved a general direction for them to follow. I see this game experience as being an interesting contribution to the old theological and philosophical debate regarding people's ability to make choices on their own, measured against being victims of circumstance or the will of God. This is the power of the *BioShock* mono-myth embedded within an interactive experience.

I hope these examples demonstrate the important difference between the shortcomings of a game like *Left Behind: Eternal Forces*, and the successes of the game *BioShock*. Games that trust the experience and thoughts of the participant, through the use of subtle messages, become far more powerful and meaningful than didactic ones that set out to overtly teach particular concepts. In *Left Behind*, knowledge is imparted, while in *BioShock* the learning is lived.

Good video games value choice and freedom. Reviews of video games frequently discuss whether the game is linear or nonlinear. A nonlinear game is usually valued as being more open-ended, allowing players to make choices about in which direction to lead their characters. A balance is usually struck between this open-ended quality of a game and the level of linear structure needed to actually tell the story the game presents. Nonetheless, video game designers frequently remind each other that the game belongs to the player, and not the designer.[12] A good game designer allows the player to lead the story. An inferior game designer traps the player in the direction in which the game designer wants to go.

With this in mind, video games can help us understand and articulate the ongoing debate of free will versus predestination. Video game designers struggle with the same issue that theologians do, albeit in a more rudimentary way. *BioShock*, which has won praise for its fusion of the genre of the first-person shooter game with the more complex genre of the role-playing game, exhibits this clearly. Designer Ken Levine discusses the tension: "*Bio-Shock* just flows differently than other shooters. We wanted to let the player drive, to set the terms of combat, and to make the rules. Shooters are generally very designer controlled. We wanted to give the rudder to the player. . . . *BioShock* is all about choice."[13] The surprising, widespread success of *BioShock* suggests that players long for intelligent design and considerable freedoms. Levine concluded, "When people say console gamers are mouth breathers who don't care about story, deep gameplay, and stuff like that, I think that puts a lie to that. And I think it's told the publishers to some degree, I hope, that maybe the audience is ready for a little more. Maybe you should trust them a little more."[14]

Levine's instinct to trust the player has led the world of gaming in some interesting new directions. One surprising lesson of *BioShock* is that players are drawn to games that allow them to play the role of the villain as well as the hero. The ironic thing about this is that when I have informally surveyed people who play these games, I've found that most people play these games as the hero first. Later, they will replay the game as the villain so they can see "what it would have been like to be the bad guy." Given the choice, most people still choose to be the hero, but they want villainy as a possibility.

This point raises interesting moral questions. If we have no choice but to be the hero, are we really being noble? If our end goal is to identify with the hero, shouldn't adding the temptation to do wrong bring more value to the player choosing to do right? Video games like *BioShock* suggest that evil must be available as an option in order for someone to be able to choose to do good. A true hero is tempted, but is able to overcome that temptation. It echoes the insights of Paul, "No testing has overtaken you that is not common to everyone. God is faithful, and he will not let you be tested beyond your strength, but with the testing he will also provide the way out so that you may be able to endure it" (1 Cor. 10:13).

Great games leave choices open to the participant. Rather than taking direction from textbooks and spelling out ideas in a literal fashion, games that capitalize on the strength of the medium allow the gamer to experience ethical dilemmas and draw one's own conclusions. These vivid scenarios have the potential to stimulate our minds and speak to our souls. Games such as *BioShock* reveal the opportunities this medium has to teach ethics, philosophy, and theology.

SECTION 3

Avatars

10

'Til Disconnection Do We Part

The Initiation and Wedding Rite in Second Life

JASON SHIM

When I first arrived, I didn't know the local language or the cultural mores of the community. I didn't know exactly how the economy worked, how to exchange money, or even what the exchange rate was. In fact, I felt pretty helpless in this strange new land, but the friendly locals took me in, invited me to their get-togethers, and taught me the local customs. As time went on, I became a member of the community.

I was in a new country. I was in the virtual world of *Second Life*.

When discussing online virtual worlds, a certain amount of sensationalism dominates the mass media. Headlines that highlight game addiction and online infidelities garner much attention, but they overlook the more nuanced daily lives of the people who participate and an economy that is comparable to that of a small country. I have had the opportunity to be part of *Second Life* since it was officially launched in 2003 and have watched it go from relative obscurity to media sensation, and eventually become a part of the mainstream modern culture. *Second Life*'s big break came in 2007 when an entire episode of the TV series *CSI: New York* was dedicated to the virtual world.

For the most part, *Second Life* reflects the lives of those who participate, but people ultimately have control over what is reflected and how. Individuals build communities, hold events, and run businesses. Others engage in romantic relationships, and some elect to wed online. However, when I speak on the topic of online weddings that are enacted within the virtual world of *Second Life*, I am often asked, "Is it real?" Well, that begs the question that philosophers have struggled for time immemorial: what is "real"?

Is a wedding rite conducted in another country or another language any less real? Is a wedding on a beach any less real than a wedding in a church?

When you write someone a love letter, is it real? When you express "I love you" over the telephone, is it less real than if you'd said it in person?

It can certainly be debated how meaningful sacred rites may be when performed over the Internet and how much may be lost in translation. But rather than regarding the *Second Life* wedding rite as merely a digital representation of a First Life[1] ceremony, it may be helpful to frame *Second Life* as we would any other culture—a community with its own unique perspectives and ways of doing things. With this understanding, the rites may be regarded as sacred not in and of themselves, but by virtue of what they aim to accomplish.

In this chapter, I argue that wedding rites performed in *Second Life* can be as real and meaningful as those enacted in one's First Life. I also suggest that wedding rites enacted on *Second Life* may even be more real, as they encourage a serious reflection on the process of marrying and require the conscious construction of the ceremony. I also address the messy possibilities that arise at the intersection of First and Second lives.

A BACKGROUND TO *SECOND LIFE*

Second Life is commonly identified with a genre of computer programs known as massively multiplayer online role-playing games (MMORPG).[2] These types of computer programs have existed since the early 1990s, when they were primarily text-based, and have since evolved to the modern graphics-intensive immersive environments we see today. The most distinguishable characteristic of MMORPGs is that the action continues within the online environment whether or not individual users are online.

Second Life is an online environment released by Linden Labs in June 2003. The personal goal of the founder, Philip Rosedale, was to fashion a shared creative space in which the world would be built by its residents.[3] By the end of the 1990s, the advent of faster processors, video cards, and broadband Internet made this possible. With the advent of three-dimensional spaces, *Second Life* has become a vibrant realm for personal expression and artistic experimentation.[4]

For the most part, *Second Life* resembles most traditional MMORPGs, but it differs significantly in one respect—while most MMORPGs typically have a specific goal for the user, such as the attainment of experience points, defeating an enemy, or completing quests, *Second Life* has none. Scholar Tom Boellstorff distinguishes between virtual worlds and video games (while still respecting their points of overlap). Users cannot "win" at *Second Life*. But *SL* is also a more than a social network. As an anthropologist, Boellstorff notes how "One connects relationships 'through' networks, but lives relationships 'in' places" (like *Second Life*).[5]

So what is the *point* of *Second Life*?

In *Life on the Screen: Identity in the Age of the Internet*, Sherry Turkle studied users of multi-user dungeons (MUDs), which were precursors to MMORPGs, and concluded that from a postmodern perspective, online interactions are indeed quite *real*.[6] For Turkle, the online interactions in MUDs are understood to be part of an integrated self rather than an identity that is fragmentary, distinct, and privileged from others.

Though *Second Life* is classified as an MMORPG, it would be erroneous to simply dismiss it as a "game," with connotations of insignificance, as there are indeed real people, interactions, and emotions involved. If online interactions may be regarded as just as legitimate as those in First Life, the question, "What is the point of *Second Life*?" becomes very broad indeed.

It can be a virtual playground, a place to try on personas, a chance to practice social interactions. Some of the acting out is sexual in nature, and it is estimated that almost one-fifth of the relationships on *Second Life* involve some sort of master/slave/bondage scenarios.[7] But plenty of users are also developing enduring relationships, rooted in love and commitment. This chapter examines two elements of *Second Life*—the initiation and wedding rites—and explores the implications of online practices that have emerged.

AVATARS

In *Second Life*, all interactions are mediated through the avatar. Avatar is derived from the Sanskrit word *avatara*, which means "the descent of god" or, more simply, "incarnation." In *Second Life*, each resident possesses an avatar that is customizable. It is not uncommon to see people customize their avatar to be representations of themselves, though it is common to hear people admit that they have taken a few liberties with regard to their appearance. While users can customize their avatars into supernatural creatures or animals, they must nonetheless define their gender as male or female.[8] This determines basic body shape, most notably the appearance of breasts in females. However, it also inscribes certain societal expectations that carry over from the real world, such as the way an avatar sits—female avatars sit with their knees closer together than male avatars. Author Mark Stephen Meadows asked 130 users whether their avatars resembled themselves in height, weight, and charisma. Seventy percent said "yes" in each of those categories. Reflecting upon his activity within *Second Life*, Meadows concluded, "The main thing avatars are good for is practicing for real life. . . . An avatar can be seen as a rehearsal mechanism we can use to figure out the important stuff in real life."[9] This can include job searches and mating rituals. Baby steps first, though—learning how to walk!

A FAILED INITIATION

On November 10, 2003, I was prematurely "born" into *Second Life*. I stood naked in the middle of an unknown land and started jumping uncontrollably. A small group of people looked on in amusement, while I watched myself in embarrassment. This was the consequence of failing to follow through with my initiation rite.

After registering for *Second Life*, individuals are brought to Orientation Island, a land mass that is set apart from the "mainland." The first message that an individual receives reads as follows:

> Welcome to your Second Life!
> To walk around, press the arrow keys on your keyboard (or WASD).
> Follow the path down the hill for a short orientation course. We'll teach you how to chat, move and use objects, change your appearance—even how to fly!
> At the end of the path, we'll transport you to the mainland, where your Second Life awaits!

I briefly skimmed the message and discarded it. In a moment of hubris, I noted that the controls for *Second Life* were similar to some computer games I had previously played, so there would be little need to go through training—besides, I could always come back later, right? I pressed the button labeled "fly" and haphazardly guided myself through the air to the temple that stood at the top of the island. From there, I teleported to the mainland.

I appeared near a small group of avatars who stood talking among themselves. While trying to get closer, I inadvertently began rising into the air, unable to determine which keys controlled my body. I started pressing all the keys on the keyboard and found myself plunging through the air until I landed with a resounding thump in the middle of the group. Somewhere along the way, my clothes had fallen off and now I was being told by one of the members that I was violating the community standards and would get in trouble if I did not promptly dress myself. I would have thanked them for telling me this, except that I had no idea how to communicate. I simply jumped up and down repeatedly.

My first day in *Second Life* was riddled with problems. The residents had to teach me how to dress myself, how to speak, and how to remove a motorcycle that I had inadvertently attached to my head. These were skills that I would have learned on Orientation Island, had I completed the training. When I asked how I could return to the island, I was told it was impossible.

The irony of this anecdote is not lost on me. As a student studying rituals in *Second Life*, I had decided to forgo the most important rite of passage: the initiation. In *Deeply into the Bone*, Ron Grimes cites *The Encyclopedia of World Problems and Human Potential*, which asserts that without rites of passage, "Society has no clear expectation of how people should participate in [their] roles and therefore individuals do not know what is required by society."[10]

However, in the above situation, was it the ritual or the individual that failed? To place the blame on the ritual would imply that a more effective one would have overcome human agency. In *Ritual Criticism and Infelicitous Performances*, Grimes summarizes a typology of "infelicitous performance" used to describe and critique ritual failure. My own experience would be classified as an "'omission' . . . where the rite did not fail; rather, one fail[ed] to perform it."[11] My failure to undergo this initiatory rite of passage rendered me figuratively (and literally) naked and vulnerable.

REFINING THE RITE OF PASSAGE: THE HISTORY OF ORIENTATION ISLAND[12]

When *Second Life* was first released, new users were simply teleported directly into the mainland. They would land in an area that was surrounded by a shopping district, a boardwalk, a disco, and a casino. The original hypothesis of Linden Labs was that these places would develop as activity centers where new users could congregate and socialize.

However, much to the chagrin of Linden Labs, newcomers would be swarmed by existing members upon arriving in *Second Life* for the first time. People would wait by the welcome area and every time a new user arrived, the avatar would be swarmed with solicitations to buy from a certain store or to trade calling cards.[13]

In addition, many of the new users did not know how to chat or move, and people were taking advantage of this. Linden Labs removed the welcome area from the mainland and placed it on a separate island. Christened with the theologically loaded moniker of "Eden," it contained four paths with eight to ten activity stations on each. A staff member from Linden Labs was stationed to welcome all new users, and there was an obstacle course and a course for evaluating one's flying skills. However, feedback from participants made it clear that Linden Labs had assumed too many things.

First, the designers had assumed that people wanted guides upon entering. Much to the surprise of Linden Labs, the guide was often ignored; people made it clear that they did not desire to chat. A second mistake was that Linden Labs had assumed that people wanted a great deal of training. The users found that the activity stations were far too complicated and frustrating; they simply wanted to learn basic skills in a safe environment.

In response, Linden Labs reduced the number of stations and rebuilt the island to allow users to guide themselves through their initiation. It was shortened to a twenty-minute experience containing only the bare essentials. Also, the name was changed to Prelude, because Eden possessed too many religious overtones.

The Prelude name was short-lived, however. Some users would arrive on Prelude and mistakenly believe that the island was all that *Second Life* had to offer. It was renamed Orientation Island and a message was added to remind users that this was to train them in basic skills. After receiving feedback that suggested that the island was effective, Linden Labs focused their efforts on the mainland welcome area, to ensure that people generally knew that help was available to them. To this day, the activity stations

---

Rand Miller on Second Life

Rand, I've wondered—Myst was so meditative and allowed people to wander around at their own pace. Do you think you made Second Life *possible? Is that an extension of what you and your brother, Robyn, were creating?*

Rand: I think to a certain extent, they're almost at opposite ends of the pole. *Myst* was a story that you could walk around in or a history that you could walk around in. *Riven* was even more so. Every element of it was meticulously placed there because it represented some part of the story or history and had a reason for being there. And as you walked around, you uncovered that story. And it was meticulously designed that way from a creator, sub-creator perspective.

Second Life is a chaotic mess. There is no cohesive sub-creator, so you get in and you're just trying to find anything that might have some meaning or something to do that might be purposeful. It's kind of interesting. You feel like everything in *Riven* has purpose and in *Second Life* you're looking for it. That's why it's called *Second Life*; it's a lot like life. You're just looking for those elements that have something that are a little bit deeper.

From *Myst*'s point of view, we did the story and wrapped the game play around that. And I think typically in games it's the opposite way around, you do the game play and then you wrap the story around it. But either way it's fine. I don't think there is a right and wrong. It's interesting what you can do. . . . It's a very flexible medium. It's still being defined. There's gonna be these huge spurts of innovation and then large lulls, doldrums of copies. And that's what we look forward to—more innovation.

remain. Although they are not often used, mentors and liaisons are there to guide and to give tours.

Linden Labs initially attempted to structure the experience of new users with the belief that they first needed to be integrated with the community. However, their failure to successfully orient new users demonstrated that this model did not work. New users were being exploited by existing ones. In *Deeply into the Bone*, Grimes states, "In the absence of rites of passage, major transitions become ritualized. Bereft of the explicit framing of rites, unconscious and unintentional activities displace conscious and intentional ones."[14] Indeed, new users were pounced upon for their initial cash allowance, and the exploited who remained would later become the exploiters.

Linden Labs refined its initiation rite after realizing that people did not need to be first integrated with others, but equipped with basic skills to enable interaction with the community. Though it may seem self-evident, it is not always easy to recognize the need to orient individuals with themselves prior to orienting them to the community at large. Despite the fact that I never successfully completed my initiation, I still managed to acquire the skills that are taught on Orientation Island through the aid of sympathetic residents. Though the initiation rite is intended to transform the individual, the transformation may still occur despite the absence of the rite. Grimes asserts, "The primary work of a rite of passage is to ensure that we attend to such events fully. . . . Unattended, a major life passage can become a yawning abyss."[15] But it would be an oversimplification to dichotomize rituals into merely successes and failures. What about the rites of passage that are partially attended to by the participant? They may not fully transform the individual, but they do not necessarily leave a person dangling over the void either. Grimes makes it clear that he believes that rituals cannot be judged to be failed or flawed in absolute terms. While Linden Labs put forth an initiation rite that spanned the void, I inadvertently chose to construct my own. It may not have been as efficient, or as effective, but it got the job done.

THE WEDDING OF GARTH FAIRLIGHT AND PITUCA CHANG

I was sitting at the organ at St. Isidore's when the bomb went off. The church had been filled with people getting ready for the wedding, and suddenly there was nothing. Everything was in disarray. When the smoke cleared, the culprit was identified as someone who wanted to go out with a bang. But the bride and groom were undeterred. We all found one another and had the wedding on an airport runway. On this day, November 20, 2003, Garth Fairlight and Pituca Chang were married in *Second Life*.

Garth and Pituca had first met at a Fourth of July party in 2003. The chemistry was evident between them. Two months later, they had moved in together, and in November, they were married in *Second Life*. Ron Grimes describes the wedding as a rite "that effects a transition from the social state of being single to that of being coupled."[16] Are *Second Life* weddings simply the ceremonial union of avatars? Or do they touch upon something deeper?

Weddings in *Second Life* are not legally binding, but they do establish expectations and express emotion. Anyone can go through the motions of a wedding, but only the effective ones truly establish a meaningful bond. How is a meaningful bond to be defined in *Second Life*? Relationships that are conducted online are not as ethereal as popular media often depict them to be. When you are "with" someone on *Second Life*, it typically means that you spend the majority of your time with him or her online and genuinely care for the person whom the avatar represents. Typically, when they say, "I love you," serious consideration is not given to its form. Whether it is communicated in person, in a letter, over the telephone, in an instant message, or in an e-mail, the sentiment remains the same.

WHY A *SECOND LIFE* WEDDING?[17]

In First Life, people are defined in relation to others. I am the son of my mother and the brother of my sister, and these are recognized as biological, incontrovertible facts. However, upon entering *Second Life*, an individual has no prior affiliations with anyone. Grimes, in *Marrying and Burying*, describes the wedding rite "as a ceremonial realignment."[18] When people enter *Second Life*, for the most part, they truly exist unto themselves—but the wedding rite in *Second Life* establishes in-world partners.

When asked why they decided to get married in *Second Life*, two couples—Garth Fairlight and Pituca Chang, and Johnny Bunderfeld and Malana Spencer—responded that they simply felt a need to do so. Though it is not legally binding, the wedding ceremony is described by Garth Fairlight as a "cement . . . not unbreakable, but a tighter bond." He went on to say that "it also announces your . . . intentions . . . [and] dedication to that person to the world." Johnny Bunderfeld responded, "All I know is that for Mal & I it just seemed right." The *Second Life* wedding may retain much of the architecture of a real-life wedding, but it must be understood that it carries different meanings. The *Second Life* wedding does not tend to significantly alter relationships in terms of how they were carried out: when both couples were married, they were already living together in *Second Life* and spent a considerable amount of time with one another online. The *Second Life* wedding affirms a relationship before the online public and establishes commitment between two individuals.

THE ENGAGEMENT AND CEREMONY

Though diamonds are merely polygons with a diamond texture affixed, they nonetheless remain integral as a prelude to a wedding. When asked about his proposal to Malana, Bunderfeld said, "Can't even think of doing that without a ring . . . I don't care what life it is, the girl wants to see a ring." In *Cinderella Dreams*, Cele C. Otnes and Elizabeth H. Pleck detail the advertising campaigns of De Beers and the increasing popularity of the diamond engagement ring as a symbol of love and devotion. This symbolism is not lost in *Second Life*, as both Pituca and Malana received "diamond" engagement rings. As Bunderfeld attests, it is not the ring itself that is important in the engagement, but what it symbolizes.

As with the engagement ring, the *Second Life* wedding is more recognizable than it is different from "real" weddings. *Second Life* weddings often take weeks to plan. When compared to systems like the *Sims Online*, which can take only a matter of hours, the highly customizable nature of *Second Life* makes the coordination of a wedding a highly complex task. And just as in First Life, where complex rituals require specialized or trained guides (Grimes describes these as "ritual plumbers," people who use the resources available to make rites effective), *Second Life* rituals need experienced helpers. Baccara Rhodes is such a person.

At the time of Garth and Pituca's wedding, Baccara Rhodes was a well-known wedding planner in *Second Life*. When I first met Baccara, she was flying outside the reception area for Garth and Pituca's wedding, ensuring that everything was set up and ready to go. In First Life weddings, the couple must book the church; in *Second Life*, the couple must either build the church themselves or find someone who will. In Garth and Pituca's case, Baccara took care of it all.

Second Life has its own currency, the Linden Dollar, which is used by residents to buy and sell goods and services. Linden Dollars are also exchangeable for U.S. dollars on the in-world Lindex exchange with the currency typically valued between L$260 and L$300 to $1 U.S.[19] Indeed, there are some residents whose primary source of income is drawn from business conducted in *Second Life*.[20] Currently, basic accounts are free and residents who have registered under this plan receive a signup bonus of L$250. Residents who register a premium account, which starts at USD $6 per month, receive a signup bonus of L$1,000 and a weekly stipend of L$300. The economy in *Second Life* is structured in such a way that someone cannot simply enter the world and expect what has been defined as a "decent" wedding without an additional contribution of money. The average *Second Life* wedding costs between L$20,000 and L$40,000, and Garth and Pituca's wedding was approximately L$25,000.

When I first met Pituca and Garth, they mentioned that they were planning their wedding and invited me without hesitation. They simply remarked that I would have to arrive early in order to secure a spot. The day of the ceremony, I arrived an hour early and sat in front of the cathedral with several other individuals. I remarked that I had neglected to go shopping for a tuxedo and I was promptly given one to wear by someone who appeared to be distributing them. Wedding attire in *Second Life* echoes its First Life counterpart: in *Cinderella Dreams*, Otnes and Pleck state the transformation is not limited to the bride on the wedding day, but that other participants may feel entitled to this experience.[21] Indeed, I share the sentiments of Stanley Elkin regarding tuxedos:

> [There is] something possessive in the feel of the thing, something hospitable and generous, father-of-the-bride, say, founder-of-the-feast, chairman-of-the-board, leader-of-the-band, master-of-ceremonies, maitre-d'. Something patrician, the long, deep bloodlines of first families and old money. I didn't want to take it off. I never wanted to take it off.[22]

In retrospect, I realize that the ceremony was not just for Pituca and Garth, but it was for me, too. It made me feel as though I was truly a part of their group of friends and their *Second Life*.

As time went on, more people arrived until something went wrong. I was kicked out of the program and could not get back into the cathedral. It was soon revealed that it was because someone had set off a script bomb, a piece of code that used up a significant part of the server resources. In *SL*, this kind of hassle or disruption is known as "griefing," as in causing people grief. Yes, boorish and obnoxious behavior extends into virtual worlds. I tracked down the individual who had coded it and the following conversation ensued (NB: My username is PerpetualJ Valkyrie):

Vlade Statosky: are they really getting married

PerpetualJ Valkyrie: On SL, yes.

PerpetualJ Valkyrie: There's about 45 people.

Vlade Statosky: i mean, are they actually being married, in holy matramony [*sic*], and all that crap

PerpetualJ Valkyrie: They are having a ceremony.

Vlade Statosky: im asking you are they really married or is it a virtual marriage because i'm not apologizing if it's fake.

Vlade Statosky: and i'm also not apologizing to the idiot who thought up having their marriage in a video game.

PerpetualJ Valkyrie: You dont think that this could be just as real?

Vlade Statosky: what the hell are you talking about.

Vlade Statosky: this is a game.

PerpetualJ Valkyrie: A game?

Vlade Statosky: a game.

PerpetualJ Valkyrie: How so?

Vlade Statosky: game, "virtual" reality, not reality

Vlade Statosky: game.

Vlade Statosky: it's on your computer

Vlade Statosky: i'm quitting SL, and i'm going out with a bang, you see

PerpetualJ Valkyrie: Why?

(end of conversation)

Evidently, weddings in *Second Life* are not universally recognized. To Vlade, the notion of an online marriage was ridiculous. He regards *Second Life* purely as a game, which may be attributed to the lack of language used to describe this virtual environment. As detailed earlier, up until this point, most interactive programs have been games, and *Second Life* is unique in that it does not designate any specific purpose for its participants. For Vlade, the definition of a wedding, or as he put it, "being married," conflicts—and his opposition, from his point of view, is quite legitimate. He is under the impression that a *Second Life* marriage is a poor replication of one that is legally binding. So what is the difference in its meaning?

Let us examine the vows. Following the script bomb, the wedding was held on an airport runway that Garth owned. Pituca and Garth used vows from a traditional religious wedding service:

> We are gathered here today in the presence of friends and loved ones, to celebrate one of life's greatest moments, to give recognition to the worth and beauty of love, and to add our best wishes and blessings to the words which shall unite Garth Fairlight and Pituca Chang in holy

matrimony. Marriage is a most honorable estate, created and Instituted by God, signifying unto us the mystical union, which also exists between Christ and the Church; so too may this marriage be adorned by true and abiding love.

Pituca and Garth's ceremony continued as adapted from the Episcopal Book of Common Prayer, containing such familiar phrases as "forsaking all others" and an exchange of wedding rings. As in First Life weddings, the crowning moment is the declaration of vows and the affirmation, "I do." J. L. Austin's *Speech Act Theory* describes indicative sentences such as "I do" as statements that *do* things; they do not just express sentiment. Thus, when the vows were exchanged between Pituca and Garth, they not only expressed, but created, a new bond.

Within the context of *Second Life*, it is impossible to care for someone "in sickness and in health," but the words are not intended to be taken literally. Though neither Pituca nor Garth professed to be religious, the structure of their vows nonetheless retained the holiness of a Christian ceremony that focuses on establishing a sacred union. When further questioned about the ceremony, the couple did not place as much importance on the words themselves as the fact that they had taken the time to consciously decide on their inclusion. Garth and Pituca desired to have a ceremony that catered specifically to their needs and their relationship.

As a wedding gift, Linden Labs granted a new last name to Garth and Pituca, uniting their surnames of Fairlight and Chang to become FairChang. To date, I am not aware of other instances of this occurring. Since I began my examinations of online weddings in *Second Life* in 2003, there have been some significant changes. In the past there was no formal indication that one avatar was "partnered" with another; however, Linden Labs has introduced a form to officially register a partnership that is displayed in the user profile.[23]

FROM *SECOND LIFE* TO FIRST LIFE

Is it infidelity if you're involved with someone on e-mail?
Kathleen Kelly, You've Got Mail *(1998)*

While *Second Life* draws upon First Life, in turn, First Life reinterprets itself through *Second Life*. When you have already married someone and committed to them online, what happens in "real life"? If we accept Turkle's postmodern approach, those who have real, meaningful interactions online make commitments that are then integrated as a facet of their whole life. To this end, Garth and Pituca met, fell in love, and married in *Second Life*, as we've seen. They then got engaged in First Life as well and were married on May 6, 2006, nearly three years after their virtual wedding.

Whether weddings take place in the First or *Second Life*, the rituals we enact need to be consciously thought out, or Vlade's comments about a wedding being merely a game, with connotations of triviality and insignificance, may indeed come true. But worse yet, if we do not consciously reflect on our interactions online and the power that they hold, we may be doing ourselves and others a disservice, because it would not be *Second Life* we would be treating as a game, but our First Life.

Indeed, Turkle affirms, "Our experiences [in virtual worlds] are serious play. We belittle them at our risk. . . . Without a deep understanding of the many selves that we express in the virtual we cannot use our experiences there to enrich the real."[24] I would also offer an inversion of Turkle's statement: that without a deep understanding of the selves that we express in our First Life, we cannot use our experiences there to enrich our *Second Life*. Though some may regard *Second Life* as an escapist fantasy, for others, it has offered an opportunity to construct perhaps *more* meaningful interactions as it may require the thoughtful negotiation of one's worldview.

Such interactions also require the thoughtful negotiation of relationships and sensitive feelings. Some of the messy possibilities of online relationships were detailed in a romantic comedy, *You've Got Mail* (1998), starring Tom Hanks and Meg Ryan as two business competitors who unknowingly fall in love with one other online. *You've Got Mail* was based on the 1940 film *Shop around the Corner*, starring Margaret Sullivan and James Stewart, which centered the love story around anonymous penpals. Is it infidelity if you're involved with someone over letter mail? While online weddings in *Second Life* may seem novel, when regarded as a practice within a distinct culture we may draw some useful parallels when assessing questions of ethics.

Is it infidelity if someone is married to different people in their First Life and *Second Life*? From a Christian theological perspective, is it possible to sin in a virtual world? Do Christ's words in Matthew 5:28 still apply? "But I say to you that everyone who looks at a woman with lust has already committed adultery with her in his heart." Would an individual be looking lustfully at a computer screen? Or another individual? When dealing with the intersections of First Life and *Second Life* relationships, communication is crucial to ensure that the expectations and responsibilities with all parties are clearly understood. Infidelity, like the wedding rite, is a social construction and though some may find this approach disheartening, for Christians, it may serve to strengthen faith as it encourages a thoughtful reflection on personal boundaries and spousal responsibilities.

While there have been articles in the mass media detailing jilted spouses who cite *Second Life* as the reason for the disintegration of a marriage,[25] these accounts appear to overlook underlying issues, such as Internet addiction. There are numerous support groups for "widows" of individuals who play online games compulsively, the most notable of which was created in 2000. EverQuest Widows currently has over seven thousand members[26] and has been a model for other related groups, such as World of Warcraft Widows.[27] In these cases, an online relationship that jeopardizes a real-life marriage may be a symptom of a greater problem surrounding impulse control and a failure to negotiate meaning between one's First and Second lives.

In a virtual world like *Second Life*, users must create not only day-to-day objects and buildings, but also *meaning*. When it comes to First Life practices such as weddings and notions of love and relationships, it requires a certain amount of thoughtful deconstruction before it can be re-created in *Second Life*. I argue that this process of re-creation renders practices and meaning more real by virtue of their design—the ideal form, as conceived by residents of *Second Life*. Keeping this in mind, an ideal, and more "real," notion of romantic and meaningful love can certainly be constructed within *Second Life*. For some, this may be a fruitful exploration of Christian love within the context of a virtual world. However, these explorations in *Second Life* must be tempered with a thoughtful negotiation with one's First Life, especially when a marriage is involved. While the avatars in *SL* may be virtual, the people and emotions behind the keyboard are not. Just as expressions of love in a letter or over the telephone can be significant and powerful sentiments, so can the interactions that take place in *Second Life*.

The approaches that people have in *Second Life* may find some parallels to one's First Life. It may be a game, a competition, a journey, and for some, one in the service of God. Between wood, under stones, and across circuits, the continued study of practices in *Second Life* and other virtual worlds is a mirror and lens from which we can enrich and engage our First Lives.

※※※※※

For better or for worse, for richer or for poorer, in sickness and in health, Garth and Pituca FairChang loved and cherished one another 'til disconnection did they part. On September 6, 2009, Garth FairChang died of pancreatic cancer. In her blog, his wife, Pituca, wrote, "He was like a comet in my life, speeding through and touching every corner of my life and soul. I will miss him so much, but I know that he is at peace now and waiting for me on the other side." This chapter is dedicated to the memory of Garth FairChang.

11

Role Playing

Toward a Theology for Gamers

DANIEL WHITE HODGE

As I unpacked my recorder, microphone, and notepad to begin my first interview with a gamer, I began to realize how deep gaming runs. As a person who grew up with Atari and Super NES, I underestimated how immersive this gaming phenomenon had become. The young man in front of me was anxious to discuss his passion and even more excited to have someone listen to him. I finally got everything together and began the interview. After we got through the preliminary demographic questions, I told him that I was attempting to see a spiritual and theological connection through gaming. His response reminded me why video game culture deserves further study. He stated,

> You know, I really feel that . . . gaming has really helped me see God better. Through playing these games, I can really see God's love for me and just how the creative talent he's given me runs through these games. I know parents and sometimes preachers don't really understand this, but I see God almost every time I play games. . . . I've just never thought about it like that until now. . . . It's a trip man![1]

I knew at this point that I was on the right path to enter into gamers' world.

This chapter gives respect and context to gaming culture and provides qualitative insight from gamers as it relates to their spirituality. I discuss how theology shows up in video games and provides deeper meaning for a generation immersed in media culture. I use qualitative semi-structured interviews, participant observations, and video game analysis to arrive at my conclusions. I pay special attention to the spiritual, theological, and even christological implications of video games—particularly role-playing games (RPG).[2]

This study included thirty-five qualitative interviews with gamers between the ages of nineteen and thirty-eight: To be considered gamers, they had to play video games, on average, between twenty and forty hours a week (about three to six hours per day) for at least five years. These thirty-five interviewees were then observed playing video games in their natural habitat, and the interviewer would only observe and ask clarifying questions. Several surprising insights resulted. While some may consider gaming as an isolating, sensation-driven activity, gamers' experience suggests otherwise. They consider video games a highly communal, story-driven medium that can actually create spiritual spaces within participants' lives. While games can offer a simplistic perception of life as solvable or winnable, the virtual worlds created by game designers have also created a generation comfortable with mystery, eschatology, and the numinous.

STORY AND MYTH MAKING

According to my interviews, the top reason that gamers buy and delve into games is story. Ninety-five percent of all the gamers I interacted with commented on how much a good story line matters. Narratives, allegories, and fables are essential to the gaming experience. Story sets the mood, tone, and overall strategy for the game. There are several recurring stories in gaming that relate to theology:

> Narratives of quest
> Narratives of companionship
> Narratives of social problems (a virus spreading, machines taking over)
> Narratives of judgment day
> Narratives of postapocalyptic
> Narratives of heroism
> Narratives of victory

In role-playing games, these stories often take the form of legends or mythology. *God of War* is rooted in Greek mythology. *Too Human* draws upon Norse legends. *Tomb Raider: Legend* takes Lara Croft on a search for King Arthur's sword. *Prince of Persia* springs from Aladdin and the Arabian Nights.[3] Most religions are also steeped in legends and myths. Game designers capitalize on that, which gamers realize.

Gaming narratives can be seen as a "second naïveté."[4] Theologian Veli-Matti Kärkkäinen states, "In this scheme, the story of Christ is not read from a distance by an objective researcher, but from inside the community of participation in the narrative of Christ." As they recount the stories behind

Halo, BioShock, or even *Grand Theft Auto,* gamers are putting their meaning-making skills to work. Pastors mired in a modern mind-set may not grasp the importance of connecting God's story to epic gaming narratives, yet gamers born into a postmodern era need stories and nonliteral references at times for Scripture. By engaging in narrative, gamers are able to experience God in an entire new dimension and are allowed to find God on their own terms within that story—not within the confines of a prepackaged salvation formula. Gaming narratives can become a form of hermeneutic to interpret and analyze Scripture within community.

Many gamers find spiritual and theological meaning in metanarratives within games such as *Halo 3,* which allow them to play games where they are the hero or heroine, save the world from holocaust/disaster, and explore new worlds, therefore allowing them to find connection with spiritual elements. These grand narratives revive the self in a consumer-driven culture. Players take on qualities of strength, valor, and love, characteristics that—in many different ways—connect back to their core identity and the symbolic superstructure within both the game and real life. *Halo 3* offers a chance to say, "Yeah, I'm good, I just beat this game, and saved lives while doing it!" Without such role-playing games, the narrative is lost along with their identity, which leads to a disengagement for the gamer.

Although narrative is far and away the most important aspect of gaming for veteran participants, several other facets of gaming cropped up often in my interviews. The first recurring theme that arose from my observations is the concept of sacred space, as games are thought to offer an "escape route"[5] or "supernatural release."[6] Games create a safe space for friends, community, and people deemed "companions" to discover new realms of spirituality. Often those routes are through an immersive game such as *EverQuest* or *World of Warcraft.* Players may discover multiple ways to master a quest, which may have a spiritual implication in that they may resonate with the idea that there are multiple paths to God. As John Beck and Mitchell Wade contend, gaming "has always been an escape route, a technology that lets them transport themselves away from the boring and restrictive world inhabited by their parents and other authority figures, and to a place that those older people—who wouldn't 'get it' anyway—simply cannot follow."[7]

This brings to mind a second theme, which is community. My observations suggest that although media stereotypes emphasize gaming as a loner experience, community is everything for gamers. Gamers "hang" with those with whom they feel a connection and whom they deem as "one of us." Community is a large part of the gaming experience, and even more so when the game is played in multiplayer mode. Real-time strategy allows players to cooperate across continents to defeat a common foe. It is not uncommon to lose the sense of self within that gaming community while playing a game. As one gamer, Allen, put it to me, "Games are best played with other people. . . . That's one of the biggest reasons I play."[8]

A final aspect of gaming is the strong emotion it tends to evoke. When playing games, it is only natural to get emotional and want to win the game while playing, yet this goes deeper than a mere in-the-moment excitement. For many gamers, the emotional part of the game is similar to that feeling they get when they smell Mama's home-baked apple pie or Christmas dinners. For gamers, certain memories are locked into the gaming experience. They may have bonded the "first time" they played a game. As one interview said, "Forget booty and food, it's all about that first time you played *Donkey Kong* and *Super Mario Brothers*! That's the way to a man's heart!" For gamers, the emotions behind games are just as real as the game itself, and are not to be ignored.

Within these broad areas, what deeper theological significance can be seen within gaming? For many gamers, life becomes part of the gaming experience and symbolic superstructure—not in a reclusive loner fashion, but in a healthy and natural way of engaging life, interpreting and solving problems, quantitative reasoning, and figuring out "life's issues." At their best, video games can become a lens through which participants see life. For some of us, it is difficult to put on the gamers' lens. We do not see the larger metanarrative connection within role-playing games. The gamers' number-one complaint was: older people just don't understand us.[9] They felt that adults are too suspicious of, and prejudiced against, gamers.[10] This suggests a virtual divide that supersedes race and class. In other words, gamers tend to see other gamers in solidarity as "one." The struggle to be understood becomes universal.[11] Can we follow their stories, join their community, come alongside their spaces, and affirm their emotions? Surely, we can enter into their experience rather than isolating ourselves from their unifying activities. Social change and theological movements have often begun on the margins of society. From playing consoles around the world, we attempt here to forge a theology of gaming. I focus upon three major themes that dominate video game narratives, including (1) judgment days and postapocalyptic scenarios, (2) violent battles, and (3) heroic victories.[12] We consider each narrative strand, followed by its theological implications.

JUDGMENT DAYS

Video games often focus on apocalyptic scenarios. *Resident Evil* (the whole series), *Call of Duty: World at War*, *Gears of War*, *FallOut 3*, and the *Halo* series all depict the final days of earth and humankind as bleak, militarily driven, and survivor-based. In their apocalyptic settings, some force is often attempting to take over the world. Since many major religions have theological teachings about "final days" and the end of the world, it is not surprising that we find this type of schema within video games. Moreover, gamers love it.

The end time is represented within games in several ways:

> *Mutant Based*: A deadly virus, poison, or illness has spread throughout the world, annihilating most of the human race. In some cases, there is only a "remnant" left that must save all of humanity. (Example: *BioShock*)
>
> *Machines Gone Wild*: Television and film typically depict a future with artificial intelligence (AI) or cyborgs as uncontrolled and untamed. Such stories typically end with the machines gaining self-awareness, which results in their revolt against their masters—humans. Games are no different, featuring robots or cyborgs gone awry who are bent on the destruction of humanity. (Example: *Halo*)
>
> *War Is Inevitable*: In this scenario, humanity is thrust into war—typically nuclear—and forced into a fight that demands creative thought, team effort, and new technology to generate a new world and better society for humans. Games like this often tend to demonize a group of people; during the 1980s it was the Russians, during the 1990s it was extremist groups, and currently it is people of Middle Eastern descent. (Example: *Resident Evil*)

Apocalyptic games explore issues of power and autonomy: someone or something is attempting to control or overpower humankind. It is typically up to a small group of people to stop them. Will this community rally in time to rescue humanity? Apocalyptic games never depict the end of the world as a pleasant picture. For gamers, this is, of course, all myth. It is the game creator's imagination of a world that has lost civility and now has created an apocalyptic ending for itself. But for many gamers, even this is too close to home. Mike stated,

> Games like this make you think of what governmental schemes are going on that we don't even know about and have no clue. It sort of makes you paranoid about what is happening in our world today. I mean, the games are great, don't get me wrong, but it does make you paranoid and insecure about the world around you—but it's *awesome!*[13]

For Mike, along with other gamers, virtual eschatology, while frightening and partly based in conspiracy theory, is welcomed. Moreover, some gamers see virtual judgment days as reminders of humanity's plight and ultimately how it all "might end." Virtual eschatology is yet another part of overcoming and "winning" the game—not just in virtual worlds, but also in real life. Gamers are aware of the science fiction behind the game, but when theatrical and realistic clips combine fact and fiction, the overall experience causes them to think, *Is this really happening?*

INESCAPABLE VIOLENCE

Our world is violent. Do video games reflect this violence or inspire greater violence? Many games place players at a moral crossroads: they must resort to violence in order to restore peace. This leads to several questions, particularly for Christians. Is it appropriate to view violence as fun? Should we feel guilty about shooting people (even within a game)? When is violence right? When is it wrong? When is it necessary?

For some gamers, even Christian ones, violence in video games is just another part of life. It is the "norm," as a gamer named Larry put it, a part of life in which we all engage. Larry states,

> I mean, we all take part in violence every day. . . . If we follow the mandate of Christ in Matthew where he says if we talk about people then we murder them. . . . Come on, we all do that, we sarcastically respond to someone we don't like, we snub others, we talk about those we hate, and ultimately, we love violent movies when the "hero" kicks everyone's ass in the end. . . . Come on, violence is all around, the games just reflect back what is going on in our society today.[14]

For Larry, violence takes on a subtle form: snide discourse, subtle snide looks, and even the enjoyment of watching James Bond kill the bad guy. He is not overly concerned about violence in the games he plays. In fact, when it comes to understanding violence, most gamers are much like Larry. Eighty-five percent of my interviewees viewed violence as "a part of life" and did not see anything wrong in killing the "enemy" within a game. They also expressed little moral conflict with certain games that allow gamers to be the bad guy and take out the good guy within the game—a postmodern twist. Violence in video games is, in many ways, a reflection of the violent society in which we live. For video game manufactures and designers, a violent video game only makes fiscal sense. But does violence in games then in turn create more violence in society? Perhaps. Mike, a dedicated gamer, feels that video violence desensitized him to other violence within his societal frameworks. He states,

> I honestly believe that gaming has caused me to be desensitized to a level of violence. Games which put you into a fantasy role of killing other people have certainly caused me to be less shocked by movies

that depict similar events. I like to believe that I can easily delineate the difference between fantasy and real life. If I see a scene of violence on TV which I am informed is real, these scenes disturb me. If I see an episode of *Law & Order* on TV, it is not likely to bother me as much.[15]

For Christians, there is another component to this. Video games reflect the violence within not just our society but the Bible as well. We cheer David on as he takes out those nasty Philistines. We gladly cheer for Moses when the thuggish Egyptians chase after the children of Israel. Theologically speaking, violence is all over the Bible. Yet we recoil in fear and bewilderment when our children pick up a video game controller and release some negative energy in a game that has them killing zombies or drug dealers. Christians in general need to take a closer look at violence as it relates to our own theology. Biblical violence raises important questions, including: Can a God who condones killing children in the Bible do the same in contemporary times? How can God allow such violence to occur? Can we grow closer to God despite (or even through) the violence in the video game?

Such questions will continue to plague not just gamers but theologians as well. Moreover, there may not be any clear-cut answers, and that is often why games are played: to seek some type of comfort in an ambiguous world.

ULTIMATE VICTORIES

Epic games like *Halo 3* and *Gears of War* have a special meaning: the defeat of evil and the vanquishing of all "bad" things. In these two games (among many!), players conquer a foe—whether it be a mutant spider or zombie robots. The enemy is a nuisance, a pest, a hindrance to humanity. For the gamer, victory is at hand and the enemy must be destroyed. These games, in essence, become a type of *protoevangelium* for victory, the ultimate "good news."

Protoevangelium is considered by many scholars to mean "the first gospel." The *Oxford English Dictionary* defines "protoevangelium" as "The promise concerning the seed of the woman implied in the curse upon the serpent (Genesis 3:15)."[16] Some biblical interpreters see this passage "as predicting the defeat of evil by the victory of Jesus Christ and thus as the first promise or 'gospel' of a coming redeemer."[17] The *protoevangelium* is the hope, vision, and desire for the final destruction of evil. For Christians this would mean Christ redeeming the world and destroying the devil once and for all.

Games tap into a similar ideal of final victory. The "good news" for many gamers is that victory can be had through conquering the game. Many games offer a form of ultimate victory, a *protoevangelium* that the heroes embody within each narrative. As an interviewee named Doug told me, "Sometimes you just stay up and play and play trying to figure out the game and win. You know . . . you need to win, 'cause if the game can't be beat, what's the point of playing, if you can't defeat an enemy that is threatening mankind?"[18] Winning the game and defeating the enemy is a type of *protoevangelium*. Many gamers see life through the lens of the game, which emphasizes winning the good fight against an evil power, winning the battle for ultimate good, and defeating an enemy that was considered to be undefeatable—all battles that have echoes in the Christian story.

What's more, the victory does not have to occur in isolation. Games like *Halo 3* and *Call of Duty: Modern Warfare 2* offer the player a chance to engage in this epic quest and struggle for good with multiple friends and in community. You can, in essence, experience the *protoevangelium* with friends and other gamers as you defeat evil for good—in some sense, almost participating with Christ in the ultimate defeat of evil.

FANTASIES FULFILLED: IN GAMES AND RELIGION

Video games can offer a "religious experience" because of the fantasy involved, the role playing that occurs, and the camaraderie between participants in that world. For gamers, role playing becomes what scholars refer to as "hyper-real society."[19] Part of what the technological revolution has done, socially speaking, is to create a world of too much information and stimulation.[20] Philip Mellor observes that "the 'social' is displaced by a simulation of the social, just as the real has given way to the hyper-real. Here, there is no ontological basis upon which to ground any notion of the real, or any form of knowledge about anything, since there is only radical, chaotic, meaningless contingency."[21]

For gamers, problems that cannot be solved in "real life"[22] may build up and lead to frustration, pessimism, and ultimately depression. One outlet for them to retain their sanity is through a game, which offers an attainable goal, a fantasy fulfilled, and a chance to be an agent of change. Anthony states,

> Well, I love playing the FIFA soccer series, which is similar to the Madden Series for the NFL. The experiences you have in FIFA are extremely competitive and you can experience dramatic feelings caused by winning and losing in the comfort of your own living room. Primarily gaming is a way for me to relax and be actively involved in a sport that I really enjoy without having to go outside and get a game

started with people who are really busy or when there is no soccer on television.[23]

Here, Anthony discusses how life can be overwhelming and tiring. A good game can provide positive outlets for people like him, who look to games for relaxation.

For other players, games provide a sense of relief and disconnect from hardships that come on a daily basis. Jake states,

> When playing video games, I am intrigued and motivated by a game that rewards your success with accomplishments and further game play. Good video games within the genres of my own personal interests are entertaining. Day-to-day work, parenting, life, etc., is often mundane in the sense that it is often repetitive. A good game can allow me to vicariously experience something that would be otherwise dangerous or life threatening from the safety of my own home. . . . The more popular games to me are the ones that do allow me to escape, forgetting, for a short time, about other real-life dilemmas.[24]

For Jake, the "real-life dilemmas" can become overwhelming, while the hyperreal society, which exists within the game, allows him to relax and "refuel" for the next day. Fantasy games provide a deep emotional satisfaction and the opportunity, as Jake puts it, to "vicariously experience" scenarios that might be too dangerous or are unlikely to occur in real life.

Before we dismiss fantasy as adolescent, let us consider the connection between faith and fantasy. Fantasy is part of religion and religion is part fantasy. We hope to have a better life through ritualistic prayer. We envision a better tomorrow by having faith. We wish for a society that puts God first every day. We desire to live in a world that has utopian qualities and idealistic morals and values. Fantasy arises when people live in that state of idealism and romanticism constantly and refuse to see societal issues outside of that box.

For example, at some church services, there is a sense of wanting to escape to a realm that is free of sin, anger, lust, and the basic problems of this world. For a brief moment in time, via candles, music, and preaching, a worshiper can be transported to another place without ever leaving the building. Gaming does the same thing for players. It elevates them into a certain level of fantasy, taking them into a world that allows them to rise above their circumstances.

It is easy to criticize and judge gamers. They may be written off as naïve, immature, adolescent, and inexperienced, yet many churchgoers who rely on religion to get them through the day engage in the same types of behavioral patterns. Allow me to make some comparisons:[25]

Churchgoers' Experience as Fantasy	Gamers' Experience as Fantasy
Religion and church as a form of escape	The game as a form of escape
The belief or notion that religion will make bad things better	The belief or notion that more gaming will help relieve bad days
Religion explains elements of life and society	The game helps in explaining certain elements of life, especially problem solving[26]
Religion is a form of nonmaterial culture	Gaming is a source of nonmaterial culture
Religion as the hope for what life might be like one day	Games become a vision for better things to come
Religion can become a crutch and an all-encompassing element to life	Gaming/games can become a crutch and an all-encompassing element to life
Religion takes the place of reality	Games take over the gamer, whose life is consumed with gaming and the nonreality of avatars and second lives

Within this table, we see some of the comparisons between the fantasy within religion and within games. In my research, all of the gamers I spoke with understood the difference between reality and fantasy. For example, as one gamer put it, "I mean, yeah, you know that you can't just go and shoot someone on the street like you do in the game. That would be stupid, come on! You gotta use some common sense here."[27] All of the gamers I interviewed recognized the escape from reality they received when playing. This is similar to some who might use religion as a sort of outlet for life and hard times. This same person might see church as a way of escape and dealing with life's hard issues. This escape would be the same for gamers who see the game and playing the game as that escape. For them, an almost religious ritual experience also occurred every time they played certain games, especially games that challenged them and made them think.

PROBLEMS SOLVED? LIVING WITH MYSTERY AND AMBIGUITY

For gamers, answers are paramount. Each game offers a puzzle to be solved or a quest to be fulfilled, yet the most committed players ignore manuals and user guides, preferring to adopt trial and error. If a strategy fails or an avatar is killed, players simply push the reset button. But what works in virtual worlds may not translate into real life. What happens when gamers encounter intractable problems, where no escape routes or cheat codes are available? John Beck and Mitchell Wade list some characteristics of many gamers' personalities.[28]

How the Game World Works	How Gamers Relate
There's always an answer.	It's all about competition.
Everything is possible.	Relationships are structured.
The world is a logical, human, friendly place.	In the game, we are all alone. The game is the goal, and even while in community, your task is to figure that game out.
Trial and error is always the best plan. (Most gamers would agree that after a worthwhile try, if the game still does not work, the problem is not with them, it is with the software/game.)	Young people rule.
Things are unrealistically simple—games can be figured out, completely, but attempt that in real life and you have problems.	People are simple—personalities within games can be multidimensional in skill and complex in user configurability, but personality types and behaviors are simple.

If Beck and Wade are correct, gamers have some major issues when life does not work out as expected. For some gamers, people are just "too hard to deal with . . . I'm better off with my game where people make sense, and if they don't, I can get rid of them."[29] Mystery and ambiguity are not seen as values and assets for many gamers. Most of them want answers and solid conclusions when it comes to both their game and real life—hence, the "escape" within the game.

Many Christians also want clear and solid conclusions. Much of modern evangelicalism seeks to explain and answer life's problems, via resources like the Bible Answer Man. If life proves particularly vexing, biblical answers are just a Google search away. However, the Bible is not a convenient cheat code. Following God does not always work that way.

Mystery and ambiguity provide discomfort for gamers and Christians, yet God lives in the mysterious intersection between reason and chaos. The Bible is filled with as many questions (see Job or Ecclesiastes) as answers (see Proverbs). God continues to operate in a realm many of us cannot even begin to comprehend. For gamers and Christians (and gamers who are Christians), the mystery of God is something that invites more exploration.

However, the key difference is that gamers are often willing to plunge into mystery and ambiguity within the game. Grand narratives such as *Halo 3* and *Final Fantasy* all have a mystical quality about them that allows gamers to enjoy a certain amount of mystery. A puzzle like *Myst* allowed players to explore a virtual world at a contemplative pace.

For dedicated gamers, God can remain a mystery. Ambiguity becomes just part of life. With so many questions left to be answered, one can only hope to arrive at some type of conclusion that offers a clearer picture of God. That "clearer picture" may come in the form of a game. Sociologist Gerry Coulter suggests,

> The gamer exists on the margins of political economy and is understood by some to be an example of the élan of the system in capturing everyone. The gamer, however, attempts to gain an escape velocity from the system of political economy. Some gamers feel their virtual worlds are the opposite of political economy and its hard currencies on which they frown. The currency of the gamer is simulacra, and simulacra now exist in abundance.[30]

What Coulter describes as "simulacra," the *Oxford English Dictionary* defines as "A material image, made as a representation of some deity, person, or thing." This is the mysterious and often elusive notion of an avatar.

THE NUMINOUS: TRANSCENDENCE IN THE GAME

While some games attempt to re-create our world, most games approximate another time and place. Virtual worlds are rooted in the imagination, often in things unseen. The numinous encompasses elements in the experience of life that are holy, sacred, fascinating, and mysterious. These are all elements of the gaming experience. For gamers, the numinous can give rise to a sense of the spiritually transcendent, especially in art or media, or evoke a heightened sense of the mystical or sublime. Gamers may experience this heightened sensibility in an awe-inspiring game, such as a complex role-playing game, where the player is surrounded by the numinous. Games like this can elicit the sense of some other being—namely, God. God shows up in many ways in games, which can be unexpected, surprising, wondrous, and amazing. John stated,

> It's kinda hard to really put a finger on how God shows up in my gaming experience, but I know he's there, I can feel him in games like *Halo 3* sitting next to me just being happy for me. . . . I get lost in that. . . . I get lost in the game. Sometimes you can go all day and not even realize it, but, in all that, I know that God is still there, it's kinda funny that way.[31]

Three elements within the gaming experience create the *numinous* for gamers:

1. *Sacred time*. Ninety-eight percent of the gamers I interacted with considered time spent on a game with friends as "sacred." That time was "holy": a place to unwind, relax, and meditate. That time was off limits for outsiders

and it was considered a major offense if someone were to either walk in front of the game or interrupt them while playing. In this sacred space, gamers were often taken into another realm and some even reported finding a deeper relationship with God.[32]

2. *Transcendent games*. Games that help create a stronger sense of the unknown, the unreachable, and the unexplained only reinforce the notion that there is something else beyond our own lives here on earth. Transcendence in games is nothing new, nor is it something that gamers take for granted; it is almost something to be expected within a good game. Games such as *Halo 3* offer to take the player into a world where the player is the hero attempting to save the world from evil and also give the player the opportunity to ponder life's issues regarding death and family.

3. *Quests and epic mythology*. Within every myth, there exists some truth. Therefore, for many gamers the quest within a game becomes mythological, having a storybook quality. Quests and epic mythology are prerequisites of a good game. Take, for example, the description of *Halo 3*: "Master Chief returns to finish the fight, bringing the epic conflict between the Covenant, the Flood, and the entire human race to a dramatic, pulse-pounding climax."[33] These elements suggest many correlations between Christian theology and the game itself.[34]

Most gamers are aware of the numinous, but cannot explain it. It is another reality that takes them into a place of discovery.

CONCLUSION

Games remain loaded with eschatology and violence. They offer an opportunity to claim victory over evil forces, to experience a foretaste of the *protoevangelium*. Games offer an escape and the promise of tangible rewards. But gamers must also learn to embrace the ambiguous and unsolvable aspects of life. When the concrete and the numinous are combined, they create a very strong and plausible way to understand God, life, religion, and a gamer's place in the world.

Like the technology used to create the games, video gaming theology is a brave new frontier. It is not a traditional model for understanding God, but a new mode and path in which God is discovered through virtual extremities and alter egos. Gaming is a life filled with adventure, struggle, alternate ego formation, perils, fragmentation, and the reality that it could all blow up at any given time. New paths in theological thought must be forged in order to continue building connections between digital worlds and God's kingdom. Video games play an essential role in that journey.

12

Cybersociality

Connecting Fun to the Play of God

JOHN W. MOREHEAD

I grew up in the 1970s in northern California, and like many of my generation I had a lot of fun with video games that were just beginning to become fixtures in popular culture. I still remember the thrill of going with my family to the pizzeria and asking my parents for a few quarters to play the handful of video games at the restaurant. As I grew a little older, I enjoyed the first home video game consoles, the Ataris, in the homes of my friends. Like many of my teenage male peers, I also spent a great deal of my school breaks each summer at the video arcades in the malls. With the passing years into my adulthood, new technologies such as the Internet have developed, and the previous technologies like video games have become more sophisticated, resulting in hours of fun that I could never have imagined in my teens.

Over the years, as the digital technologies moved from laboratories to become the tools and toys of popular culture, they have been explored with various levels of interest and user ability. Those users who are a little older might be called Digital Immigrants, people who moved from more familiar landscapes of previous technologies into the new digital world. They have learned how to use e-mail and the Internet, but tend not to engage the digital world in much depth. Then there are the Digital Settlers, those who share my generational time frame and experiences with digital technologies. We are more comfortable with the digital world than the Immigrants, but even so we are very different from the growing group of Digital Natives. The members of this group were born after 1980,[1] and their relationship with the digital world is natural, intimate, and immersive as a central facet of their lives. In their experience, all of the "major aspects of their lives—social interactions, friendships, civic activities—are mediated by digital technologies."[2]

The increasing interpenetration between our lives and the digital technologies, and the impact of them upon millions of people, represents a significant phenomenon. We must understand it, and do so accurately, even as we take it seriously and seek to engage it. This may mean dropping some of our stereotypes and misconceptions. For example, we must recognize that this is not a phenomenon restricted to young males. The average age of video gamers is approximately thirty-three, but 25 percent of gamers are over the age of fifty-five, and male game players under eighteen are outnumbered by women over eighteen.[3] We might also consider that digital technologies often have the greatest appeal to "early adopters," the "most active and influential user types"[4] who are usually the first to gravitate toward new forms of technology.

It might be tempting to dismiss this as mere game play and meaningless escapism, perhaps even a great danger and "assault on reality,"[5] but such sweeping generalizations are a mistake. For many involved in digital exploration and creation, "what happens in virtual worlds is just as real, just as meaningful, to participants"[6] as what takes place in the nonvirtual world. Digital technologies are changing our perceptions of ourselves as individuals, how we relate to each other, and our understanding of cultures themselves.[7] These changes are occurring in negative as well as positive ways, and careful and even-handed analysis is needed to understand this phenomenon appropriately. It must also be examined proactively. Rather than playing catch-up in responding to an aspect of popular culture after it is well established, a practice all too common in Christianity in the West, it's time for Christians to take a deeper look at the phenomenon of video games and digital cultures.

The focus of this chapter relates to theological reflections on "cybersociality,"[8] a term that refers to the result of the personal immersion and social interaction that comes from certain types of video games, particularly the massively multiplayer online games (MMOGs) such as *World of Warcraft*, as well as digital worlds and cultures such as *Second Life*. In this chapter, I consider a few of the significant theological issues related to the new forms of sociality and community that arise from these components of the digital world.[9]

Before I begin my exploration, I need to say a few words about my theological approach. For theology to be practical in this context it must draw upon an appropriate theological method to assist in the understanding and critique of popular culture.[10] In the discussion that follows I utilize a theological approach informed by the work of sociologist Peter Berger in his book *A Rumor of Angels*.[11] In this small but significant book, Berger said that he wanted "to show how the intellectual tools of the social sciences, which had contributed greatly to the loss of credibility of religion, could be turned on the very ideas that had discredited supernatural views of the world."[12] He described his method as "a very rough sketch of an approach to theologizing that began with ordinary human experience, more specifically with elements of that experience that point toward a reality beyond the ordinary."[13] This involved an inductive approach[14] informed by anthropology as well as sociology, which resulted in a "search for 'signals of transcendence' in order to 'transcendentalize. secularity.'"[15] By these signals of transcendence Berger meant "phenomena that are to be found within the domain of our 'natural' reality but that appear to point beyond that reality."[16] Berger provides theologians with an important theological method for our time. As Fitzgerald has noted, "In a pluralistic and secularized modernity, we should begin by looking at the human experience of the divine, the 'signals of transcendence,' and then move to religious affirmations about the nature and truth of reality."[17]

By applying Berger's approach to theologizing, I argue that aspects of the cybersociality experienced in video games and digital cultures represent signals of transcendence that can be understood as an expression of human beings in their reflection of the divine image. The biblical concept of the *imago Dei* (humanity created in God's image) is expressed through our activities as *homo cyber* (the virtual human), including *homo ludens* (human at play), *homo fantasia* (the fantasizing and imaginative human), and *homo faber* (the human as maker—in this discussion, the maker of cultures). My theological reflection in these areas will be dialogical as well as self-critical as I bring theology and popular culture into dialogue and consider not only what theology may "say" to digital technologies, but also what these technologies may "say" back to the church. Such a dialogical and self-critical posture is crucial, because as Gordon Lynch reminds us, "Judging popular culture on the basis of our own preformed religious and cultural assumptions, without allowing the possibility for these to be challenged or changed in some way by our study of popular culture, will not help us become better cultural critics or more thoughtful theologians."[18]

HOMO LUDENS: SACRED PLAY AND DIGITAL WORLDS

Science fiction has served as a tool for the exploration of important cultural issues in the West.[19] This point is illustrated in the television series *Star Trek: The Next Generation* (STNG) in ways that relate to the subject matter of this book. One of the features of the futuristic starship *Enterprise* was a piece of technology called the "holodeck." This computerized device drew upon computerized, three-dimensional imaging technology, a form of holography, that allowed the user to create realistic and immersive environments based upon

Impression Management on Facebook

Social networking has turned making friends into a game. Cybersociality involves a form of keeping score. Facebook users have incredible latitude regarding what they choose to reveal on their pages—the information they share, the pictures they upload, and so on. Such information can shed light on how individuals see themselves and how they would like to be perceived. Because Facebook relies entirely on self-disclosure, it allows users, in a sense, to create personas for themselves—who they would like to be and how they would like to be perceived. Girls who want to be seen as desirable may post flattering or even suggestive pictures of themselves. Guys who want to appear edgy and iconoclastic may list bands that no one else has ever heard of. Few people mention their flaws, no matter how glaring they may be in real life. Thus, Facebook provides not so much a snapshot of who people are—though there are certainly elements of that on every profile—as much as who they would like to be.

These techniques can all backfire, however. Just as people use social cues to sense peculiarities in the people they meet in real life, such cues also exist on Facebook. A user may post self-promoting content or a suggestive profile picture in order to seem desirable or attractive, but such behavior is often perceived as narcissistic by viewers and is even associated with narcissistic tendencies in real life.* People may "friend" everyone they know, as well as people they don't, in order to appear popular—but an overabundance of Facebook friends can make people question how popular or desirable those users really are.**

In sum, what Facebook seems to present is not a snapshot of the user as much as an idealized picture—a virtually airbrushed one, perhaps, with flaws hidden and strengths highlighted and magnified. Yet flaws can still make themselves apparent on Facebook; the ways in which people try to package themselves can reveal tendencies that they would probably rather not project. Thus, conveying and discerning reality on Facebook is a nuanced, tricky issue. The opportunity to create a public identity begs additional questions, too. Will it make people less genuine or more self-conscious? The consequences have yet to be seen in full.

—Liz Lin is a clinical psychology student at Fuller Theological Seminary.

*L. E. Buffardi and W. K. Campbell, "Narcissism and Social Networking Web Sites," *Personality and Social Psychology Bulletin* 34 (2008): 1303-14.
**S. T. Tong, B. Van Der Heide, L. Langwell, and J. B. Walther, "Too Much of a Good Thing? The Relationship between Number of Friends and Interpersonal Impressions on Facebook," *Journal of Computer-Mediated Communication* 13 (2008): 531-49.

the user's specifications. Holodeck scenarios were sometime used for conducting experiments or training simulations, but most often the crew of the *Enterprise* used the holodeck for recreation as a form of digital vacationing. Imagine the ability to create any world of your choosing in ways that seem completely real. Instead of just entering the realm of imagination through literature or television or film, the holodeck enabled its users to actually enter a place of play of their own imaginative construction to experience fun at its most realistic and immersive. With the fun potential of the holodeck, it's a wonder anyone got any official business done on the *Enterprise*.

Unfortunately it is not possible with present technology in virtual reality to create digital worlds as close to reality as the holodeck, but we're not far away. The reason the holodeck was so enchanting to its users on the *Enterprise* (and why it was used as a narrative device in so many of STNG's episodes) is the same reason that so many people are involved in video games and digital cultures. Whether it involves playing games of mental strategy, racing at breakneck speeds, shooting alien invaders, or creating various virtual worlds, video games and digital cultures are a lot of fun and filled with great possibilities.

The fun aspect of video games and digital cultures should not be underestimated. Edward Castronova has called attention to the "time and attention" that is "migrating from the real world into the virtual world" through an exodus of increasing numbers of people, which has resulted in a literal "fun revolution."[20] This revolution poses serious ramifications in the areas of public policy, economics, and other societal issues and relationships.[21] Play in relation to the digital world needs to be added to the agenda for our consideration of social (not to mention theological) issues. Tom Boellstorff has stated, "From one perspective it could be argued that the information age has, under our noses, become the gaming age, and thus that gaming and its associated notions of play could become master metaphors for a range of human social relations."[22]

Game designers keep fun and play at the forefront of their agenda in the creation of new games. After all, a boring game won't keep its buyers interested for very long, and it certainly won't result in much by way of sales. Play is also a large part of digital cultures as well. Consider the example of *Second Life*, created by Philip Rosedale (a.k.a. "Philip Linden"), a man described as having attended "a born-again Baptist school" but who later discarded "traditional religion" while still "yearning to visualize the absolute."[23] In 1999, he attended Burning Man Festival,[24] an annual alternative cultural event and art festival in Nevada, which he described as a "huge playspace" and a "wonderland of creative projection."[25] This experience provided the inspiration for *Second Life*, which Rosedale considers a "virtual Burning Man."[26]

Since we are in the midst of a fun revolution, the concept of play needs to be considered from a theological perspective as we seek to understand video games and digital cultures. What does play mean in our overall expression of what it means to be human? What is the theological significance of our play in the digital realm?

At times play may be superficial, but at other times it expresses the human desire for the sacred dimension of life. We might recall that experiences of the transcendent in connection with play were part of C. S. Lewis's discovery of spirituality that eventually led to his embrace of Christianity.[27] Peter Berger, in his discussion of signals of transcendence in human experience, mentions the "argument from play"[28] and connects it to conceptions of sacred time and human religiosity:

> One aspect of play . . . is the fact that play sets up a separate universe of discourse, with its own rules, which suspends, "for the duration," the rules and general assumptions of the "serious" world. One of the most important assumptions thus suspended is the time structure of ordinary social life. . . . In playing, one steps out of one time into another.[29]

Berger's mention of time, and the important distinction between play time and ordinary time, dovetails with the thinking of Mircea Eliade, who distinguished between profane and sacred time in the celebration of religious festivals.[30] According to Eliade, religious rituals conducted during festivals recapture a sense of sacred time. Playing video games and digital cultures should not be construed as a religious festival or religious ritual, but they do involve a high level of personal immersion and a sense of game time distinct from real time that often results in the loss of perceptions of connection to real time. This brings together Berger's notion of play time and Eliade's observations regarding play and its relationship to sacred time and human religiosity. With the notion of sacred time related to ritual and play in mind, play in video games and digital cultures represents far more than the activities of the young and not-so-young pursuing meaningless escape from the "real" world, although at times that certainly can be the case. Rather, considered alternatively, play in the digital world can be understood at times and in a sense as a context wherein participants enter into a sacred time of expression that "appears as if one were stepping not only from one chronology into another, but from time into eternity."[31] In other words, the experience of play in video games and digital cultures can be considered as a form of spiritual experience and a hint of transcendence as the player steps out of the real world of time and into the sacred space and time of the play environment.

At this point in the discussion we should not only recognize that play is an important dimension in video games and digital cultures, but also that it represents a significant theological issue for engagement rarely addressed by Christian theologians.[32] Of the few who have explored this area, David Miller's work provides a concise overview and some helpful considerations as to the relationship between Christianity and play.[33] His work provides a summary and overview of theology and play studies that were going on in the late 1960s and early 1970s, and he references the work of play theologians such as Hugo Rahner, as well as that of Sam Keen, Harvey Cox, and Robert Neale.[34] Miller refers to the gravity of the subject matter and reminds us that the term "play" has been used "as a metaphor to explain serious cultural meaning."[35]

Sensitive to concerns about the orthodoxy of play theologies in various religious traditions, he states,

> It is one thing to use "play" and "game" terminology to construct academic theories about nature, the social order, and the self, but it is an altogether different matter to speak of religious matters, indeed, of the gods and God himself, in these terms. It may seem to some even blasphemous. Of course, it *is* true that some contemporary studies of religion which have adopted the game/play metaphor are far from orthodox in their viewpoint. But what may seem surprising to some is the quite blatant fact that the greatest number and the finest quality of "game" and "play" theologies have been written by very orthodox scholars who themselves stand squarely in the front doors of the religious traditions they are interpreting.[36]

Miller also connects games and play to the Judeo-Christian tradition where they surface through the metaphor of the child at play. He says this is applied not only to conceptions of an Eden-like paradise in the Genesis story, "but also to Utopia and the Day of the Coming of God's Kingdom. Doctrines of eschatology as well as doctrines of creation found the metaphor of play appropriate."[37] In support of this thesis he cites Zechariah 8:3–5, and also mentions that "on at least two occasions the Gospels credit Jesus as comparing the Kingdom of God with children and their game and play,"[38] referencing Matthew 18:2–4 and Mark 9:36–37. Miller then moves to a discussion of a theology of play, and he refers to an example developed by Catholic scholar Hugo Rahner, where "the interpretation of traditional religion as play—would view God as a player, man as a player, the church as the community of play, [and] salvation (both now and in the life to come) as play."[39] Miller also touches on the connection between play as an expression of the kingdom of God:

> The church of the Western tradition lives in that period after the Fall into a life of labor as its Scripture in fact indicates. But the same church has not been able to anticipate the heavenly Kingdom, to which its Scriptures also refer, a Kingdom of the Spirit which, like paradise before the Fall, is pictured as a spirited life of play, where play is not laborious, as work is, but labor is playful just as games are.[40]

In light of the "exodus to the virtual world" fueled in large measure by a desire for play, it would seem that the theological assumptions concerning the Protestant emphasis on work must be reexamined. As Hockett states, "The Protestant work ethic elevates work in industrial society to the realm of the sacred while relegating play or leisure to the profane."[41] The Protestant work ethic is important, but it must be balanced against other important theological considerations, such as the significance of play which, according to several theologians, represents an expression of the reflection of the divine nature in humanity.

With the theological significance of play in mind as expressed by *homo ludens*, the human at play, I now turn to consideration of video games and digital cultures as expressions of *homo fantasia*, the fantasizing human seeking escape from the mundane and movement into the sacred realms of the imagination.

HOMO FANTASIA: SACRED IMAGINATION AND DIGITAL WORLDS

If play is a significant aspect of video games and digital cultures, then imagination provides the fuel for the engine of fun. Surely some of the imagination and play associated with digital entertainment and cybersociality may be understood as superficial forms of escapism, but I believe that much of it is far more meaningful. Many times the use of imagination and the immersion into the fantasy stories of video games and digital cultures through "purposeful play"[42] represents a migration from daily experience into alternative fantasy worlds that are representative of the imaginative ideal.

I take this view of the imagination and apply it to select digital technologies through consideration of Pierre Bourdieu's idea of the *habitus*, and Roger Aden's suggestion that imaginative narratives in various forms serve as a means of escaping the habitus and engaging in a symbolic pilgrimage into promised lands. Bourdieu described the habitus as "our collective, cultural sense of place that is forged through the reproduction of history. In other words, our sense of where we are, culturally speaking, depends largely on where we've been."[43] Our habitus is our understanding of who we are and how the world functions around us based upon our previous experience of the way things are. Aden goes on to say that not only does our daily experience of the routine and mundane tend to confirm our sense of habitus, but also that the repetition of narratives or stories within Western cultures reinforces such perceptions. But human beings are not satisfied with the mundane and desire something more. Imaginative stories "allow opportunities to transcend habitus, making possible the envisioning of—and symbolic escape to—alternative social worlds."[44] Aden goes further in his argument, stating that such experiences may be construed as "symbolic pilgrimages, those purposeful, playful, repeated journeys in which we imagine ourselves leaving the material world of habitus to enter the symbolic world of promised lands."[45]

Imaginative stories have a long and intimate connection to human history, expressed in various forms including folklore, fairy tale, and myth. They have inspired and entertained human beings in oral, literary, and visual forms, and some commentators argue that fairy tales are the "precursors of virtual worlds."[46] In more recent times in the Western world, the literature of speculative fiction has been a significant expression of the worlds of imagination. It has also been influential in the development of virtual worlds "throughout the last century, [as] science fiction and fantasy literature have been fundamental to [their] imaginings."[47]

Here Christians should pause to consider that in his discussion of the impact of science fiction and fantasy literature on contemporary virtual worlds, Boellstorff mentions the work of C. S. Lewis and J. R. R. Tolkien as "most crucial," with Tolkien's *Lord of the Rings* trilogy being "the single most important influence on virtual worlds from fiction."[48] Part of what makes Tolkien's work in particular so significant is connected to what Tolkien called "a special skill, a kind of elvish craft . . . [that] produces a Secondary World into which both designer and spectator can enter."[49] Tolkien called those who possessed such skill at creating Secondary Worlds of fantasy "sub-creators."

With the idea of sub-creators of Secondary Worlds in mind, it is interesting that Boellstorff's research on *Second Life* refers to "creationist capitalism" in the West wherein "production is reinterpreted as creation," and that those engaged in the activities of capitalist production may be understood as "creators of their own worlds."[50] This concept is surely applicable to Linden Labs, the creators of *Second Life*, as well as the creators of other digital cultures such as *Habbo Hotel*, *Gaia Online*, *Lineage*, and *World of Warcraft*. Those associated with bringing these digital cultures and games to life have as sub-creators created realistic worlds that have captured the imaginations of millions of people.

Returning to Aden's idea of imaginative stories as escape from the habitus and entry into promised lands through symbolic pilgrimage, Aden supports his argument with a number of illustrations of imaginative stories that function in this way, from the television program *The X-Files* to the motion picture *Field of Dreams*. The impact of fantastic narratives like these upon those experiencing escape from the habitus can be quite profound, as exemplified by Aden's quotation of a source referring to "devoted" and "avid" television fans whose experience with their favorite programs becomes "a major source of self-definition, [and] *a kind of quasi-religious experience.*"[51] The Western world is currently undergoing a period of reenchantment[52] in response to the secularizing process of modernity, and virtual worlds, digital cultures, and video games are playing a major part in providing yet another medium for the reenchanted imagination in this process. Like the social revolution fueled by play, the imagination revolution holds great potential for impact on society. As Castronova states,

> This aspect of virtual worlds may be their most powerful for social transformation. In virtual worlds, we are consciously resurrecting the notion of myth and directly embedding it in human societies. In thinking about what this might mean for happiness, I return again and again to the notion of a coming "Age of Wonder." Wonder, in the sense of miracle, mysticism, and faith, may well be the single most important contribution of virtual worlds to human experience.[53]

As we have seen, many times video games and digital worlds serve an imaginative function similar to fairy tales and the literature of science fiction and fantasy. They immerse "20 or 30 million people in worlds of perpetual fantasy"[54] that not only provide forms of entertainment but also "offer a mythical cosmos in which a personality can find a reason to exist,"[55] and in so doing individuals escape from the mundane aspects of life and find entry and immersion into alternative worlds of promise. Given this scenario, Christians might consider the promise of a fantastic and mythic apologetic for our time in the West.[56] The increasing experience of *homo fantasia* (humanity as agent of fantasy and the imagination) seems filled with possibilities for those who wish to engage the coming Age of Wonder.

Yet another dimension of this discussion needs to be considered. The expression of play through imaginative worlds is a phenomenon pursued individually as well as collectively. Aden says that "our movement toward alternative promised lands that transcend habitus suggests a quest for community,"[57] which brings me to the third aspect of my theological reflections on cybersociality. Through the activities of *homo cyber* (the virtual human) exploring *homo ludens* (the human at play) and *homo fantasia* (the imaginative human), human beings come together as *homo faber* (humanity as maker) to create new forms of community.

HOMO FABER: SACRED COMMUNITY AND DIGITAL WORLDS

In developing this section of my analysis, I consider three concepts: Putnam's thesis about the rise of individualism in connection with the rise of technologies, Oldenburg's thesis of new "third places" of social interaction, and the concept of "postmodern neo-tribes." These concepts are then applied to the social aspects of MMOGs to assist in an understanding of the social function of video games and digital cultures that produce new forms of community.

Many times technology has not been construed as a tool that facilitates community. Some have argued that technologies result in greater isolation of individuals from social groups. Robert Putnam put forward this thesis in his classic text *Bowling Alone*,[58] which suggests that with the rise of various technologies, most notably television and mass media, American concepts of community have shifted toward individualism and away from community as defined in previous generations. Over time this has resulted in declining civic involvement, whether through bowling leagues, Rotary clubs, or church membership.

In addition to Putnam's thesis, Ray Oldenburg's[59] concept of "third places" is important for this discussion. He identifies three primary social spheres of interaction, the first being the home, and the second being the workplace. In addition to these there are "third places," which are "the core settings of informal public life" that refer to "a great variety of public places that host the regular, voluntary, informal, and happily anticipated gatherings of individuals beyond the realms of home and work."[60] Oldenburg's research suggests that third places in the form of coffee shops, bars, and bookstores now serve an important social function as forms of community.

Another element of the late modern situation needs to be considered. Since at least the late 1960s with the rise of the counterculture, there has been a changing concept of self-identity and its relationship with others that continues into the period of late modernity. It has resulted in a change in how people understand themselves and how they relate to and participate in social groups. This process has been referred to as the retribalization of Western culture, which has brought about the rise of various "postmodern neo-tribes":[61] an increasing identification of individuals with various subcultures which share a set of interests, beliefs, and an ethical consciousness that functions as a form of social identity.

With these three ideas in place, they can be considered in application to video games and digital cultures. Putnam's thesis is important in that technology has resulted in the increasing individualism of Americans, but at the same time we seem to want the paradox of, if you will, "individual community": we want our individualism but we also want community, only with greater personal autonomy and in somewhat individualist terms. As we will see, digital technologies have provided a means to accomplish this. Beyond this, Oldenburg's concept of third places has direct application to online gaming and digital cultures. Steinkuehler and Williams argue there is a structural similarity between Oldenburg's concept of third places and online gaming.[62] In their view, various digital environments serve as new forms of third places for community. They state that "By providing spaces for social interaction and relationships beyond the workplace (or school) and home, such virtual environments have the potential to function as new (albeit digitally mediated) third places similar to pubs, coffee shops, and other hangouts."[63] They go on to state that "such feelings of rootedness within MMO[G]s help create a shared sense of home, and with it the sense of support and warmth that some folks may very well lack in their own 'real world' households and work places."[64] Although Oldenburg dismisses the idea that a group of individuals playing video games represents a valid third place,[65] Steinkuehler and Williams's research indicates that "this conclusion is uninformed."[66]

Putting the three pieces of our puzzle together then, the rise of technologies and mass media has resulted in a greater sense of individualism, but people are still seeking out various forms of community beyond the social spheres of home and work and they do so through new third places. As Steinkuehler and Williams argue, multiplayer online games can rightly be considered third places of social interaction, which results in the formation of neo-tribes of community, people coming together through their shared interests in video games and digital cultures.

Finally, in terms of online gaming and digital cultures in regard to community, a certain irony is at work. While Oldenburg's thesis describes civic decline as a result of technology and mass media, we have seen that "various online forms of community" have created *new* forms of sociality and serve as "a mechanism for its maintenance (if not restoration)."[67] Online communities provide the tools for the "individualized community" that many now seek in the Western world.

The common stereotype of a lone gamer sitting in front of the television screen idling away hours of productivity in isolation from others may at times be the case, but as I've discussed above, video games and digital cultures are often now resulting in the creation of alternative expressions of community and cultures, new third places that rival other institutional structures as forums for social interaction. The activities of the virtual human engaging in play in the creation of alternative worlds of imagination results in the creation of new forms of community.

CONCLUSION

In this chapter, I have suggested a few items for theological reflection that flow from the social implications of video games and digital cultures. Christians often tend to engage popular culture first and foremost in terms of critique, stating what they disagree with and find wrong without due consideration for finding balance between critique and positive interaction. I recognize that video games and digital cultures, like every aspect of culture, popular or otherwise, need to be understood in terms of their neutral as well as negative and positive aspects. But I prefer to focus on the positives and the possibilities of the virtual world. I leave it to others to reflect carefully on the negative aspects and to provide an appropriate critique.

In my view the presence of video games and digital cultures represents an opportunity for Christians to consider how human beings created in the image of God express that image in the digital world. Growing numbers of people are captivated by the fun the virtual realm provides, and they are expressing the reflection of their Creator in play, in constructing Secondary Worlds of imagination, and in the creation of new forms of community.

What does all of this say back to the church? The reader might recall that in my introduction I expressed a desire to take a dialogical and self-critical posture. In the preceding pages I have dialogued with aspects of video games and digital cultures, and with my concluding thoughts I move to a brief process of self-criticism where I seek to consider what all of this might mean for Western Christians in the twenty-first century. I present the following for consideration.

First, millions of people want to have fun through video games and digital cultures. If we're honest, perhaps we might acknowledge that many times Christian churches are not exactly the first places people think of as forums for the expression of play. We might counter this by imagining the ways in which we can seek balance between work and play, how play is also a divine attribute to be expressed in God's human creatures, and how the church can become a community and space for godly play.

Second, Christians continually look to C. S. Lewis and J. R. R. Tolkien as those gifted visionaries who created realistic worlds of fantasy through their literary works. They continue to provide an example for us in charting new ways forward for a Western world starved of fun and imagination. We might be thinking about raising up a new generation of Inklings who can draw upon the mythic and fantastic reservoirs of Lewis and Tolkien and thus serve as sub-creators for the twenty-first century.

Third, a host of third places vie for the time and attention of busy people. We must recognize that the church is but one of many social spaces where community is found. With so many people playing and imagining in virtual realms, we might be thinking about ways in which the church can serve as an alternative community, a countercultural one where sacred space is made for creative expression and exploration of the best of what video games and digital cultures have to offer.

As I mentioned in the introduction to this chapter, many times in history the church has had to play catch-up in terms of responding to cultural change and trends. I am pleased to be part of a project that engages a cutting-edge cultural phenomenon as the wave continues to crest. The stakes couldn't be higher. As Castronova writes, "Virtual worlds are on the path to becoming the most powerful source of personal meaning in the contemporary world. The changes that result might well be compared to the ones unleashed by Luther's 95 Theses: not just a fun *revolution*, but a fun *reformation*."[68] My hope is that the church will help produce a group of digital Martin Luthers to draft these theses to post in the forums of the digital world.

Conclusion

Born to Play

CRAIG DETWEILER

Thank you for joining us on this journey through interactive entertainment. We have endeavored to find spiritual spaces within virtual worlds. But rather than focusing solely upon stories, we've also discussed the architecture of video games. From the cathedrals of Europe to the islands of *Second Life*, the spaces we inhabit shape our spirituality.

More people are spending more time playing more games. Psychologists, educators, and parents are all rightly concerned about the effects of such activities. Rather than bemoaning the games' growing influence, we have endeavored to discover the religious possibilities within video games. Movies are being unseated by games as our primary cultural metanarrative. We've pointed out how the structure of games like *Ultima IV* can encourage virtue. While some corners of the Muslim community have jumped into gaming in an effort to counterprogram stereotypical portrayals, Christians have remained hesitant to manipulate Jesus within games. The *Left Behind* video game attempts to graft faith onto a format that reinforces conflict, separatism, and sexism. We must think deeply about how games operate in order to understand what they communicate about humanity, divinity, and eschatology. We've noted how the rise of the Wii corresponds to a hunger for a more embodied faith.

How do we ensure that we're not settling for *simulacra*, for the appearance of artistry, accomplishment, or imagination? We've highlighted how the smartest game designers help us appreciate the complexity, fragility, and interdependence of the world we live in. Playing God can be an exhausting task. The finest games simulate real-world dilemmas and encourage creative problem solving. They grant us freedom and responsibility.

We're still figuring out what this new era of cybersociality will yield. Our first lives and second lives are blurring. We're finding individual expression within communal gaming, which provides an easy way to try on personas, to taste victory in a world of often banal defeats. As games continue to professionalize, we must forge a robust theology of play that gets us back to the garden, where life itself is a delightful, God-given gift.

Faith has been translated across eras and cultures. Gaming represents yet another culture loaded with revelatory possibilities. Jesuit scholar Antonio Spadaro wrote in Rome's *La Civiltà Cattolica*, "Deep down, the digital world can be considered, in its way, mission territory. *Second Life* is somewhere where the opportunity to meet people and to grow should not be missed."[1] I conclude with a brief reflection on the opportunities and challenges that may arise for a generation born to play.

NO INTEREST IN THE MANUAL

Gamers are driven to participate. They don't want to *read* about a game; they simply plug and play. They dive in, figuring out the navigation as they go. In video games, the more you play, the smarter you get. Wisdom grows via experience. Consequently, video games are an inherent threat to all manner of textbooks. There isn't much interest in reading about how things work. Gamers prefer to click first, read later. So how can such an essential sacred text like the Bible be reintroduced to the gamer generation?

Perhaps we should describe the Bible as a user's guide for life. It is for consultation on how to play the game better (but only after you've been frustrated by the game). Gamers may be genuinely surprised when people do not behave in a predictable or maneuverable manner. When they bring their questions, problems, and frustrations to the Bible, they'll find plenty of empathy in the psalms of David or the struggles of Job. The game didn't always work for them either.

Instead of convincing kids to start their day with a devotion, perhaps we have to shift the emphasis to the end of the day—looking back. The questions become, "What have you seen/learned/heard?" and "How might Scripture enhance and deepen that?" God's word speaks into our life based upon our experience. Perhaps the Proverbs could be seen as a cheat code. And Ecclesiastes is what you consult after you've made your mistakes. While parents would undoubtedly like to spare kids the pain of bad decision making, a pattern of risk taking followed by reflection may prove their chosen route.

The nonlinear and episodic nature of the Bible could make it even more attractive. Rather than trying to explain it as a single dramatic through line, perhaps gamers would be attracted by sixty-six chapters, each with its own particular characters, background, and adventures. Gamers are used to jumping around, going back and forth, from scenario to scenario. The whole may only come together when they've sifted through the various parts.

FREE PLAY

Games are designed with remarkable ingenuity and precision. They have a clear set of rules and protocols pointing to a tangible goal. Once the parameters are set, players are offered a wealth of options. In fact, after the puzzle within the game is solved, players are often granted "free play." They can exchange personas when they've demonstrated a certain level of mastery (or maturity).

Games approximate the ancient tension between predestination and free will better than any other form of entertainment. The next generation may not be troubled by the seemingly irreconcilable truths of an omniscient Creator and a humanity granted ample freedom. They may appreciate the connections between an intelligent designer and more sophisticated game play.

In god games like *SimCity*, you decide what is healthy, what is "winning." Great simulations leave ample room for users to roam. They are rife with "what if" scenarios. A game like *Civilization* is about learning to share and manage resources. Issues of stewardship, particularly of the environment, are easily translated into game scenarios. Gamers will appreciate their God-given calling in Genesis 2 to till and keep the garden.

Educator James Gee notes how a strategy game like *Full Spectrum Warrior* "suggests that freedom requires constraints and that deep thinking requires a framework. Once the player adopts the strong values and identity the game requires, these serve as a perspective and resource from which to make decisions about actions and with which to think and resolve problems."[2] Games provide the structure and the freedom to help us grow in our thinking.

The more time and ingenuity invested by the creator of the game, the more pleasurable, complex, and empowering is the resulting game play. A benevolent creator challenges players to make the right decisions. Choice flows from generous design.

BORN AGAIN (AND AGAIN)

Gamers are used to dying and rising. Multiple selves and multiple lives are assumed in game construction. Consequently, the theological idea of being

born again will seem increasingly mild and mundane to the gamer generation. Rebirth, respawning, and reincarnation are all part of resetting a game.
It happens so often, with so little thought or consequence, that it has lost most
of its meaning. As business professors, John C. Beck and Mitchell Wade note
how casually the gamer generation handles bankruptcy and defeat. They are
willing to take risks, because they assume that "game over" is a temporary
setback that can be rectified with a quick click.

So how should ministers talk about discipleship? What does it mean to
ask for forgiveness? To atone for our sins? Perhaps iPastors can recover the
ancient rite of catechesis. Catacombs and hidden rooms are familiar to dedicated gamers. So Jesus' promise to prepare a place in his Father's mansion
with many rooms may resonate (John 14:2). James Gee suggests that deep
learning is "not just about 'belief' (what the facts are, where they came from,
and who believes them) but also strongly about 'design' (how, where, and why
knowledge, including facts, are useful and adequate for specific purposes and
goals)."[3] The keys to God's kingdom are unlocked only after plenty of trial
and error.

Gamers understand the need for proper netiquette, for earning your way
into higher (or deeper) levels. In virtual worlds like *Second Life*, you are not
invited in until you know the rules. Newbies are dependent upon others to
learn how to walk and talk (and fly). In most games, as you solve puzzles and
obtain artifacts, you get additional friends and avatars. But it is usually impossible to skip levels or jump ahead. You must earn your place/position. Is this
a graceless system, or a journey rooted in genuine interest and investment?
Games do not give things away quickly. They challenge you. They ask, "How
committed are you?"

How might we inspire devotion and discipleship? By withholding information or at least doling it out in a creative and systematic fashion. In games,
essential info often arrives just as it is needed. Once gamers have mastered a
section, they want to move on. Can we structure the discipleship process as a
sequence of wisdom to be grasped before we can advance? Following Jesus can
be like obtaining keys to unlock hidden secrets (Easter eggs within a game![4]).
It takes time, just like the work catechists put into Easter initiation rites.

MULTIPLE ROADS

Gamers appreciate multiple ways to solve a problem and win a game. Real-
time strategy games like *Age of Mythology* offer different routes to achieve
status. The freedom and self-determination inherent in interactive entertainment present significant challenges to the unique claims of Christianity. Jesus

may have identified himself as "the way, and the truth, and the life" (John 14:6), but gamers are likely to bristle at the notion of only one way to reach heaven. But the "many dwelling places" in "my Father's house" (John 14:2) are likely to inspire much more fascination. Questions of pluralism will only rise as the gamer generation comes of age.

Rather than reducing faith to a formula (like the Four Spiritual Laws), an interactive faith will appreciate how uniquely Jesus addressed each person he met. Jesus offered a blind man a mud pie for his eye. Zacchaeus needed a hand down (from the tree) rather than a hand up. The cost of discipleship also changed depending upon a person's value systems. The woman at the well needed to stop sleeping around, while a rich young ruler was asked to sell all his possessions. The gospel was particularized for each individual.

We should not necessarily, though, proffer a self-centered message. Games put the player in charge, asking, "What do you want to do today?" Surely, following Jesus has become a far too solitary endeavor. Individual battles against a computer can be challenging, but games are best enjoyed in community, with others. Those companions may be online or in the same room. The greatest pleasures and joys in gaming come from shared experiences—taking turns with a Wii bowling match, working as a team in *Halo*, or winning the Mushroom Cup in *Super Mario Kart*.

Gamers anticipate pitfalls and blind alleys. They often prefer playing with a friend who can offer wisdom informed by prior experience. My son learned how to navigate *Lego Star Wars* and *Indiana Jones* from those who'd gone before. Gaming is profoundly communal and bonds players together via a shared accomplishment. It is a passion passed on by mentors who've been through a (virtual) war.

Gamers Speak

Arnold, fourteen years old, Hispanic, 3.4 GPA

- Why do you play? *Because I like feeling some sort of accomplishment from the game.*
- If I asked your parents about the effects of video games on you and your relationships, what would they say? *My dad says that when I play "Roller Coaster Tycoon," it gives me a perspective on real life. I used to play it excessively and he used to say I played it too much, and now I play in moderation.*
- What do you wish your parents realized about video games? *That some of them help me mentally and physically, or at least provide me with some entertainment.*
- What else would you want to say about video games? *Usually when I finish a game, I really feel a sense of accomplishment.*

KEEPING SCORE

Gaming is a reward-based system. As you succeed, you get more clues, more insight, more passwords, more rewards. It is like being ushered into a secret society. But in research geared toward businesses, John C. Beck and Mitchell Wade note, "The game generation sees competition everywhere. . . . They have largely grown up in a place where just about the only way to relate to any other character, living or silicon, is through competition. So they believe, quite literally, that competition is the law of nature."[5]

Yet the acceptance of competition does not necessarily result in more self-centered behavior. Beck and Wade were surprised to discover that "Despite digital games' focus on the individual, despite the constant competition, despite the hints of Machiavellianism in some gamer attitudes, growing up with games does not seem to systematically increase individualism. . . . When it comes to real-world professional attitudes, it seems that even heavy long-term exposure to games hasn't made players more rebellious, iconoclastic or even independent."[6]

The biggest problem with score-based thinking is that it produces performers. Some people may willingly lean on cheat codes just to get ahead. Games are merit-based, while the historic Christian faith is rooted in grace. No amount of high scoring earns Christians a key to the kingdom. Life is not something to be mastered and dominated. Grace arrives as a gift of unmerited favor. Perhaps a generation raised on numerical evaluations (and test scores) will be uniquely attracted to a faith system that undercuts scorekeeping. Thankfully, human salvation does not depend on our performance: "For by grace you have been saved through faith, and this is not your own doing; it is the gift of God" (Eph. 2:8). We are released from the burden of trying to get our initials on the high score.

JESUS: THE ULTIMATE AVATAR?

Avatars are rooted in the Hindu notion of divine descent. So how does this connect with the historic Christian faith? When our digital stand-in drops into a battle, we experience a bit of what Jesus may have experienced in the incarnation. Games are filled with invigorating risks and heroic possibilities. Our avatars must learn to move within the limitations of any given virtual world or game. But if they get it right, untold riches and rewards await.

While people may worry about the fragmented selves we spread across multiple systems (our Facebook profiles, our Miis, our Second Lives), they still represent legitimate expressions of our essential nature. While no single space may hold all of our true self, they all point to a more complete version of ourselves. All these virtual selves suggest that I am much more than a body. My—and our—influence extends into worlds and eras and games that continue with or without us. Our absence may not always be noticed, but our presence changes the dynamics of the game with every choice we make.

Jesus dropped into the game of our world with both remarkable (even divine) skills and crippling limitations (of humanity). He explored many corners of his Middle Eastern "island." Among his contemporaries, he made both friends and enemies. A tightly knit, dedicated community arose around him. Jesus and his clan experienced plenty of grief from aggressive and uncooperative rivals. He was eventually fragged during a deathmatch on an unexpected field of battle. He submitted to the rules of engagement, even while resisting them, proposing an alternative way to play. After three days, Jesus respawned, took his place as Administrator, and redefined the way the game is played.

Consequently, we are all invited to play, to enter the kingdom like children. Thank God it is not about achieving the high score. As followers of Jesus, we can reset and respawn, having learned new ways to navigate. We can even share the biblical and experiential cheat codes we have gathered along the way.

Appendix: Beyond "Turn that Thing Off!"

Elevating the Gaming Conversation between Parents & Kids

KARA POWELL AND BRAD M. GRIFFIN

I (Kara) had taken out the trash thousands of times as a teenager, but this time was unique. In the midst of the banana peels, eggshells, and milk cartons lay some of my most prized possessions: my cassette tapes (yes, I am that old).

As a teenager, my mom hated the music that I listened to. I hid many of my cassette tapes and records from her so that she wouldn't know how much I actually had (for you younger readers, records contain music and are shaped like really big CDs). My mom used to complain about the "loud, stinkin' secular music" that came from my bedroom stereo, which was the size of a large suitcase. She begged me to get rid of my "secular" music for years but I stubbornly refused.

The turning point came not from my mom's pleas, but during a teaching series our youth pastor did on music and its influence in our lives. During those several weeks of teaching, I heard a well-reasoned, balanced, biblically inspired approach to selecting and listening to music that made sense to me. As a result, both my brother and I decided to sort our records and cassette tapes and throw away albums that didn't align with the love, joy, peace, and hope that come from kingdom living.

My mom was thrilled, but also a bit mystified. Why had we all of a sudden become critical music listeners? How had we moved from arguing that "the music doesn't affect us, we just like the beat" to analyzing the lyrics of every song we owned?

Something clicked in me as a high school sophomore, and over twenty years later, I still find myself constantly analyzing songs and their effects on my feelings, thoughts, attitudes, and even behaviors. What I gained from my youth pastor was not a narrow list of bands to be listened to and bands to be avoided. Instead, I gained a broader vision of how God wants me to interact with music in such a way that my mind is stretched, my relationships are strengthened, and God is glorified.

The parallels between my process as a fifteen-year-old grappling with music and today's teenagers grappling with video games are many. Whether you're a parent, a youth leader, or a church member who cares deeply about the kids in your congregation, you can play a part in helping teenagers thoughtfully interact with video games.

DEEPER INTERACTION WITH KIDS AND GAMES: A PROCESS OVERVIEW

At the Fuller Youth Institute, our mission is to leverage research into powerful resources that equip leaders, kids, and families (visit our Web site at www.fulleryouthinstitute.org for our free resources). All of our research and writing is geared toward helping parents and leaders make a deeper impact on teenagers in all areas, ranging from video games to short-term missions to their decisions about relationships and sexuality. As practical theologians, we are committed to a thorough exegesis of current practices, a diligent examination of relevant research, and a broad survey of adults doing exemplary work in the lives of kids. Because of this, many of our initiatives follow a four-step methodology called the Deep Design.[1]

The first step of the Deep Design invites us to consider ways that adults are *now* trying to engage with kids and gaming. Having understood the strengths and weaknesses of our current approaches, the second step calls us to consider *new* and more effective ways of engagement. In order to flesh out these new ideas, the third step profiles parents and leaders *who* are already a few steps ahead in living out the new paradigms. Finally, the fourth step provides a series of prompts that help us identify *how* we will now interact differently with the kids we care about.

STEP 1: NOW—BALANCE IS SOMETHING WE SWING THROUGH ON OUR WAY TO THE OTHER EXTREME

Across the country, parents and mentors are following my mom's example and are begging their kids to play fewer video games and shelve games that glorify violence and sexual objectification. More often than not, these adult pleas fall on deaf ears.

Marty O'Donnell on Parenting and Games

I remember a point where I was in junior high or something and I was listening to Led Zeppelin. And you know my mom was classically trained and wanted me to be a classical musician and all the rest of it. But she saw the record and she listened to it. She looked at all the words. I came home from school and she was like, "Hey, I was listening to this thing and what does this all mean? This 'Stairway to Heaven' thing? Hey, what do you think that means?" And I'm like, on one hand, "Mom, come on, get out of my stuff," 'cause I had no idea what it meant, of course. But what I still remember from that is that it was a legitimate loving interest that she was taking in me because I was her son.

There are so many parents that are in my generation. I'm now in my early fifties, and I've been in games for twelve years. And I can't tell you how many people my age, when they hear I do games, they're like, "Oh, yeah, well, my kids play games. I don't know what any of that is." And I'm like, "Hey, how many hours a week do your kids play games?" Because don't you think you'd take some sort of interest in something your kids are interested in? I mean, don't just dismiss this stuff.

I think a lot of these people think this is something their kids are growing out of. And when you hear the politicians talk about games, you can tell they know nothing about games. When you hear parents talking about games or punishing their kids because they're playing games, it's just such a ridiculous reaction. Don't you want to understand what your kids love? Because you love your kids—that's why you're going to look at what they're doing and show an interest? I just encourage all these parents, hey, pick up a controller, spend some time when your kid isn't there. See if you can make heads or tails out of these games and maybe you'll find some common interest. 'Cause the kids are sure finding it with their friends. Those communities are huge.

Yet on the other end of the continuum are parents and mentors who figure video games and any negative messages they promote are "here to stay." They figure that trying to curb their influence on kids is a bit like standing under an umbrella during a tidal wave. The umbrella inevitably breaks, leaving its holders all wet despite their best intentions and efforts. One group of adults shouts themselves hoarse. The other whispers and mumbles, never to be heard.

One of our life mantras is that balance is something we swing through on our way to the other extreme. In between these two extremes, adults who care about kids need to find the more balanced middle ground.

There are certainly a host of risks incurred when teenagers game, from isolation to addiction. The National Institute on Media and the Family, an organization whose aim is to help families make healthier media choices, has identified the following negative effects of video games on kids:[2]

- Overdependence on video games, especially those played alone, can foster social isolation.

- Women in video games are often portrayed as weaker characters who are helpless or sexually provocative.
- Games are often centered around plots of violence, aggression, and gender bias.
- Many games revolve around weapons, killings, kicking, stabbing, and shooting.
- There's some evidence that playing video games may be linked to aggressive behavior.[3]
- Many games do not offer action that requires independent thought or creativity.
- Games can confuse reality and fantasy.
- In many games, players must become more violent in order to win.
- In first-person video games, players may be more affected because they control the game and experience the action through the eyes of their own character.

Yet in a spirit of balance and academic integrity, the National Institute on Media and the Family also highlights a host of video games' positive effects on kids:[4]

- Video games introduce players to computer technology.
- Games can give opportunities to practice following directions.
- Some games provide chances to problem solve and use logic.
- Games can help develop fine motor and special skills.
- Games give opportunity for social interaction among peers and between kids and parents (more on this later).
- Games are entertaining and fun.

Wise adults who want to engage with gaming kids will keep in mind both the opportunities and the costs of gaming. Instead of silence or screaming, they'll have real conversations about gaming with kids they care about. They'll move beyond despair at one extreme, and denial at the other, into a healthier middle ground of true dialogue.

STEP 2: NEW—ASK QUESTIONS, DON'T LECTURE

Acclaimed philosopher Dallas Willard writes, "But now let us try a subversive thought. Suppose our failures occur, not in spite of what we are doing, but precisely because of it."[5] Now that we understand mistakes we've made in the past, it's time to identify *new* paths of engagement with kids. So, the most importance sentence we will share in this chapter is this: *never explain something to a kid if you can ask a question instead.*

Why is this so important? Picture the teenager(s) who are on your mind and in your heart currently. Do they know what you think about video games?

Do they know what you would want to say to them about video games? Odds are good that the answer to both questions is "yes." Because they already know what you think and what you'd want to say, they will likely close their mind as soon as you open your mouth. One noted psychologist who is also a dad recently relayed the story of talking to his sixteen-year-old son about a behavior that the dad felt should be changed. After the dad's long and well-reasoned list of reasons the son should change, the son shrugged and said, "Are you done yet?" Note that the question was are "you" done yet, not are "we" done yet. So instead of lecturing teenagers, ask questions.

Good Questions to Ask

As we have surveyed teenagers and parents and asked them about ingredients of good conversations, a common theme is nonthreatening questions. Here are some great springboards that parents, youth workers, or adult mentors can use to dive into deeper conversations with kids:

- What are your favorite games? What do you like about them?
- What characters do you tend to become? Why do you choose those characters?
- Who do you like to fight against? Why?
- Do you prefer to play against just one competitor or lots? Why do you think that is?
- Do you like to compete with a team or on your own? Why?
- How is video game competition similar to sports competition? How is it different?
- How does gaming make you feel? What different feelings do different games raise in you?
- How do you feel when you win a game? What about when you lose?
- If I asked your parents about the effects of video games on you and your relationships, what would they say?
- What do you wish your parents or other adults realized about video games?
- How would your life be different without video games?
- In what ways do you think gaming impacts your life with God?

Raising Issues without Lecturing

But what if you want to raise a specific issue with a gamer? Perhaps you notice that your teenager tends to be moodier after playing games, and the open-ended questions we suggest above aren't likely to lead to a conversation about moodiness.

When that's the case, try phrasing the question this way: "I've heard that video games can make kids your age really moody. What do you think about that?" Some kids will be able to identify and admit their moodiness at that point. Others will deny that gaming affects their emotional state, and at that point you as a caring adult would likely want to volunteer what you've observed. But you're sharing your observations in a spirit of dialogue, not lecturing.

The Importance of Baby Steps

Research from the field of communication studies brings up another important quality in our dialogues with kids about their gaming habits. According to social judgment theory,[6] the more a person cares about something, the more firmly he or she will stand against a differing opinion. Every person (adult and adolescent) brings to every discussion a nuanced system of beliefs, attitudes, and values. *Beliefs* are what we think is true, *attitudes* are our reflexive responses to a given situation, and *values* are what we cling to as important. The more strongly and deeply someone holds particular beliefs, attitudes, and values, the harder it is to suggest change. In a conversation (or series of conversations) about video games with a young person, determining how strongly they hold to their current beliefs, attitudes, and values will go a long way in helping you effectively discuss potential change.

Every time we hear a persuasive message, we have to make a choice, or actually a series of choices. We have to first decide whether we will allow this person or message to impact us. We then need to decide how much of our own opinions and feelings we are going to let get involved. Finally we need to decide how much of our personal perspectives and commitments we will allow to be confronted by the message and whether or not we are open to consider changing our minds.

Given this series of choices inside kids' minds when you bring up video games, your task as the persuader is to help them consider saying "yes" at all three points of decision (without being manipulative in the process) rather than putting up their defenses and shutting you out.

Here's where baby steps become so important. Another element to consider in talking with kids about gaming (or any subject) is the assimilation-contrast effect. Let's say you want to talk with Tina, a fifteen-year-old, about her gaming habits (which you think are excessive). If Tina already has strong opinion commitments about her gaming, she will feel threatened if the new position you are suggesting is too far away from her current position. As a result, your message may push Tina even *further* from your desired change than when you started (this is called the "contrast effect").[7]

But if instead Tina feels like the new message respects her and only tries to get her to move a little toward you, she is more likely to move closer to your position (the "assimilation effect").[8] The key is Tina's initial attitude and how open she is to changing her mind. The best way to picture this is on a seven-point scale that measures initial attitudes:[9]

Attitude of Rejection			Attitude of Noncommitment		Attitude of Acceptance	
1	2	3	4	5	6	7
Extremely Unfavorable	Unfavorable	Slightly Unfavorable	Neutral	Slightly Favorable	Favorable	Extremely Favorable

In other words, if Tina's initial attitude toward your new position is somewhere between a 1 and a 3, the best way to persuade her is not to try to push to 7, but to help her consider, talk about, and maybe even pray about moving one point forward (1 to 2, 2 to 3, or 3 to 4). If these seem like baby steps, that's exactly what they are. Having respect for Tina means we are willing to care for her over the long haul, even if it takes a number of conversations over a number of months—or even years—to move her toward accepting a different perspective regarding her gaming practices.

Of course, God can do instant and holistic transformation that is literally off the chart, but given the way people normally respond, this probably shouldn't be the goal or method of all of our communication—about gaming or anything else.

STEP 3: WHO—INSIGHTS FROM A PARENT AND A SON

In order to understand how these principles are lived out in a parent/teenager relationship, we interviewed Mark Lau Branson and his son, Noah Lau Branson. Mark, who has spent almost forty years in ministry in churches, education, student work, and community outreach, is a professor of practical theology at Fuller Theological Seminary. Noah, the older of Mark and Nina's two sons, is a church pianist and a university freshman, with a double major in psychology and music. We caught up with Mark and Noah while Noah was still a senior in high school. Here's what we learned:

> Q: *Noah, in what ways did Mark and your mom help you navigate through technology as a younger child, as a junior higher, and now as a high school student?*

> Noah: When we were younger, we wouldn't have much screen time compared with all the other kids that I would go to school or

church with. But we were still watching about an hour a day after school, and during the weekend we would maybe watch a family movie. But in fifth grade, our parents decided to limit us to one half hour of screen time during the week and an hour during weekends, and that's ended up being mostly computer and video games. Now we've added more time, and we watch more movies around the weekends.

Q: *So listening to Noah talk, Mark, it sounds like there has been kind of an evolution in how you have set limits. What was behind that shift for you and your wife?*

Mark: The main concern for us was how sedentary their lives could be and what they would become interested in or have time for. And we wanted them to give more energy to pour into other aspects of their lives, other kinds of recreation, even other time with friends. We knew that if their first agenda after school was to head for the TV, that would cut into their creativity. We also noticed that their emotional moods were often unhelpful after screen times. Once we made that change, they both became engaged readers.

Noah: Yeah, I read a lot. And it really jumped more when I didn't spend as much time watching TV. It's also given me time where I can just talk to my friends on the phone. As we've gotten more lenient with the TV and movie rules, I've noticed how those different choices bump into each other.

Q: *Noah, in some of our previous conversations we've talked about a point at which your parents did get a little bit more involved in your online conversations. Can you talk about that?*

Noah: Yeah, as I started getting more into e-mail, IM [instant messaging], MySpace, and Facebook, I was asked to give my parents passwords so they could have access. That wasn't actually a real problem for me because they didn't talk about it at dinner like, "Oh you were talking about this online . . . ," so for the most part I just really didn't notice. And I always could talk on the phone or at school when I needed more privacy.

There were times when my language would get out of control and I'd start swearing, and so my dad would just note that and say, "Is this who you really want to be?" And I would say, "No." And so, as I've gone through high school I've really worked on that.

Q: *Mark, when Noah started swearing, how did you try to approach that conversation with Noah? What were your goals?*

Mark: We had already verbalized, "We know you have private conversations. You can do that at school or on your cell phone." Those conversations were not monitored. So we were only monitoring part of his communication by using access to his pages and our protective Internet software. It was funny at times because Noah would let his friends know that his dad had access, so in the middle of some running IM there would be a "Hello Mark!" from one of his friends. So there was no desire to hide or to be sneaky.

In that conversation with Noah after reading a lot of IMs, I noticed a number of times that his language raised questions for me. I just wanted him to be able to say, "That's who I want to be. That's the language I want to use." Or to be able to say, "No, that's not who I want to be." I was interested in the dialogue more than in saying, "If you keep doing this, you can't have IM." I don't think I would have done that. His response was terrific. He said, "No, that's not what I want to be. And I need to watch that." We already had a good relationship for being able to discuss topics.

Q: *Noah, I know that you have friends and a brother who are more into video games than you. What are some of the positive effects about gaming on other kids or your brother that you've seen?*

Noah: I think the biggest thing is it that it just brings people together. It's something to talk about. It's something to do while you hang out. Since we got an Xbox recently and my brother and I have been playing that, we actually do more together. It can lead to arguments, but usually it's a really good experience. In excess, though, they can be a problem. Like yesterday I found myself sitting there for two hours without anybody else, just playing.

Q: *Mark, from your perspective as a parent and as one who studies culture, what are some of the positives about gaming? And what do you look for in a game?*

Mark: We were always most positive about software games that pushed creativity, problem solving, and narratives, or that allowed for some interaction other than clicking your fingers and yelling at each other.

Early on we were aware that we wanted the games that pushed narratives because we learned the more arcade-ish or battle-oriented they were, that after the game both of our sons were less capable of good relational dynamics. So they were more apt to get in fights with us or with each other after gaming.

One of the most frustrating issues for us is that so much of game creation goes into violence, especially human violence. It's been good to hear from both my sons that at times they get bored with that. We have sometimes set limits on violent games, although we are aware that when they are at friends' homes, there are limits we can't set. We may ask them about it, but we don't set limits on what they can do if they are at a party. Part of it is knowing what makes for awkward socialization, especially for boys. To be at a party among friends and say, "Sorry, my mom and dad won't let me play this," just doesn't work. We would much rather either of them of their own accord say, "I don't like that game. I'm going to do something else for a bit"— for them to figure out, as we all have to do, how they want to embody their values as they go out into the world.

Q: *Noah, what do you wish parents—not necessarily your own, but parents in general—knew about gaming?*

Noah: Part of it is just that kids are not going to go crazy because they are playing these bloody games. And a lot of kids are moving away from those and playing more *Guitar Hero* or sports games. I think another thing that could really bring understanding between kids and parents is just playing—both the parents and the kids playing together even if the parents don't totally understand what's going on.

Q: *Or like it.*

Noah: Or like it.

Mark: Talk about lame . . . I was playing with my younger son the other day, who had invited me into a game, and it was all I could do, with his guidance, to simply stay behind him as he raced through. It was just totally beyond my capacity to perceive what was happening, but it was still fun.

Noah: I was talking with my brother today about why he likes it when our parents play with him. He said, "Because I get to tell them what to do."

Mark: It doesn't happen often. It's a good thing.

Some Gaming Guidelines for Parents

All this talk about talking is helpful, but what if you're a parent struggling to figure out boundaries and practical issues like, "Is it okay to game until 2 a.m. on the weekend"? Here are a few concrete suggestions for setting house rules about gaming. But one huge caveat: Be sure to talk with your kids about any drastic changes in the way you approach gaming in your home before attempting to actually make changes. Get their ideas and suggestions for livable alternatives that respect their desire to game as well as your desire for more balance and health.

1. No gaming consoles in their bedrooms so your chances of observing their true gaming habits are improved. Set up gaming in a central family location instead.

2. Limit daily and/or weekly gaming time.

3. Let gaming time be a reward for completing homework or chores, or for good attitudes around the house—and give permission cheerfully!

4. Do your homework on games (check game ratings and online reviews from more than one source).

5. When possible, encourage multiple-player games since they foster more social interaction.[10]

6. Play *with* them—not just when they are little, but as teenagers, too. Usually adolescence brings with it more violent and racy games. Yet unfortunately, parents seem to be relatively out of the picture when it comes to teen gaming. Sixty-nine percent of parents report rarely or never playing video games with their children.[11]

7. Give them other outlets for fun and creativity. Game together, but also go out to eat or for coffee, and give them ways they can do creative and active things on their own that don't involve staring at a screen.

STEP 4: HOW—ACTION STEPS TO MOVE FORWARD IN OUR CONVERSATIONS ABOUT GAMING

By now you have probably placed yourself somewhere along the continuum of reactant versus avoidant adults when it comes to helping kids think harder about video games and faith. The questions below can help you move toward a more balanced approach in your conversations. You may want to think about them on your own, with a trusted friend or spouse, or with other adults who also care about kids and their gaming practices.

1. What am I doing well in the way I am interacting with kids about gaming?
2. What might I need to begin to do differently?
3. Do I agree that I should "never explain something to a kid if I can ask a question instead"? Why or why not?

4. Which of the questions given on page 201 would be best for my next conversation with a teenager?
5. Where is the teenager(s) I care about most on the communication continuum when it comes to talking about video games? What are the implications of that for the way I interact with them?
6. If you're a parent, How do I feel about Mark Lau Branson's idea that he was more interested in a dialogue with his son about the language he was using on technology than prohibiting his son from using that technology?

Conversations across the electronic divide are never easy. But we must learn to speak the language of our digital natives. We're hopeful that you and your children will communicate about, around, and even within the vibrant world of gaming.

Notes

Introduction

1. Amanda Lenart, Joseph Kahne, Ellen Middaugh, Alexandra Macgill, Chris Evans, and Jessica Vitak, "Teens, Video Games, and Civics," *Pew Internet and American Life Project*, September 16, 2008.
2. James Paul Gee, *Good Video Games + Good Learning* (New York: Peter Lang, 2007), 123.
3. Devlin Barrett, "Video Games Feature Ads for Obama's Campaign," *San Francisco Gate*, October 14, 2008, http://www.sfgate.com/cgi-bin/article.cgi?f=/n/a/2008/10/14/politics/p122935D97.DTL.
4. Donna St. George, "Study Finds Some Youths 'Addicted' to Video Games," *Washington Post*, April 20, 2009, http://www.washingtonpost.com/wp-dyn/content/article/2009/04/19/AR2009041902350.html.
5. W. David Garner, "Video Games Are Good for Kids, Experts Find," *Information Week*, September 17, 2008, http://www.informationweek.com/news/personal_tech/virtualworlds/showArticle.jhtml?articleID=210602159.
6. Chuck Klosterman, "The Lester Bangs of Video Games," *Esquire*, June 30, 2006, http://www.esquire.com/features/ESQ0706KLOSTER_66, accessed July 1, 2009.
7. Jeremy Parish, "Hallowed Be Thy Game: Where Gaming and Religion Collide," www.1up.com, March 4, 2005, http://www.1up.com/do/feature?cId=3138717.
8. Acronyms for 870 different video game terms are identified at http://www.all-acronyms.com/tag/video_game.
9. Wikipedia, s.v. "Mobile game," http://en.wikipedia.org/wiki/Mobile_game.
10. Gabriel Madway, "Big Game Publishers Muscle In on iPhone's Upstarts," Reuters, July 15, 2009, http://www.reuters.com/article/rbssSoftware/idUSN0939135420090715.
11. Alex Pham, "Women Left on Sidelines of Video Game Revolution," *Los Angeles Times*, October 21, 2008, C1.
12. A list of winners and honorees appears at www.interactive.org.

209

13. Kevin Kelly, *Out of Control: The New Biology of Machines, Social Systems, and the Economic World* (New York: Basic Books, 1995).

14. Michael Rymaszewski, *Second Life: The Official Guide* (New York: Wiley, 2006), 7.

15. Kelly, *Out of Control*, 232.

16. For a more extended discussion, see Toby Crockett, "The Computer as a Dollhouse," in *Videogames and Art*, ed. Andy Clarke and Grethe Mitchell (Bristol, UK: Intellect Books, 2007), 219–25.

17. Johan Huizinga, *Homo Ludens: A Study of the Play-Element in Culture* (London: Routledge, 1998), 8.

18. Ibid., 12.

19. Ibid., 13.

20. Ibid., 14.

21. Alex Pham and Ben Fritz, "Hollywood Game Changers," *Los Angeles Times*, June 1, 2009, B1.

22. Edward Castronova, *Synthetic Worlds: The Business and Culture of Online Games* (Chicago: University of Chicago Press, 2005), 2.

23. James Paul Gee, *What Video Games Have to Teach Us about Learning and Literacy*, 2nd ed. (New York: Palgrave MacMillan, 2007).

24. The groundbreaking collection *From Barbie to Mortal Kombat: Gender and Computer Games*, ed. Justine Cassell and Henry Jenkins (Cambridge, MA: MIT Press, 2000), has been updated as *Beyond Barbie and Mortal Kombat: New Perspectives on Gender and Gaming* (Cambridge, MA: MIT Press, 2008).

25. Henry Jenkins, *Convergence Culture: Where Old and New Media Collide* (New York: New York University Press, 2006).

26. Two of the more comprehensive early histories are Steven L. Kent, *The Ultimate History of Video Games* (Roseville, CA: Three Rivers Press, 2001), and Van Burnham's lavishly illustrated *Supercade: A Visual History of the Video Game Age, 1971–1984* (Cambridge, MA: MIT Press, 2001).

27. James Newman and Iain Simons, *100 Videogames* (London: British Film Institute, 2007).

28. Heather Chaplin, "Is That Just Some Game? No, It's a Cultural Artifact," *New York Times*, March 12, 2007, http://www.nytimes.com/2007/03/12/arts/design/12vide.html?ex=1331352000&en=380fc9bb18694da5&ei=5124&partner=permalink&exprod=permalink.

29. "The 100 Best Games to Play Today," *Edge*, April 2009, 58.

30. Janet H. Murray, *Hamlet on the Holodeck: The Future of Narrative in Cyberspace* (New York: Free Press, 1997).

31. Roger Caillois, *Man, Play and Games*, trans. Meyer Barash (Champaign: University of Illinois Press, 2001).

32. Jesper Juul, *Half-Real: Video Games between Real Rules and Fictional Worlds* (Cambridge, MA: MIT Press, 2005).

33. Tom Loftus, "God in the Console," MSNBC.com, August 20, 2003, http://www.msnbc.com/news/954674.asp?vts=082120031240&ep1=1#BODY.

34. Ian Bogost bridged the philosophical divide, combining the best of both theories in *Unit Operations: An Approach to Videogame Criticism* (Cambridge, MA: MIT Press, 2008).

35. Mark Binelli, "Inside Halo's Secret Lab," *Rolling Stone*, October 4, 2007, 30.

36. Mark Wilson, "A Counter-Strike Game That Spills Real (Fake) Blood," *Kotaku*, April 3, 2008, http://kotaku.com/375624/a-counter+strike-game-that-spills-real-fake-blood.

37. Barbican Gallery, "Game On—Tour," http://www.barbican.org.uk/artgallery
    /event-detail.asp?ID=4964.
38. Craig Detweiler and Barry Taylor, *A Matrix of Meanings: Finding God in Pop
    Culture* (Grand Rapids: Baker Academic, 2003).
39. For an extended discussion of my theological method, see Craig Detweiler,
    Into the Dark: Seeing the Sacred in the Top Films of the 21st Century (Grand Rap-
    ids: Baker Academic, 2008).

Chapter 1: From *Tekken* to *Kill Bill*

 1. John August, "Seven Things I Learned from World of Warcraft," John
    August.com, http://johnaugust.com/archives/2007/seven-things-warcraft.
 2. Steve Jones, "Let the Games Begin: Gaming Technology and Entertainment
    among College Students," *Pew Internet and American Life Project*, http://www
    .pewinternet.org/pdfs/pip_college_gaming_reporta.pdf.
 3. Amanda Lenhart, Joseph Kahne, Ellen Middaugh, Alexandra R. Macgill, Chris
    Evans, and Jessica Vitak, "Teens, Video Games and Civics: Teens' Gaming
    Experiences Are Diverse and Include Significant Social Interaction and Civic
    Engagement," *Pew Internet and American Life Project*, http://www.pewinternet
    .org/pdfs/pip_teens_games_and_civics_report_final.pdf.
 4. Seth Gilbert, "Slowing Economy Not Stalling Gaming Sales: February NPD
    Results In," Media, Entertainment & Technology, http://metue.com/03-14
    -2008/npd-february-video-game-retail-stats/.
 5. Janet Murray, "The Last Word on Ludology v. Narratology in Game Stud-
    ies," the Future of Electronic Games, http://www.lcc.gatech.edu/~murray/
    digra05/lastword.pdf.
 6. Lenhart et al., "Teens, Video Games and Civics."
 7. Doreen Carvajal, "The New Video Arcade in Spain Might Be the
    Movie Theater," *New York Times*, http://www.nytimes.com/2007/02/26/
    technology/26games.html?_r=1.
 8. Neal Gabler, *Life: the Movie: How Entertainment Conquered Reality* (New York:
    Vantage Books, 2000).
 9. David Bordwell, *Narration in the Fiction Film* (New York: Routledge, 1987), 157.
10. Ibid.
11. James Newman and Iain Simons, *100 Videogames* (London: British Film Insti-
    tute, 2007), 148.
12. Ibid., 33.
13. Roger Ebert, "Doom," RogerEbert.com, http://rogerebert.suntimes.com/
    apps/pbcs.dll/article?aid=/20051020/reviews/51012003/1023.
14. Andrew Darley, *Visual Digital Culture: Surface Play and Spectacle in the New
    Media Genres* (London: Routledge, 2000), 52.
15. Ibid., 171.
16. Philip E. Jenks, "NCC's 2009 Yearbook of American and Canadian Churches
    Reports Decline in Catholic, Southern Baptist Membership," National Coun-
    cil of Churches USA, http://www.ncccusa.org/news/090130yearbook1.html
17. Ibid.

Chapter 2: *Ultima IV*

 1. Readers who wish to play *Ultima IV: Quest of the Avatar* may download it at the
    SourceForge Web site, http://xu4.sourceforge.net/. An additional download
    called a "snapshot" eliminates a few crippling bugs in the freeware file. The
    user should understand that this freeware version of *Ultima IV* does not fully

emulate the play of the original. For example, the clock speed runs faster when meditating at shrines, temporarily hastening the game's originally intended contemplative pace. Nevertheless, the freeware version is largely faithful to the original experience of playing *Ultima IV*.

2. Following Garriott, it is now commonplace to use the word "avatar" in reference to a video game player's onscreen persona.

3. For further discussion of the explicit and implicit curriculum, see Philip W. Jackson, *Life in Classrooms* (New York: Holt, Rinehart and Winston, 1968), and Eliot W. Eisner, *The Educational Imagination: On the Design and Evaluation of School Programs*, 3rd ed. (Upper Saddle River, NJ: Prentice Hall, 2002).

4. For a technical treatment of the ludology/narratology debate, see Marie-Laure Ryan's essay "Beyond Myth and Metaphor: The Case of Narrative in Digital Media," and Jesper Juul's article "Games Telling Stories?" in the inaugural online issue of *Game Studies: The International Journal of Computer Game Research* (http://www.gamestudies.org/0101/). For the more casual reader, take a look at Henry Jenkins's article "Game Design as Narrative Architecture," http://web.mit.edu/cms/People/henry3/games&narrative.html.

5. For a brief treatment of *Ultima IV*'s place within video game history, see Frans Mäyrä, *An Introduction to Game Studies: Games in Culture* (London: SAGE Publications, 2008), 81–86.

6. Although Garriott's work on *Ultima IV* lends itself to a religious reading, Garriott maintains that his intention was to avoid the twin pitfalls of either "treading on the toes of religion" or supporting religious claims. See Shay Addams, *The Official Book of Ultima* (Radnor, PA: COMPUTE Books, 1990), 42.

7. J. C. Herz, *Joystick Nation: How Videogames Ate Our Quarters, Won Our Hearts, and Rewired Our Minds* (New York: Little, Brown and Company, 1997), 157.

8. The term "moral economy" was first coined in reference to the relationship that exists between economic behavior and social justice. See E. P. Thompson, *The Making of the English Working Class* (London: V. Gollancz, 1963). However, I reframe its use here. At the GLS 2.0 conference (2006) in Madison, Wisconsin, during a panel discussion titled "Economies of Meaning: Value, Property, Exchange," I first heard professor Thomas Malaby suggest that morality within massively multiplayer online role-playing games (MMOR-PGs) was based upon reciprocity and the accumulation of social capital. In other words, players create general social capital within the virtual world by doing good to others. In turn, this social capital affects the perception, experience, and behavior of all other players. His remarks stimulated my own thinking about a moral economy within video game worlds. Within a computer role-playing game, a moral economy is structured by the video game designer and explored by the video game player. The moral economy operates in a logical and somewhat predictable way within a largely closed system. However, I like to think of morality within an MMORPG as ecology—not economy—due to the organic, emergent, and less predictable way in which multiple human players choose to relate to each other. Interestingly, when the moral economy of *Ultima IV* shifted into the moral ecology of the MMORPG *Ultima Online* (1997), Pkillers (player killers) and other outlaws ran wild. For an interesting firsthand account of this shift, see Amy Jo Kim, "Killers Have More Fun," *Wired*, May 1998, http://www.wired.com/wired/archive/6.05/ultima.html.

9. In *Ultima IV*, Garriott's own philosophical commitments ring loud and clear. Players cannot win the game without practicing the eight virtues according to his rules. As Garriott recalls, he initially thought, "Hey, I'm going to build my

own little structure, a mathematically interrelated structure, which will build Avatarhood." See Caroline Spector, "A Conversation with Richard Garriott," in *Ultima: The Avatar Adventures*, ed. Rusel DeMaria and Caroline Spector (Rocklin, CA: Prima Publishing, 1992), 363–89. However, Garriott places as much value on the process of critical thinking as the conclusions of social ethics. Thus, he prefers the word "ethical" to "moral." Garriott explains, "I consider an ethic a rationally concludable law based upon cause and effect in social inter-action. . . . A moral, for Richard Garriott, is any other philosophical basis that lacks the rational structure." See Richard Garriott, interview by Steve Bauman, "Lord British Speaks: part VI: Violence in Games—Richard Garriott Offers His Opinion on Today's Hottest Topic," Archive.org, http://web.archive.org/web/20020828164231/www.cdmag.com/articles/023/004/garriott_interview6.html. Garriott's semantic preferences notwithstanding, he clearly conceives of video games as laboratories for ethical (or moral) exploration.

10. In *Ultima V: Warriors of Destiny* (1988), a player can hit Ctrl-K to access a visual display of one's virtue scores through the karma counter. However, that feature is not included in *Ultima IV*.

11. Alasdair MacIntyre, *After Virtue: A Study in Moral Theory*, 3rd ed. (Notre Dame, IN: Notre Dame Press, 2007), 219.

12. Spector, "Conversation with Richard Garriott," 370.

13. Ian Bogost, *Unit Operations: An Approach to Videogame Criticism* (Cambridge, MA: MIT Press, 2006), 85.

14. Ibid., 122.

15. CBS Interactive, "The Ultima Legacy: In Garriot's [*sic*] Own Words; Ultima IV: Quest of the Avatar," GameSpot, http://www.gamespot.com/features/ultima/g7.html.

16. Alfred North Whitehead, *The Aims of Education and Other Essays* (1929; repr., New York: Free Press, 1967), 12.

17. See, for example, *Super Noah's Ark 3D* (1994), *Catechumen* (1999), *Ominous Horizons* (2000), and *The Bible Game* (2005). For an interesting analysis of evangelical Christian video game designers and the theologies that motivate their work, see Jonathan Dee, "PlayStations of the Cross," *New York Times Magazine*, May 1, 2005, http://www.nytimes.com/2005/05/01/magazine/01GAMES.html.

18. Despite Garriott's concern to avoid any religious affirmation or objection in his games, he nonetheless recognizes that general religious and spiritual themes hold great potential for video game developers. He explains, "Games that treat religion realistically, weaving it into the game as it is woven into people's lives, can provide a richer and more realistic simulation. . . . Spirituality lends the game world credibility and completeness. The search for meaning in life is universal, and a shallower life of conflict and treasure collecting will never match the strength of a game that includes ethical or spiritual underpinnings." See Andrew S. Bub, "Game with God," *Computer Games Magazine*, May 2002, http://www.gamingwithchildren.com/2008-06-23/retro-game-with-god/#more-632.

Chapter 3. The Play Is the Thing

1. Henry Jenkins, "Game Design as Narrative Architecture," in *The Game Design Reader: A Rules of Play Anthology*, ed. Katie Salen and Eric Zimmerman (Cambridge, MA: MIT Press, 2006), 673.

2. Eric Zimmerman, "Narrative, Interactivity, Play, and Games," in *First Person: New Media as Story, Performance, and Game*, ed. Noah Wardrip-Fruin and Pat Harrigan (Cambridge, MA: MIT Press, 2004), 156.

3. Ibid., 157.
4. J. Yellowlees Douglas and Andrew Hargadon, "The Pleasures of Immersion and Interaction," in Wardrip-Fruin and Harrigan, *First Person*, 196.
5. *Against Heresies* 4.33.
6. Ibid.
7. *On Christian Doctrine* 1:36–37.
8. Markku Eskelinen, "Towards Computer Game Studies," in Wardrip-Fruin and Harrigan, *First Person*, 38.
9. Henry Jenkins, "Online Response" to Douglas and Hargadon, "Pleasures of Immersion and Interaction," in Wardrip-Fruin and Harrigan, *First Person*, 197.
10. Jenkins, "Game Design as Narrative Architecture," 675.
11. Marc LeBlanc, "Tools for Creating Dramatic Game Dynamics," in Salen and Zimmerman, *Game Design Reader*, 440.
12. Jenkins, "Game Design as Narrative Architecture," 673.
13. Ken Perlin, "Can There Be a Form between a Game and a Story?" in Wardrip-Fruin and Harrigan, *First Person*, 12.
14. Torben Grodal, "Stories for Eye, Ear and Muscles: Video Games, Media, and Embodied Experiences," in *The Video Game Theory Reader*, ed. Mark J. P. Wolf and Bernard Perron (New York: Routledge, 2003), 150.
15. Alison McMahan, "Immersion, Engagement and Presence: A Method for Analyzing 3D Video Games," in Wolf and Perron, *Video Game Theory Reader*, 74.
16. Miroslaw Filiciak, "Hyperidentities: Postmodern Identity Patterns in Massively Multiplayer Online Role-Playing Games," in Wolf and Perron, *Video Game Theory Reader*, 92.
17. Perlin, "Can There Be a Form?" 15.
18. Richard Bartle, *Designing Virtual Worlds* (Indianapolis, IN: New Riders Games, 2003), 154–55.
19. Ian Bogost, *Persuasive Games: The Expressive Power of Videogames* (Cambridge, MA: MIT Press, 2007), 43.
20. Wade Clark Roof, *Spiritual Marketplace: Baby Boomers and the Remaking of American Religion* (Ewing, NJ: Princeton University Press, 1999), 75.
21. Jolyon P. Mitchell and Sophia Marriage, *Mediating Religion: Conversations in Media, Religion, and Culture* (London: T&T Clark, 2003), 12.
22. Grodal, "Stories for Eye, Ear and Muscles," 149.
23. Perlin, "Can There Be a Form?" 15.
24. Grodal, "Stories for Eye, Ear and Muscles," 149.
25. Ibid.
26. Ibid., 151.
27. Douglas and Hargadon, "Pleasures of Immersion," 203.
28. To see this for yourself, visit www.catholic.org/prayers/station.php.
29. Mark Bernstein and Diane Greco, "*Card Shark* and *Thespis*: Exotic Tools for Hypertext Narrative," in Wardrip-Fruin and Harrigan, *First Person*, 178.
30. Richard Schechner, "Response" to Douglas and Hargadon, "Pleasures of Immersion," in Wardrip-Fruin and Harrigan, *First Person*, 194.
31. Ibid.
32. Bernstein and Greco, "*Card Shark* and *Thespis*," 178.
33. Ibid.
34. This game is available at http://www.onlinegames.net/games/689/running-jesus.html.

35. Cited in Katie Salen and Eric Zimmerman, *Rules of Play: Game Design Fundamentals* (Cambridge, MA: MIT Press, 2003), 74.
36. Cited in ibid., 75.
37. Ibid., 305.
38. Filiciak, "Hyperidentities," 87.
39. Posted by KFR. For those unfamiliar with the term, "griefing" is generally understood as harassment of other players through refusal to obey rules for given areas, taking advantage of other players' inexperience, engaging in virtual destruction or violence, or other forms of unacceptable online behavior.
40. Posted by "Tommyboy," March 27, 2006.
41. See the *Roma Victor* Web site, www.roma-victor.com.
42. Johan Huizinga, *Homo Ludens: A Study of the Play Element in Culture* (Boston: Beacon Press, 1955), 10.
43. Salen and Zimmerman, *Rules of Play*, 94.
44. Medine's Web site explains the purpose of the project, http://www.geocities .com/itsallok66/index.htm.
45. Jenkins, "Game Design as Narrative Architecture," 679.
46. Ibid.
47. "Vatican Pulls Plug on Sony Ad 'Blasphemy,'" Mirror.co.uk, October 1, 2005, http://www.mirror.co.uk/news/top-stories/2005/10/01/vatican-pulls-plug-on-sony-ad-blasphemy-115875-16196475/.
48. Espen Aarseth, "Genre Trouble," in Wardrip-Fruin and Harrigan, *First Person*, 52.
49. Ibid.

Chapter 4: Islamogaming

1. Left Behind Games, http://www.leftbehindgames.com/.
2. "New video game is first to star Rabbi?" ABCNews.com, http://abcnews .go.com/Technology/wireStory?id=2722583.
3. "Maverick Releases from Manifesto Games, 2007," *Wired* 15, no. 1, http:// www.wired.com/wired/archive/15.01/play.html?pg=4.
4. "Manifesto Games, The Shiva," http://www.manifestogames.com/shivah.
5. Ed Halter, "Islamogaming: Looking for Video Games in the Muslim World," *Computer Gaming World*, September 2006, http://www.1up.com/do/ feature?cId=3153332.
6. Ibid.
7. Abu Isa Games, http://www.abuisagames.com/.
8. Innovative Minds, http://www.inminds.co.uk.
9. See http://www.inminds.co.uk/islamic-thought.html
10. Ibid.
11. Description found at http://www.inminds.co.uk/islamic-fun.html.
12. Ibid.
13. Boycott Israel page, http://www.inminds.co.uk/boycott-israel.php.
14. Chris Suellentrop, "The Evildoers Do Super Mario Bros: The War on Terror's Least-Frightening Video Games," Slate.com, http://www.slate.com/ id/2124363.
15. See http://www.inminds.co.uk/islamic-fun.html. Spelling and capitalization are from the original.
16. J. Ferre, "The Media of Popular Piety," in J. Mitchell and S. Marriage, *Mediating Religion: Conversation in Media, Religion and Culture* (London: T&T Clark, 2006), 83–92.

17. C. P. Scholtz, "Religious Education and the Challenge of Computer Games: Research Perspectives on a New Issue," in Caroline Gustavsson and Rune Larsson, *Towards a European Perspective on Religious Education* (Stockholm: Artos & Norma, 2004), 256–67.
18. Nazih N. M. Ayubi, *Political Islam* (New York: Routledge, 1991).
19. Ibid.
20. John L. Esposito, *Islam: The Straight Path* (New York: Oxford University Press), 1998.
21. Special Forces demo, http://www.youtube.com/watch?v=yvmj7wj1UOw.
22. Toby Harnden, "Video Games Attract Young to Hizbollah," *Telegraph Online*, February 21, 2004, http://www.telegraph.co.uk/news/main.jhtml?xml=/news/2004/02/21/whizb21.xml&sSheet=/news/2004/02/21/ixworld.html.
23. The Stone Throwers, http://www.damascus-online.com/stonethrowers/.
24. Ibid.
25. Quote from ibid.
26. Under Ash, http://www.underash.net/en_download.htm.
27. Afkar Media, http://www.afkarmedia.com.
28. Under Siege, http://www.underash.net/en_download.htm.
29. See game description at http://www.afkarmedia.com/en/index.htm.
30. See review at http://www.digitalislam.eu/videoAndGames.do?articleId=1450.
31. Interview with Afkar Media, 2005, Omand3D.com, http://www.oman3d.com/features/interview_afkar/.
32. Matthew Moore, "'Muslim Massacre' Video Game Condemned for Glamorising Slaughter of Arabs," http://www.telegraph.co.uk/news/uknews/2776951/Muslim-Massacre-video-game-condemned-for-glamorising-slaughter-of-Arabs.html.
33. Marissa Calligeros, "Call to Ban Anti-Islam Video Game," *Brisbane Times Online*, September 14, 2008, http://www.brisbanetimes.com.au/news/queensland/call-to-ban-antiislam-video-game/2008/09/14/1221330622864.html.
34. Jonathon Schanzer, "Hypocrisy 2.0—Islamic Groups Condemn a Macabre Anti-Muslim Video Game," Israelenews.com, http://www.israelenews.com/view.asp?ID=3220.
35. Rhonda Roumani, "Muslims Craft Their Own Video Games," *Christian Science Monitor Online*, June 5, 2006, http://www.csmonitor.com/2006/0605/p07s02-wome.html.
36. Vit Sisler, "Representation and Self-Representation: Arabs and Muslims in Digital Games," in M. Santorineos and N. F. Dimitriadi, *Gaming Realities: A Challenge for Digital Culture* (Athens: Fournos, 2006), 85–92, http://www.digitalislam.eu/article.do?articleId=1423.
37. Ibid.
38. SimplyIslam.com, "Maze of Destiny," http://www.simplyislam.com/iteminfo.asp?Item=54854.
39. Suellentrop, "Evildoers Do Super Mario Bros."
40. Adventures of Ahmed trailer, http://www.youtube.com/watch?v=tiE6J9fq4VY.
41. Quraish, http://www.quraishgame.com/qe_index.htm.
42. Sisler, "Representation and Self-Representation."
43. Vit Sisler, "In Videogames You Shoot Arabs or Aliens—Interview with Radwan Kasmiya," *Umelec International* 10, no. 1 (2006): 77–81, http://www.digitalislam.eu/article.do?articleId=1418.

44. Vit Sisler, "Digital Arabs: Representation in Video Games," *European Journal of Cultural Studies* 11, no. 2 (2008): 203–20.
45. C. Steinkuehler and D. Williams, "Where Everybody Knows Your (Screen) Name: Online Games as 'Third Places,'" *Journal of Computer-Mediated Communication* 11, no. 4 (2006): article 1, http://jcmc.indiana.edu/vol11/issue4/steinkuehler.html.
46. Heidi Campbell, *When Religion Meets New Media* (London: Routledge, 2010).

Chapter 5: Wii Are In*spir*ited

1. According to John Beck and Mitchell Wade, the size of the "gamer generation" (those born after 1977) is already greater (approximately 90 million) than the baby-boom cohort was at its peak (estimated at 77 million). Beck and Wade's claim is that, based upon sheer size, the lived experiences of the gamer generation have engendered a marked shift in contemporary cultural attitudes, expectations, and abilities. See John C. Beck and Mitchell Wade, *The Kids Are Alright: How the Gamer Generation Is Changing the Workplace* (Boston: Harvard Business School Press, 2006).
2. Insofar as I am concerned here with the passions, desires, and impulses of contemporary culture and the manners in which those drives are related to the presence and work of God in the world, I am indebted to Bill Dyrness's work on theological aesthetics, especially his *Poetic Theology* (Grand Rapids: Eerdmans, forthcoming).
3. Mark J. P. Wolf and Bernard Perron, *The Video Game Theory Reader* (New York: Routledge, 2003), 14.
4. "*Graphics* . . . refers to some kind of changing and changeable visual display on a screen, involving some kind of pixel-based imaging. . . . The *interface* occurs at the boundary between the player and the video game itself, and can include such things as the screen, speakers . . . input devices (such as keyboard, mouse, joystick, trak-ball, paddles, steering wheels, light guns, etc.), as well as onscreen graphical elements . . . which invite player activity and allow it to occur. . . . *Player activity* is input by means of the user interface, and is limited and usually quantized by it as well" (Bernard Perron and Mark J. P. Wolf, *The Video Game Theory Reader 2* [New York: Routledge, 2009], 9–15).
5. I must note that, due to space limitations, I am leaving out a discussion of each console's "algorithm." According to Perron and Wolf, the algorithm is the program that contains the "procedures controlling the game's graphics and sound, the input and output engaging players, and the behavior of the computer-controlled players within the game. . . . The algorithm is responsible for the *representation, responses, rules,* and *randomness* that make up a game" (Wolf and Perron, *Video Game Theory Reader,* 15–16). While I certainly am not suggesting that the algorithm is in any way insignificant, insofar as it stands behind the video game experience, it seems to be less directly involved in the ways in which the average consumer perceives and understands the gaming experience offered by home consoles.
6. Ibid., 221–22.
7. Although the Fairchild Channel F, which also used game cartridges, preceded the 2600 (VCS), Atari perfected the production and the marketing of this technology. The Channel F was released in 1976, but was discontinued in 1980 following the overwhelming success of Atari's technologically superior VCS.

8. Leonard Herman, "Atari VCS," in Van Burnham and Ralph H. Baer, *Super-cade: A Visual History of the Videogame Age, 1971–1984* (Cambridge, MA: MIT Press, 2001), 148.

9. Due to the proliferation of third-party software, which suffered from unchecked quality issues and a distinct lack of innovation, the entire gaming industry nearly went bankrupt in the video game crash of the early 1980s. Nintendo, however, maintained control over the companies that could develop games for its console, which allowed Nintendo to demand a higher level of quality and prevent others from flooding the market with inferior games. Nintendo's model of software licensing is now the industry standard.

10. Jeannie Novak and Luis Levy, *Play the Game: The Parent's Guide to Video Games* (Boston: Thomson Course Technology, 2008), 17.

11. Ibid., 21.

12. Sony's PlayStation 3, the most powerful console ever released, has a 3.2GHz processor, an optional 160GB hard drive, 512 Megabytes of memory, and an HDMI output for 1080p resolution, which is compatible with high-definition televisions. You do get what you pay for, though; the 160GB PS 3 retails for six hundred dollars (at the time of this writing).

13. Kenji Hall, "The Big Ideas behind Nintendo's Wii," *Business Week*, November 16, 2006.

14. As of the writing of this article, the Wii had just passed the 50-million-units-sold mark. As of the same date, the Xbox 360 had sold almost 30 million units and the PlayStation 3 had sold 21 million. Some believe that part of the Wii's success is due to its price tag of $250, which is significantly less expensive than the other two systems. Although economics certainly plays a part in the equation, I am not convinced it tells the whole story of why the Wii is so appealing on a mass scale. See Chris Nuttall, "Nintendo Wii Console Sales Pass 50m," *Financial Times*, http://blogs.ft.com/techblog/2009/03/nintendo-wii-console-sales-pass-50m/.

15. Hall, "Big Ideas."

16. Thankfully, Nintendo rectified this situation by improving the durability of the wrist straps that secure the Wii remote to the user's hand. As well, they now offer silicone jackets that provide both additional grip and protection for the controller. To Nintendo's credit, who could have known that a paradigm shift would be so hazardous to our health!

17. As Andreas Gregersen and Torben Grodal suggest, interacting with video games leads to a sense of "embodied awareness in the moment of action." However, Gregersen and Grodal go on to claim that the Wii experience, especially in *Wii Sports*, actually leads to "less than ideal feelings of being an embodied agent responsible for actions portrayed on screen since input is often incongruent over several channels of sensory input." While they are indeed correct that our agency in virtual worlds is limited by the very fact of their being virtual, I remain unconvinced that a player's "feeling of agency" is construed as "less than ideal" in the Wii experience, primarily because this experience is always already understood in relation to other, more conventional gaming experiences (Andreas Gregersen and Torben Grodal, "Embodiment and Interface," in Perron and Wolf, *Video Game Theory Reader 2*, 77).

18. The philosopher and cultural theorist Charles Taylor suggests that contemporary individuals, as post*modern*, are in a continual struggle against modern

forms of rationality, which advocate a disengagement, a "setting aside," of our physical bodies in determining what is right. However, as *post*modern, contemporary persons are "vigorously combating" this move toward "excarnation" (his term). They are rejecting the modern transfer of meaning from out of bodily, somatic forms of life to a place residing "in the head." See Charles Taylor, *A Secular Age* (Cambridge, MA: Belknap Press, 2007), 288.

19. For a comprehensive listing of these specifications, see Novak and Levy, *Play the Game*, 57–60.

20. At times the graphical disparity of Wii games borders on ironic. *Wii Sports*, a game that is bundled with the system and is, therefore, the best-selling game of all time, features tennis players, bowlers, and golfers who have no arms!

21. Cultural critic Simon Frith recognizes the essentially holistic impulse present in contemporary persons' pursuit of cultural products. In his study on the cultural experience of music, he claims that music listening and music making have to do with the "mind-in-the-body," and that, to get at the peculiarity of the musical experience, we must "not study listening, which has so much in common with reading and looking, but dancing, which places music in the very center of our bodily lives." Especially as the Wii provides an expressly dancelike experience with games such as *EA Sports*, Frith's comments prove highly instructive in our understanding of how contemporary individuals perceive the Wii experience (Simon Frith, *Performing Rites: On the Value of Popular Music* [Cambridge, MA: Harvard University Press, 1996], 266).

22. Kenji Hall, "Meet Mario's Papa," *Business Week*, November 7, 2005.

23. Beck and Wade, *Kids Are Alright*, 9.

24. Ibid. Beck and Wade suggest that one of the defining aspects of the gamer generation's reality is the emotional dimension of video games.

25. Once again Charles Taylor is helpful here. Taylor suggests that contemporary culture has inherited a distinctly Romantic sensibility in which individuals construe their experiences both subjectively and in terms of emotional engagement. As an attempt to correct Kant's separation of "feeling" from "thinking" and "doing," Romanticism places "feeling" at the center of epistemology. Taylor argues that it is due in part to the rise of this neo-Romanticism that we are provided such "a rich vocabulary of interiority, an inner realm of thought and feeling to be explored" (*Secular Age*, 539).

26. Indeed, much could be said concerning the manners in which Plato's cave metaphor impinges upon the Western conception of video games. Some would find Plato's description of unenlightened youths sitting in the darkness of a cave, consumed with watching the shadows of puppets on a wall, as a fitting description of the video game experience. Thus, as it precludes people from journeying out of the cave and into the light of the "Good," the somatic and holistic nature of video games would be construed within this conceptual framework as militating against a preferably cognitive and disembodied existence. See Plato, *The Republic of Plato*, trans. Francis Macdonald Cornford (New York: Oxford University Press, 1972), esp. book 14.

27. In book 10 of *Confessions*, Augustine states, "But this sensual pleasure [i.e., spiritual affections], to which the soul must not be delivered so as to be weakened, often leads me astray, when sense does not accompany reason in such a way as to follow patiently after it. . . . Thus in such things I unconsciously sin, but later I am conscious of it" (*Confessions of St. Augustine* [Garden City, NY: Image Books (Doubleday), 1984], 261).

28. Although we are unable to develop it here, I am speaking of the presence of the Spirit in an explicitly Trinitarian fashion. Thus, the presence of the Spirit cannot be considered apart from the presence of the Father or the presence of Christ—and vice versa. As well I am approaching the Spirit's work in light of the three theologically normative categories that reflect the Trinitarian presence of God in creation that Bill Dyrness has proposed: relationship, agency, and embodiment. Although I do not address them directly, they articulate my conception of how the world and our lives are fundamentally constituted. See William A. Dyrness, *The Earth Is God's: A Theology of American Culture* (Eugene, OR: Wipf and Stock, 1997).

29. For Schleiermacher, religious "feeling" is the "sense and taste" for the Infinite and, as such, is an essential part of human nature. In describing this "sense" of the Infinite in the finite, of the Whole in the particular he states, "How now are you in the Whole? By your senses. . . . You become sense and the Whole becomes object. Sense and object mingle and unite, then each returns to its place" (Schleiermacher, *On Religion: Speeches to Its Cultured Despisers*, trans. John Oman [London: K. Paul, Trench, Trubner & Co., 1893], 43).

30. Here we are intentionally moving beyond the Neoplatonic conception of sensuality. Rather than an impediment to our relatedness with God, our sensuality (and the created order) becomes the very means by which we are related to God. Our physicality is, therefore, inherently "good." Yet, this relatedness must never be understood independent from the energizing presence of the Spirit. We are not simply bodies, but inspirited creatures in relation.

31. In chap. 6 of 1 Corinthians, Paul seems to be claiming that, through the embodied work of the Holy Spirit, we become "related" to God somatically. As the Spirit unites our bodies as members of Christ (1 Cor. 6:15), we are "united to the Lord," and thus, "one spirit with him" (1 Cor. 6:17).

32. Nicholas Wolterstorff captures this thought well when he states, "One's attitude toward the physical incorporates an attitude toward oneself. We are not angels hovering lightly over the earth. Denigration of the physical implies denigration of oneself. . . . For even if we accept the possibility of disembodied existence, we must nonetheless resist the idea that such existence is better. . . . With our bodies, among rocks and trees, among colors and fragrances, we find our fulfillment; and only thus do we find it fully" (Wolterstorff, *Art in Action: Toward a Christian Aesthetic* [Grand Rapids: Eerdmans, 1980], 71–72).

33. Jürgen Moltmann, *The Spirit of Life: A Universal Affirmation*, trans. Margaret Kohl (Minneapolis: Fortress Press, 1991), 37 (emphasis added).

34. As John Taylor suggests, "The Spirit is not averse to the elemental world of our dreams, the raw emotions of our fears and angers, the illogical certainties of our intuitions, the uncharted groupings of our agnosticism, the compulsive tides of our history. These are his *milieu*" (John Vernon Taylor, *The Go-between God: The Holy Spirit and the Christian Mission* [London: SCM, 2004], 51 [emphasis in original]).

Chapter 6: *Myst* and *Halo*

1. Jon Carroll, "Guerrillas in the Myst," *Wired*, August 1994, http://www.wired.com/wired/archive/2.08/myst.html.

Chapter 7: *Madden* Rules

1. John Madden, "2006 Pro Football Hall of Fame Enshrinement Speech Transcript," August 5, 2006, http://www.profootballhof.com/hof/release.aspx ?release_id=2178.

2. Jon Robinson, "John Madden Interview," July 28, 2006, http://sports.ign .com/articles/721/721755p1.html.

3. For a colorful overview of the various editions, see Travis Fahs, "IGN Presents the History of Madden," August 8, 2008, http://retro.ign.com/ articles/896/896893p1.html.

4. The Official Web Site of Vince Lombardi, "Quotes," http://www.vince lombardi.com/about/quotes5.htm.

5. Michael Novak, *The Joy of Sports* (New York: Basic Books, 1976), 224.

6. Robert K. Johnston, *The Christian at Play* (Grand Rapids: William Eerdmans, 1983), 41.

7. Laura Parker, "Game Addiction: The Real Story," GameSpot, April 9, 2009, http://www.gamespot.com/features/6207309/p-2.html, accessed August 12, 2009.

8. Twin Galaxies, www.twingalaxies.com.

9. For a detailed history, see Tony Ladd and James A. Mathisen, *Muscular Christianity: Evangelical Protestants and the Development of American Sport* (Grand Rapids: Baker Books, 1999).

10. This episode of *60 Minutes* originally aired on January 22, 2006, and was chronicled online by Daniel Schorn, "Cyber Athlete 'Fatal1ty,'" August 6, 2006, http://www.cbsnews.com/stories/2006/01/19/60minutes/main1220146 .shtml?tag=contentMain;contentBody.

11. Major League Gaming, www.mlgpro.com.

12. Schorn, "Cyber Athlete 'Fatal1ty.'"

13. Ryan Goldberg, "Virtual Leagues Fold, Forcing Gamers to Find Actual Jobs," *New York Times*, April 1, 2009.

14. CPL president Angel Munoz serves as the primary antagonist in the 2009 documentary *Frag* (see http://www.fragmovie.com/).

15. Mei Fong, "Don't Tell the Kids: Computer Games Can Make You Rich," *Wall Street Journal*, May 21, 2004, A1.

16. Patrick Hruby, "So You Wanna Be a Professional Video Game Player," ESPN Page 2, October 11, 2007, http://sports.espn.go.com/espn/page2/story ?page=hruby/071008.

17. Schorn, "Cyber Athlete 'Fatal1ty.'"

18. Hruby, "So You Wanna Be a Professional Video Game Player."

19. Fong, "Don't Tell the Kids."

20. Hruby, "So You Wanna Be a Professional Video Game Player."

21. Mark Lepper and David Greene, "Turning Play into Work," *Journal of Personality and Social Psychology* 31 (1975): 479–86.

22. Chuck Klosterman, "The Lester Bangs of Video Games," *Esquire*, June 30, 2006, http://www.esquire.com/features/ESQ0706KLOSTER_66, accessed July 1, 2009.

23. Johnston, *Christian at Play*, 4.

24. Ibid., 91.

25. Ibid., 110.

26. Check out the construction of the massive DreamHack network as a time-lapse video at http://vision.ameba.jp/watch.do?movie=661073.

Chapter 8: Poets, Posers, and Guitar Heroes

1. Brent Hill, "Scott Cairns Interview," *Mars Hill Review*, no. 6 (Fall 1996): 140–43.
2. It's truly fascinating participating in a *Rock Band* session with a full "band" of friends manning the instruments. I've been in bands for the majority of my life from age sixteen on, and the virtual experience has striking similarities to the real thing (socially, if not technically). The way people hold their instruments, grin at each other during synchronized parts, and generally *act* like they are a unit is the same whether the music being produced is actual or not.
3. Much like World 1.0, but more interactive, and with better-looking people.
4. Eric Steuer, "The Infinite Album," *Wired* 14, no. 9 (September 2006).
5. Ibid.
6. Tracy Fullerton, Christopher Swain, and Stephen Hoffman, *Game Design Workshop: Designing, Prototyping and Playtesting Games* (Gilroy, CA: CMP Books, 2004), 30.
7. Leo Tolstoy, *What Is Art?* trans. Richard Pevear and Larissa Volokhonsky (London: Penguin Classics, 1996), 38.
8. Gamezplay, "*Guitar Hero* Sales Pass $2 Billion with *Guitar Hero 5* Confirmed (Surprise!)," May 9, 2009, http://www.gamezplay.org/2009/05/guitar-hero-slaes-pass-2-billion-with.html.
9. Lester Bangs, *Mainlines, Blood Feasts, and Bad Taste: A Lester Bangs Reader*, ed. John Morthland (New York: Anchor Books, 2003), 53.
10. *Duende* can be loosely explained as the dark power that fuels the aesthetic experience, which everyone can understand and feel but which no one can define. Lorca comments on the nature of the *duende*, saying that "it is a power, not a work. It is a struggle, not a thought."
11. Nick Cave, *The Secret Life of the Love Song & The Flesh Made Word: Two Lectures by Nick Cave*, Mute Records, 2000.

Chapter 9: *BioShock* to the System

1. Established studies include Craig A. Anderson and Karen E. Dill, "Video Games and Aggressive Thoughts, Feelings, and Behavior in the Laboratory and in Life," *Journal of Personality and Social Psychology* 78, no. 4 (2000): 772–90; Frithjof Staude-Müller, Thomas Bliesener, and Stefanie Luthman, "Hostile and Hardened? An Experimental Study on (De-)Sensitization to Violence and Suffering through Playing Video Games," *Swiss Journal of Psychology* 67, no. 1 (2008): 41–50; Werner H. Hopfl, Günter L. Huber, and Rudolf H. Weiß, "Media Violence and Youth Violence: A 2-Year Longitudinal Study," *Journal of Media Psychology* 20, no. 3 (2008): 79–96; Elly A. Konijn, Marije Nije Bijvank, and Brad J. Bushman, "I Wish I Were a Warrior: The Role of Wishful Identification in the Effects of Violent Video Games on Aggression in Adolescent Boys," *Developmental Psychology* 43, no. 4 (2007): 1038–44; Niklas Ravaja, Marko Turpeinen, Timo Saari, Sampsa Puttonen, and Liisa Keltikangas-Järvinen, "The Psychophysiology of James Bond: Phasic Emotional Responses to Violent Video Game Events," *Emotion* 8, no. 1 (2008): 114–20.
2. U.S. Department of Health and Human Services, *Youth Violence: A Report of the Surgeon General* (Rockville, MD: U.S. Department of Health and Human Services, U.S. Public Health Service, 2001).

3. In the Surgeon General's report, this change has been attributed to a decrease in the use of firearms.
4. C. Shawn Green and Daphne Bavelier, "Effect of Action Video Games on the Spatial Distribution of Visuospatial Attention," *Journal of Experimental Psychology: Human Perception and Performance* 32, no. 6 (2006): 1465–78.
5. Steven Johnson, "Dome Improvement," *Wired*, May 2005, http://www.wired.com/wired/archive/13.05/flynn.html.
6. Steven Johnson, *Everything Bad Is Good For You* (New York: Riverhead Books, 2005).
7. Craig Detweiler and Barry Taylor, *A Matrix of Meanings: Finding God in Pop Culture* (Grand Rapids: Baker Academic, 2003), 302.
8. Andrew Rollings and Ernest Adams, *Andrew Rollings and Ernest Adams on Game Design* (Indianapolis, IN: New Riders, 2003), 95–109.
9. There are two different videos for the ending sequence, though a third ending is created by a change in the narrator's tone. This change is dependent on the number of "little sisters" harvested during game play, giving the narrator either a sad or angry tone of voice.
10. GameSpot, "*Left Behind: Eternal Forces* Reviews," http://www.gamespot.com/pc/strategy/leftbehindeternalforces/review.html?mode=web.
11. Brendan Sinclair, "Q & A: Levine Surfs BioShock's Wake," GameSpot, August 27, 2007, http://www.gamespot.com/news/6177728.html.
12. Jessica Mulligan and Bridgette Patrovsky, *Developing Online Games* (Indianapolis, IN: New Riders, 2003), 217.
13. Daniel Etherington, "BioShock Interview," BBC Collective, August 23, 2007, http://www.bbc.co.uk/dna/collective/A26191532.
14. Brendan Sinclair, "Q & A: Diving Deeper into BioShock's Story," GameSpot, September 20, 2007, http://www.gamespot.com/news/6179423.html.

Chapter 10: 'Til Disconnection Do We Part

1. The usage of the term "real life" can be problematic. Anthropologist Tom Boellstorff suggests that our real lives have always been virtual (*Coming of Age in Second Life* [Princeton, NJ: Princeton University Press, 2008], 33). I have chosen to use the term "First Life" to denote the offline world outside of *Second Life*.
2. The genre of MMORPGs includes games such as *World of Warcraft*, *Everquest*, and *Neverwinter Nights*.
3. Personal communication with Robin Harper, former senior vice president, marketing and business development of Linden Labs, March 18, 2004.
4. James Wagner Au reported on the evolution of *Second Life* from within Linden Labs in *The Making of Second Life: Notes from the New World* (San Francisco: Harper Business, 2008).
5. Boellstorff, *Coming of Age*, 247.
6. Sherry Turkle, *Life on the Screen* (New York: Simon & Schuster, 1995), 269.
7. Mark Stephen Meadows, *I, Avatar: The Culture and Consequences of Having a Second Life* (Berkeley, CA: New Riders, 2008), 98.
8. There is also the option to be a "furry," which is an asexual, or at least ambiguous, creature. However, *Second Life* does require that users initially select their gender. The body can then be edited to remove gender-specific cues.
9. Meadows, *I, Avatar*, 72.
10. Ronald Grimes, *Deeply into the Bone* (Berkeley: University of California Press, 2002), 91.

11. Ronald Grimes, *Ritual Criticism* (Columbia: University of South Carolina Press, 1990), 205.
12. Much of this section is from communication with Harper.
13. Calling cards are similar to business cards, but with tracking devices. Once calling cards are traded, a fellow user may know where you are in the world at any given time.
14. Grimes, *Deeply into the Bone*, 91.
15. Ibid., 5.
16. Ronald Grimes, *Marrying and Burying* (Boulder, CO: Westview Press, 1995), 99.
17. The weddings that I detail here are those of Garth Fairlight and Pituca Chang, and Johnny Bunderfeld and Malana Spencer. However, due to server limitations I was only able to personally attend the former. I obtained information about the latter through subsequent interviews.
18. Grimes, *Marrying and Burying*, 99.
19. As of June 2009, the Linden Dollar was trading at approximately L$265 to $1 U.S., with volumes of L$80 million per day.
20. There are many businesses in *Second Life*, but the majority fall into one of three categories: (1) retail sales of virtual objects such as clothing, vehicles, and houses; (2) services; and (3) property management.
21. Cele Otnes and Elizabeth Pleck, *Cinderella Dreams* (Berkeley: University of California Press, 2003), 83.
22. Stanley Elkin, "In Praise of Tuxedos," *Harper's*, November 1985, 34.
23. "SecondLife | Partners,"https://secure-web8.secondlife.com/account/partners .php?lang=en.
24. Turkle, *Life on the Screen*, 269.
25. Philip Victor, "Virtual Affair Ends in Real-Life Divorce," ABC News, http:// abcnews.go.com/International/SmallBiz/Story?id=6255277&page=1.
26. "EverQuest Widows: EverQuest Widows (tm)," Yahoo! Groups, http:// health.groups.yahoo.com/group/EverQuest-Widows/.
27. "WOW_Widow : World of Warcraft Widows," Yahoo! Groups, http:// games.groups.yahoo.com/group/WOW_widow/.

Chapter 11: Role Playing

1. Interview #1. As the author, I conducted thirty-five qualitative interviews with individuals who considered themselves gamers: played video games at least eight or more hours a week, interacted in a community of other gamers, and were knowledgeable of the technical terms of gaming. These interviews were conducted in the gamers' domains (e.g., home, apartment, or video game store, such as Game Stop). They took place between the months of September 2008 and December 2008 and included individuals from various racial, class, and ethnic backgrounds.
2. Statistics and factual data were also gathered from the Entertainment Software Association, Atari, Nintendo, Entertainment Software Rating Board, Academy of Interactive Art & Sciences, Video Game Voters Network, Pew Internet & American Life Project, and the International Games Developer Association. This data was then compiled and analyzed along with the thirty-five interviews to form the results and findings. The raw data, statistics, and transcripts are available at the Urban Research Center Web site, http://urbanresearch journal.org/.
3. Douglass C. Perry, "The Influence of Literature and Myth in Video Games," May 17, 2006, http://xbox360.ign.com/articles/704/704806p1.html.

4. Veli-Matti Kärkkäinen, *Christology: A Global Introduction* (Grand Rapids: Baker Academic, 2003), 216–17.

5. Taken from the interviews' most matched phrases.

6. Ibid.

7. John C. Beck and Mitchell Wade, *Got Game: How the Gamer Generation Is Reshaping Business Forever* (Boston: Harvard Business School Press, 2004), 11.

8. Taken from interview #9. The names of interviewees have been changed to protect their privacy.

9. Taken from a culmination of the interview transcripts and total phrases stated by the gamers interviewed.

10. Author's paraphrasing of phrases stated by gaming interviewees.

11. This is not to suggest that race and class are not an issue, merely, a signifying quality among gamers is that they are largely "misunderstood" and "stereotyped," which becomes rather universal beyond race and class. Race does have a factor in gaming and technology; however, the constraints of this project do not allow me to delve into that subject.

12. These three themes were present in 95 percent of the interviewees' responses and within the games that each of the gamers brought up.

13. Interview #21.

14. Interview #24.

15. Interview #30.

16. "I will put enmity between you and the woman, and between your offspring and hers; he will strike your head, and you will strike his heel" (Gen. 3:15).

17. Donald K. McKim, *Westminster Dictionary of Theological Terms* (Louisville, KY: Westminster John Knox Press, 1996), 226.

18. Interview #34.

19. M. S. Archer, *Being Human* (Cambridge: Cambridge University Press, 2000), and Philip A. Mellor, *Religion, Realism, and Social Theory: Making Sense of Society* (Thousand Oaks, CA: Sage Publications, 2004).

20. John Seely Brown and Paul Duguid, *The Social Life of Information* (Boston: Harvard Business School Press, 2000).

21. Mellor, *Religion, Realism, and Social Theory*, 29.

22. The constraints of this chapter limit my scope of the discussion regarding identity formation, reality vs. hyperrealism, and the dialogue regarding the escape world of video games. For a detailed discussion, I recommend Wagner James Au, *The Making of Second Life: Notes from the New World* (New York: HarperCollins, 2008), 70–84. Note especially his discussion of online role playing and the effects of escape and fantasy. Au describes how gamers who are free from "the accidents of birth" are able to construct new identities and become something they are not in real life.

23. Interview #12.

24. Interview #5.

25. This is derived in a comparison analysis between gamers' responses to certain religious centered questions and prior research on religion and society. Daniel Hodge, *Can You Hear Me Calling: Hip Hop/ Gangster Culture & the Future Urban Church* (master's thesis, Pasadena: Fuller Theological Seminary School of Intercultural Studies, 2004).

26. Brad King and John Borland, *Dungeons and Dreamers: The Rise of Computer Game Culture; From Geek to Chic* (Emeryville, CA: McGraw-Hill/Osborne, 2003).

27. Interview #2.

28. Adapted from Beck and Wade, *Got Game?* 12–14. There are also similar findings by Jeroen Jansz and Lonneke Martens, "Gaming at a LAN Event: The Social Context of Playing Video Games," *New Media Society* 7, no. 3 (2005): 333–55. They observed five key personality factors within gamers: competition, control, entertainment, escapism, and pastime.
29. Interview #26.
30. Gerry Coulter, "Jean Baudrillard and the Definitive Ambivalence of Gaming," *Games and Culture* 2, no. 4 (2007): 358–65.
31. Interview #4.
32. About 40 percent of the interviewees stated they were "Christian" and of that 40 percent, 20 percent stated they were able to find a deeper connection to God through gaming.
33. Expansys, "Microsoft Halo 3," http://www.expansys.com/d.aspx?i=154496.
34. In all fairness, though, these quests and epics often become escape routes out of something that actually needs attention—like work or family life. A healthy balance is needed, and not all escapism is good. Many gamers report that playing too many video games is not healthy and that too much escape can cause a detachment from reality. See Jesper Juul, *Half-Real: Video Games between Real Rules and Fictional Worlds* (Cambridge, MA: MIT Press, 2005), for a thorough treatment of this issue.

Chapter 12: Cybersociality

1. John Palfrey and Urs Gasser, *Born Digital: Understanding the First Generation of Digital Natives* (New York: Basic Books, 2008), 1.
2. Ibid., 2.
3. Edward Castronova, *Exodus to the Virtual World: How Online Fun Is Changing Reality* (New York: Palgrave Macmillan, 2007), 25.
4. Wagner James Au, *The Making of Second Life: Notes from the New World* (New York: HarperCollins, 2008).
5. C. Wayne Mayhall, "What Price Cyberspace?" *Christian Research Journal* 31, no. 6 (2008): 12–19.
6. Tom Boellstorff, *Coming of Age in Second Life: An Anthropologist Explores the Virtually Human* (Princeton, NJ: Princeton University Press, 2008), 21.
7. Castronova, *Exodus to the Virtual World*, 25.
8. Boellstorff, *Coming of Age in Second Life*, 24.
9. The social dimension of digital worlds and cultures is more easily recognized, but video games often involve this element as well. Palfrey and Gasser state that survey results indicate that "60 percent of gamers are playing with friends and 25 percent with a spouse or parent" (Palfrey and Gasser, *Born Digital*, 215). In addition, in 2006, 44 percent of video game players in console formats or computers also played online games that included involvement in "a societal dimension" (Castronova, *Exodus to the Virtual World*, 35).
10. An excellent and helpful introduction to this process can be found in Gordon Lynch, *Understanding Theology and Popular Culture* (Malden, MA: Blackwell Publishing, 2005).
11. Peter Berger, *A Rumor of Angels: Modern Society and the Rediscovery of the Supernatural* (Garden City, NY: Doubleday, 1969); expanded ed. (New York: Anchor Books, 1990).
12. Berger, *Rumor of Angels* (1990), x.

13. Ibid.
14. For a further exploration of inductive theological methods, see John Warwick Montgomery, "The Theologian's Craft: A Discussion of Theory Formation and Theory Testing in Theology," *Journal of the American Scientific Affiliation* 18, no. 3 (September 1966): 65–77, http://www.asa3.org/ASA/PSCF/1966/JASA9-66Montgomery.html. Montgomery briefly used Berger's inductive method from *A Rumor of Angels* apologetically in *Christianity for the Tough-Minded* (Minneapolis, MN: Bethany House, 1973).
15. Paul J. Fitzgerald, "Faithful Sociology: Peter Berger's Religious Project," *Religious Studies Review* 27, no. 1 (January 2001): 13.
16. Berger, *Rumor of Angels* (1969), 53.
17. Fitzgerald, "Faithful Sociology," 13.
18. Lynch, *Understanding Theology and Popular Culture*, x.
19. Ziaudden Sardar and Sean Cubitt, eds., *Aliens R Us: The Other in Science Fiction Cinema* (London: Pluto Press, 2002).
20. Castronova, *Exodus to the Virtual World*, 7.
21. See the intriguing book-length discussion of this in Castronova.
22. Boellstorff, *Coming of Age in Second Life*, 21.
23. Au, *Making of Second Life*, 15.
24. Brian Doherty, *This Is Burning Man* (New York: Little, Brown & Company, 2004); Lee Gilmore and Mark Van Proyen, eds., *AfterBurn: Reflections on Burning Man* (Albuquerque: University of New Mexico Press, 2005); John W. Morehead, "Burning Man Festival as Life-Enhancing, Post-Christendom 'Middle Way'" (master's thesis, Salt Lake Theological Seminary, 2007).
25. Au, *Making of Second Life*, 31.
26. Ibid.
27. See his discussion of this in *Surprised by Joy* (New York: Harvest Books, 1955).
28. Berger, *Rumor of Angels* (1969), 57.
29. Ibid., 58.
30. Mircea Eliade, *The Sacred and Profane: The Nature of Religion* (New York: Harcourt Brace & World, 1959).
31. Berger, *Rumor of Angels* (1969), 58.
32. For one notable exception, see Robert K. Johnston, *The Christian at Play* (Grand Rapids: William B. Eerdmans, 1983).
33. David Miller, *Gods and Games* (New York: World Publishing Company, 1970).
34. Ibid., 349. It is interesting to note that the majority of the academic explorations of play theology were written in the 1960s and early 1970s. It appears that the counterculture and death-of-God theology provided the motivation for theological reflection in this area, but with the demise of these forces, theological reflection on play has largely disappeared. Perhaps increased awareness on the part of theologians and missiologists of the significance of play in the late modern West, particularly as it relates to video games and digital cultures, will provide the inspiration for new theological exploration of this topic.
35. Ibid., 19.
36. Ibid., 80 (emphasis in original).
37. Ibid., 101.
38. Ibid.
39. Ibid., 158.

40. Ibid., 112.
41. Jeremy Hockett, "Burningman [*sic*] and the Ritual Aspects of Play," http://www.msu.edu/~hockettj/Play.htm.
42. Roger C. Aden, *Popular Stories and Promised Lands: Fan Cultures and Symbolic Pilgrimages* (Tuscaloosa: University of Alabama Press, 1999), 9.
43. Ibid., 3. Cf. Boellstorff, *Coming of Age in Second Life*, 72.
44. Aden, *Popular Stories*, 5.
45. Ibid., 10.
46. Castronova, *Exodus to the Virtual World*, 203.
47. Boellstorff, *Coming of Age in Second Life*, 37.
48. Ibid.
49. J. R. R. Tolkien, "On Fairy Stories," in *Essays Presented to Charles Williams* (Grand Rapids: William B. Eerdmans, 1981), 70–71.
50. Boellstorff, *Coming of Age in Second Life*, 209.
51. Aden, *Popular Stories*, 8 (emphasis added by Aden).
52. For a good discussion of reenchantment and the place of literature, film, and music in this process, see Christopher Partridge, *The Re-Enchantment of the West: Alternative Spiritualities, Sacralization, Popular Culture, and Occulture*, vol. 1 (London: T&T Clark International, 2004).
53. Castronova, *Exodus to the Virtual World*, 201.
54. Ibid., xiv.
55. Ibid., 201.
56. For consideration of these possibilities, see John Warwick Montgomery, ed., *Myth, Allegory and Gospel: An Interpretation of J. R. R. Tolkien, C. S. Lewis, G. K. Chesterton, Charles Williams* (Minneapolis, MN: Bethany House, 1974); Royce Gordon Gruenler, "Jesus as Author of the Evangelium: J. R. R. Tolkien and the Spell of the Great Story," in *New Approaches to Jesus and the Gospels: A Phenomenological and Exegetical Study of Synoptic Christology* (Grand Rapids: Baker Book House, 1982); Colin Duriez, "The Theology of Fantasy in Lewis and Tolkien," *Themelios* 23, no. 2 (1998): 35–51; Philip Johnson, "Apologetics and Myths: Signs of Salvation in Postmodernity," *Lutheran Theological Journal* 32, no. 2 (July 1998): 62–72.
57. Aden, *Popular Stories*, 49.
58. Robert D. Putnam, *Bowling Alone: The Collapse and Revival of American Community* (New York: Simon & Schuster, 2000).
59. Ray Oldenburg, *The Great Good Place: Cafés, Coffee Shops, Community Centers, Beauty Parlors, General Stores, Bars, Hangouts, and How They Get You through the Day* (New York: Marlowe & Company, 1999).
60. Ibid., 16.
61. Michel Maffesoli, *The Time of the Tribes: The Decline of Individualism in Mass Society* (London: Sage Publications, 1996). See also Ethan Watters, *Urban Tribes: Are Friends the New Family?* (London: Bloomsbury, 2004).
62. Constance Steinkuehler and Dmitri Williams, "Where Everybody Knows Your (Screen) Name: Online Games as 'Third Places,'" *Journal of Computer-Mediated Communications* 11, no. 4 (2006): article 1, http://jcmc.indiana.edu/vol11/issue4/steinkuehler.html.
63. Ibid.
64. Ibid.
65. Oldenburg, *Great Good Place*, 31.
66. Steinkuehler and Williams, "Where Everybody Knows Your (Screen) Name."
67. Ibid.

68. Castronova, *Exodus to the Virtual World*, 207 (emphasis in original).

Conclusion: Born to Play

1. Cited in Mark Stephen Meadows, *I, Avatar: The Culture and Consequences of Having a Second Life* (Berkeley, CA: New Riders, 2008), 70.
2. James Paul Gee, *Good Video Games + Good Learning* (New York: Peter Lang, 2007), 79.
3. Ibid., 172–73.
4. An overview of Easter eggs hidden within games can be found at http://www .gamespot.com/features/6131572/index.html.
5. John C. Beck and Mitchell Wade, *The Kids Are Alright: How the Gamer Generation Is Changing the Workplace* (Boston: Harvard Business School Press, 2006), 81.
6. Ibid., 85–86.

Appendix: Beyond "Turn that Thing Off!"

1. For a more thorough explanation of the Deep Design, please see Chap Clark and Kara E. Powell, *Deep Ministry in a Shallow World: Not-So-Secret Findings about Youth Ministry* (Grand Rapids: Zondervan, 2006).
2. National Institute on Media and the Family, "Effects of Video Game Playing on Children," www.mediafamily.org/facts/facts_effect.shtml.
3. Craig A. Anderson and Karen E. Dill, "Video Games and Aggressive Thoughts, Feelings, and Behavior in the Laboratory and in Life," *Journal of Personality and Social Psychology* 78, no. 4 (2000): 772–90; and Douglas A. Gentile, Paul J. Lynch, Jennifer R. Linder, and David A. Walsh, "The Effects of Violent Game Habits on Adolescent Hostility, Aggressive Behaviors, and School Performance," *Journal of Adolescence* 27 (2004): 5–22.
4. National Institute on Media and the Family, "Effects of Video Game Playing on Children," www.mediafamily.org/facts/facts_effect.shtml.
5. Dallas Willard, *The Divine Conspiracy* (San Francisco: Harper Collins, 1998), 40.
6. C. Sherif, M. Sherif, and R. Nebergall, *Attitude and Attitude Change: The Social Judgment-Involvement Approach* (Philadelphia: Saunders, 1965). Also see Chap Clark, "Deep Communication: Why Doesn't Our Teaching Change Kids' Lives?" in Clark and Powell, *Deep Ministry*, 149–71. This section adapts some of the authors' well-nuanced thoughts from the research.
7. Ralph Rosnow, "Magnitude of Impact," in *Experiments in Persuasion*, ed. Leon Festinger et al. (New York: Academic Press, 1967), 399–408.
8. Richard M. Perloff, *The Dynamics of Persuasion* (Hillsdale, NJ: Lawrence Erlbaum Associates, 1993).
9. Sarah Trenholm, *Persuasion and Social Influence* (Englewood Cliffs, NJ: Prentice Hall, 1982).
10. A 2008 report indicates that teen gaming typically involves social interaction and is even connected with civic engagement. In fact, most teens say gaming is an important part of their overall social experience, and a majority game with others or around others. Those who play games with others in the room seem to be more engaged in civic awareness and participation (volunteering, giving to charity, political action) than others who game primarily alone (Pew Internet and American Life Project, "Teens, Video Games, and Civics," released September 16, 2008. See www.pewinternet.org).
11. Ibid., 37–38.

Contributors

Kutter Callaway is a PhD candidate in theology and culture at Fuller Theological Seminary. Prior to his studies at Fuller, he logged innumerable hours as a youth pastor playing *Halo* with high school students; he later developed his axe-shredding skills while playing *Guitar Hero* with twenty-somethings as the pastor of an emerging church in Colorado Springs. His dissertation will investigate the theological significance of music in film.

Heidi Campbell is assistant professor of communication at Texas A&M University, where she teaches in the areas of media, religion, and culture. She has a PhD in practical theology and computer-mediated communication from the University of Edinburgh–Scotland. Books she has written and/or edited include *Exploring Religious Community Online* (Peter Lang, 2005), *A Science and Religion Primer* (Baker Academic, 2009), and the forthcoming *When Religion Meets New Media* (Routledge).

Craig Detweiler directs the Center for Entertainment, Media and Culture at Pepperdine University. His books include *A Matrix of Meanings: Finding God in Pop Culture* (coauthored with Barry Taylor) and *Into the Dark: Seeing the Sacred in the Top Films of the 21st Century* (Baker Academic). As a filmmaker, Detweiler cowrote the high-energy, teen road trip *Extreme Days*, and codirected the comedic documentary *Purple State of Mind*.

Brad M. Griffin is the associate director of the Fuller Youth Institute (FYI), where he develops research-based training for youth workers (www.fulleryouthinstitute.org). He regularly speaks and writes for youth workers, and is the coauthor of *Deep Justice Journeys*. After fifteen years in youth ministry, he now volunteers in worship ministries at NewSong Church.

Chris Hansen is an award-winning filmmaker and the director of the Film & Digital Media program at Baylor University. He holds an MFA in script and screenwriting. His first feature, *The Proper Care & Feeding of an American Messiah*, screened in twenty national and international film festivals, including AFI's Dallas International and the Virginia Film Festival.

Mark Hayse is associate professor of Christian education at MidAmerica Nazarene University outside Kansas City. In 2009, he received the PhD in educational studies from Trinity International University in Deerfield, Illinois. His dissertation was titled "Religious Architecture in Videogames: Perspectives from Curriculum Theory and Religious Education."

Matthew Kitchen grew up in Arizona playing video games and dreaming of a future as a professional athlete. Unfortunately, the best he could do was a job in production at ESPN headquarters in Bristol, Connecticut. After nearly twenty years of grinding, he has still never beat *Mike Tyson's Punch-Out*, but he keeps on trying.

Andrew McAlpine is a writer and musician living in Nashville, Tennessee. His band, the Coalition of the Willing, released their first album, *All's Well That Ends*, in 2008.

John W. Morehead is the director of the Western Institute for Intercultural Studies (www.wiisc.org). He has an MA in intercultural studies from Salt Lake Theological Seminary and is involved in the study of new religious movements. John blogs on theology and popular culture at www.theofantastique.com.

Kevin Newgren works as a psychologist in Pennsylvania. He received an MS in marriage and family therapy, an MA in clinical psychology, an MA in theology, and a PsyD in clinical psychology, all from Fuller Theological Seminary.

Kara Powell, PhD, is the executive director of the Fuller Youth Institute (FYI) and a faculty member at Fuller Theological Seminary (www.fuller youthinstitute.org). She speaks regularly at youth ministry conferences and is the author or coauthor of numerous books, including *Essential Leadership*, *Deep Justice Journeys*, and the *Good Sex* youth ministry curriculum.

Jason Shim is an independent researcher who specializes in Internet culture and trends. He holds a degree in religion and culture from Wilfrid Laurier University and has presented papers on wedding and funeral rituals in *Second Life*. Connect with Jason at http://www.jasonshim.net.

Lisa Swain is associate professor of mass communication at Biola University. Lisa worked as production coordinator on major Hollywood feature films, including *Big Fish*, *Varsity Blues*, and *Three Kings*. She is a member of the Producers Guild of America.

Rachel Wagner is assistant professor of religion and culture at Ithaca College in Ithaca, New York. She is cochair of the Religion, Film, and Visual Culture Group of the American Academy of Religion. She is currently working on a book on religion and virtual reality.

Daniel White Hodge is a theologian, Tupac Shakur scholar, and racial bridge builder. Dr. White Hodge has been an active member of the hip-hop community for over twenty years, both studying and living the culture. Dan's latest book is *The Soul of Hip Hop: Rims, Timbs, and the Theology of a Culture* (IVP, 2009).

Index